# Shakespeare and Adaptation Theory

ARDEN SHAKESPEARE AND THEORY

Series Editor: Evelyn Gajowski

AVAILABLE TITLES

*Shakespeare and Economic Theory*, David Hawkes
*Shakespeare and Psychoanalytic Theory*, Carolyn Brown
*Shakespeare and Ecocritical Theory*, Gabriel Egan
*Shakespeare and New Historicist Theory*, Neema Parvini
*Shakespeare and Ecofeminist Theory*, Rebecca Laroche and Jennifer Munroe
*Shakespeare and Cultural Materialist Theory*, Christopher Marlow
*Shakespeare and Feminist Theory*, Marianne Novy
*Shakespeare and Posthumanist Theory*, Karen Raber
*Shakespeare and Queer Theory*, Melissa E. Sanchez
*Shakespeare and Postcolonial Theory*, Jyotsna G. Singh
*Shakespeare and Reception Theory,* Nigel Wood
*Shakespeare and Textual Theory*, Suzanne Gossett

FORTHCOMING TITLES

*Shakespeare and Presentist Theory*, Evelyn Gajowski
*Shakespeare and Performance Theory*, David McCandless
*Shakespeare and Film Theory,* Melissa Croteau
*Shakespeare and Race Theory*, Arthur L. Little, Jr.
*Shakespeare and Close Reading Theory,* Kent Cartwright
*Shakespeare and Political Theology Theory,* Sandra Logan
*Shakespeare and Legal Theory*, Karen J. Cunningham
*Shakespeare and Transgender Theory,* Alexa Alice Joubin

# Shakespeare and Adaptation Theory

*Sujata Iyengar*

**THE ARDEN SHAKESPEARE**
LONDON • NEW YORK • OXFORD • NEW DELHI • SYDNEY

THE ARDEN SHAKESPEARE
Bloomsbury Publishing Plc
50 Bedford Square, London, WC1B 3DP, UK
1385 Broadway, New York, NY 10018, USA
29 Earlsfort Terrace, Dublin 2, Ireland

BLOOMSBURY, THE ARDEN SHAKESPEARE and the Arden Shakespeare logo
are trademarks of Bloomsbury Publishing Plc

First published in Great Britain 2023

Copyright © Sujata Iyengar 2023

Sujata Iyengar has asserted her right under the Copyright, Designs and
Patents Act, 1988, to be identified as author of this work.

For legal purposes the Acknowledgements on p. xi constitute an extension
of this copyright page.

Series design by Sutchinda Rangsi Thompson
Cover image © Antonio Iacobelli /Getty Images

All rights reserved. No part of this publication may be reproduced or transmitted
in any form or by any means, electronic or mechanical, including photocopying,
recording, or any information storage or retrieval system, without prior
permission in writing from the publishers.

Bloomsbury Publishing Plc does not have any control over, or responsibility for, any
third-party websites referred to or in this book. All internet addresses given in this
book were correct at the time of going to press. The author and publisher regret
any inconvenience caused if addresses have changed or sites have ceased to
exist, but can accept no responsibility for any such changes.

A catalogue record for this book is available from the British Library.

A catalog record for this book is available from the Library of Congress.

ISBN:  HB:     978-1-3500-7358-6
       PB:     978-1-3500-7357-9
       ePDF:   978-1-3500-7360-9
       eBook:  978-1-3500-7359-3

Series: Shakespeare and Theory

Typeset by RefineCatch Limited, Bungay, Suffolk
Printed and bound by CPI Group (UK) Ltd, Croydon, CR0 4YY

To find out more about our authors and books visit www.bloomsbury.com
and sign up for our newsletters.

*For my teachers and my students*

# CONTENTS

*Series Editor's Preface* ix
*List of Figures* xii
*List of Tables* xiii
*Acknowledgements* xiv
*Note on Texts and Sources Used* xvi

**Introduction:** Much ado about adaptation 1
    What or whom are we adapting? 2
    Metaphors we adapt by 10
    Adaptation as annotation in *Much Ado* 17

**1** Plants, off-shoots, genes: Rhizomes 23
    Plants 23
    Off-shoots 27
    Genes 32
    Rhizomes: Plantation in some *Tempest*s 33

**2** Art, property, theft: Appropriation 45
    Art 47
    Property 52
    Theft 54
    Appropriation as revisioning: *Othello* without Othello (and Desdemona) 59

**3** Fidelity, families, ethics: Derivatives 67
    Fidelity 69

Families: *Lear* among the editors 70
Ethics and editing 76
Derivatives: *Lear*'s progeny 82

## 4 Transfer, remediation, broadcast: Intermedia 87

Transfer 89
Remediation 93
Broadcast and podcast 100
Intermedia: Audio *Hamlet*s 103

## 5 Memes, networks, fans: Transformations 109

Memes 111
Networks 114
Fans 117
Transformations: A gender-agenda in *Twelfth Night* 118

## 6 Relocation, translation, hybridization: Tradaptation 131

Relocation 134
Translation 140
Hybridization 145
Tradaptation: The peregrinations of *Pericles* 148

## 7 Accidents, remains, traces: Accommodations 155

Accidents 157
Remains 162
Traces 167
Accommodations: *Romeo and Juliet* 169

# Glossary of selected terms 177

*Notes* 187
*References* 189
*Index* 229

# SERIES EDITOR'S PREFACE

'Asking questions about literary texts – that's literary criticism. Asking "Which questions shall we ask about literary texts?" – that's literary theory'. So goes my explanation of the current state of English studies, and Shakespeare studies, in my never-ending attempt to demystify, and simplify, theory for students in my classrooms. Another way to put it is that theory is a systematic account of the nature of literature, the act of writing and the act of reading.

One of the primary responsibilities of any academic discipline – whether in the natural sciences, the social sciences or the humanities – is to examine its methodologies and tools of analysis. Particularly at a time of great theoretical ferment, such as that which has characterized English studies, and Shakespeare studies, in recent years, it is incumbent upon scholars in a given discipline to provide such reflection and analysis.

We all construct meanings in Shakespeare's texts and culture. Shouldering responsibility for our active role in constructing meanings in literary texts, moreover, constitutes a theoretical stance. To the extent that we examine our own critical premises and operations, that theoretical stance requires reflection on our part. It requires honesty, as well. It is thereby a fundamentally radical act. All critical analysis puts into practice a particular set of theoretical premises. Theory occurs from a particular standpoint. There is no critical practice that is somehow devoid of theory. There is no critical practice that is not implicated in theory. A common-sense, transparent encounter with any text is thereby impossible. Indeed, to the extent that theory requires us to question anew that with which we thought we were familiar, that which we thought we understood, theory constitutes a critique of common sense.

Since the advent of postmodernism, the discipline of English studies has undergone a seismic shift. The discipline of Shakespeare studies has been at the epicentre of this shift. Indeed, it has been Shakespeare scholars who have played a major role in several of the theoretical and critical developments (e.g. new historicism, cultural materialism, presentism) that have shaped the discipline of English studies in recent years. Yet a comprehensive scholarly analysis of these crucial developments has yet to be done, and is long overdue. As the first series to foreground analysis of contemporary theoretical developments in the discipline of Shakespeare studies, *Arden Shakespeare and Theory* aims to fill a yawning gap.

To the delight of some and the chagrin of others, since 1980 or so, theory has dominated Shakespeare studies. *Arden Shakespeare and Theory* focuses on the state of the art at the outset of the twenty-first century. For the first time, it provides a comprehensive analysis of the theoretical developments that are emerging at the present moment, as well as those that are dominant or residual in Shakespeare studies.

Each volume in the series aims to offer the reader the following components: to provide a clear definition of a particular theory; to explain its key concepts; to trace its major developments, theorists and critics; to perform a reading of a Shakespeare text; to elucidate a specific theory's intersection with or relationship to other theories; to situate it in the context of contemporary political, social and economic developments; to analyse its significance in Shakespeare studies; and to suggest resources for further investigation. Authors of individual volumes thereby attempt to strike a balance, bringing their unique expertise, experience and perspectives to bear upon particular theories while simultaneously fulfilling the common purpose of the series. Individual volumes in the Series are devoted to elucidating particular theoretical perspectives, such as adaptation, close reading, critical race theory, cultural materialism, ecocriticism, ecofeminism, economic theory, feminism, film theory, legal theory, new historicism, performance, political theology, postcoloniality, posthumanism, presentism, psychoanalysis, queer theory, reception theory, textual theory, and transgender theory.

*Arden Shakespeare and Theory* aims to enable scholars, teachers and students alike to define their own theoretical strategies and refine their own critical practices. And students have as much at stake in these theoretical and critical enterprises – in the reading and the writing practices that characterize our discipline – as do scholars and teachers. Janus-like, the series looks forward as well as backward, serving as an inspiration and a guide for new work in Shakespeare studies at the outset of the twenty-first century, on the one hand, and providing a retrospective analysis of the intellectual labour that has been accomplished in recent years, on the other.

To return to the beginning: what is at stake in our reading of literary texts? Once we come to understand the various ways in which theory resonates with not only Shakespeare's texts, and literary texts, but the so-called 'real' world – the world outside the world of the mind, the world outside the world of academia – then we come to understand that theory is capable of powerfully enriching not only our reading of Shakespeare's texts, and literary texts, but our lives.

\* \* \*

I am indebted to David Avital, publisher at Bloomsbury Academic, who was instrumental in developing the idea of the *Arden Shakespeare and Theory* series. I am also grateful to Margaret Bartley and Mark Dudgeon, publishers for the Arden Shakespeare, for their guidance and support throughout the development of this series.

Evelyn Gajowski
Series Editor
University of Nevada, Las Vegas

# FIGURES

0.1. Much Ado About Nothings Shakespeare Sticky Notes. Screen capture by the author, Amazon.co.uk, 10 July 2021.    7

2.1. Google Books Ngram search, http://books.google.com/ngrams, 'cultural appropriation'. Screen capture by the author, 1 November 2021.    55

2.2. Jeffery Quaiyum, Postell Pringle, and Gregory Quaiyum as Female Backup Singers, *Othello: The Remix*. Image ©Steve Reynolds/CultureWorks.    65

4.1. 'Hamlet if Hamlet had a gun', TikTok microvideo, @ivcapvlet. Screen capture by the author, TikTok, 20 January 2022.    96

5.1. 'It absorbs right up!' *She's the Man*, DVD, USA: Paramount, 2006. Screen capture by the author.    124

5.2. 'When People Think Twelfth Night is a Straight Play', TikTok microvideo, @nofearshakesqueer. Screen capture by the author, TikTok, 17 January 2022.    126

6.1. Christophe Grégoire as Périclès, from *Périclès, Prince de Tyr* (2018). Image ©Patrick Baldwin, photographer.    151

7.1. 'Dhankor Baa amputates Deepika's finger with a nutcracker', *Goliyon Ki Raasleela Ram-leela* [*Ram-leela*], DVD, India: Eros International, 2013. Screen capture by the author.    166

# TABLES

| | | |
|---|---|---|
| 4.1. | The Four Laws of Media Applied to NFT Artworks. | 92 |
| 4.2. | Popular *Hamlet*-related hashtags on the micro-video sharing site TikTok. | 95 |
| 5.1. | Productions of *Twelfth Night* and *Romeo and Juliet*, 2021, 2020 and 2015. | 128 |
| 6.1. | Selected characters as named in Gower, Steinhöwel, Twine, and Shakespeare. | 137 |
| 7.1. | Humanagrams: K. Silem Mohammad vs. Deep-Speare. | 159 |

# ACKNOWLEDGEMENTS

This book has been much delayed, first by the untimely death of my intended co-author, Christy Desmet, and then by the COVID-19 pandemic. My first thanks go to David Schiller, Christy's widower, for his support and friendship. I am grateful to the editorial team—series editor Lynn Gajowski, Bloomsbury editors Mark Dudgeon, Lara Bateman, and Ella Wilson—for their patience and firmness. Lynn's steadfastness sustained me from first to last.

A remote fellowship at the Folger Shakespeare Library uplifted me in 2020, as did remote faculty writing retreats convened by Lindsey Harding and Elizabeth Davis under the auspices of the University of Georgia Provost's Office. I am grateful for financial or infrastructural support from the University of Georgia Department of English, especially the grace extended by department head Michelle Ballif, and to funds from the Willson Center for Humanities and Arts. Thanks to the University of Georgia libraries and librarians, especially Anne Meyers DeVine at the Hargrett, Cindy Flom at Interlibrary Loan, Elizabeth Durusau in the Music Library, and Kristin Nielsen, Head of Reference and Instruction. Thanks also to the Folger's *Shakespeare and Beyond* blog, where portions of Chapter 6 first appeared.

Many discussants shaped my thinking. Carla Della Gatta, Alexa Joubin, Ginger Vaughan, and Bruce Smith read individual chapter drafts. Lynn Gajowski, Louise Geddes, and Philip Gilreath valiantly read the whole thing. At UGA, I chewed over translation theory with Drew Zawacki, race and performance with Lesley Feracho, and all things early modern with Miriam Jacobson and Fran Teague. Students in my Renaissance Disability, Shakespeare, and Shakespeare and

Media classes challenged me in fruitful ways. Weekly Zoom meetings with Matt Kozusko, Louise Geddes, and Geoffrey Way, my fellow editors at *B&L*, became chances to mull over new theoretical frames. Among the international community of Shakespeareans Steven Buhler, Sarah Hatchuel, Peter Holland, Krystyna Kujawinska-Courtney, Florence March, Fiona Ritchie, Katie Santos, Lisa S. Starks, Nathalie Vienne-Guerrin, and too many others to name joined me in remote and in-person conversations that jogged my memory or stimulated my ideas. I alone, however, am responsible for any errors or omissions.

# NOTE ON TEXTS AND SOURCES USED

References to the works of Shakespeare come from the Arden Shakespeare, Third Series, general editors Richard Proudfoot, Ann Thompson, David Scott Kastan, and H. R. Woudhuysen, London and New York, Arden Bloomsbury, unless otherwise indicated.

Given the propensity of digital links to 'rot' or become inaccessible, I have wherever possible striven to cite the most stable form of a website, to offer a printed counterpart if one is available, and to cite open-access links.

In accordance with recent discussions in scholarly ethics, where I cite fan- or user-generated work it is either already widely circulating online, made by 'brands' or 'prosumers' who desire a commercial presence, or I have made every effort to ask permission from the creators. Whenever I cite student work, I have received permission. In at least one instance I received permission to discuss and to paraphrase the work but neither to share a link publicly nor to reproduce an image. Readers will, I hope, understand why I choose to document this work despite the challenge of reproducing it: such recreations are where we find, and will continue to find, new Shakespeares and new worlds.

# INTRODUCTION

## Much ado about adaptation

This book reconsiders, after over twenty years of intense critical and creative activity, the theory and practice of adapting Shakespeare to different genres and media. Students coming to the field of Shakespeare and adaptation studies find themselves faced with an array of competing schools of thought and meta-critical debates, often couched in elaborately metaphorical terms. Adaptation or Appropriation? Derivation or transformation? Ancestor or sibling? Export or import? Off-shoot or rhizome? In many cases, such metaphors have become what cognitive scientists George Lakoff and Mark Johnson call 'dead' – clichés that seem transparent to us or even no longer to serve as metaphors, and yet that, they argue, fundamentally shape our understanding of emotions, objects, directions, and even our own bodies, making them (in the title of their germinal book) *Metaphors We Live By* ([1980] 2003). Unlike many earlier treatments of adaptation, *Shakespeare and Adaptation Theory* contextualizes Shakespearean adaptation in light of these cognitive theories of metaphor and of changing media and publishing environments.

Organized around clusters of key metaphors, the book explicates the principal theories informing the field of Shakespearean adaptation and surveys the growing field of case studies by Shakespeare scholars. Focusing each chapter around a different play, *Shakespeare and Adaptation Theory* contrasts comic, tragic, and tragicomic modes in Shakespeare's oeuvre and within the major genres of adaptation (for example film, stage-production, novel, digital media). Each chapter seasons its theoretical discursus with a lively sprinkling of allusions to Shakespeareana ranging from fan-fiction, teatowels, and coffee mugs to quartos, operas, and fine art. Each chapter concludes with a case-study of three or four significant and interesting adaptations from different genres or media. Here I begin with a brief history of the critical thinkers whose arguments underpin present-day debates within adaptation studies before considering Lakoff and Johnson's theory of 'framing discourses' or conceptual metaphors.

# What or whom are we adapting?

Isn't it simple? Aren't we adapting a script or a play-text taken from an early printed edition to a stage performance, a television show, a feature film, a podcast, a vlog, or rewriting bits of the story and the words to make a novel? Modern adaptation studies, however, is as much about the adaptation as it is about the Shakespeare, and in order to explain why, and how we got here, we will need to take a quick detour through the history of ideas and especially the modes of study called 'structuralism' and 'poststructuralism'.

In the late nineteenth and early twentieth centuries, structuralist thinkers such as Sigmund Freud, Karl Marx, Ferdinand de Saussure and Vladimir Propp identified a 'deep structure' or base that underpinned and gave form and sense to various visible 'super-structures' in the world. Freud identified an 'unconscious' mind as the motivator for human words and actions ([1899] 2010: 522–615); Marx identified the movement and ownership of capital as the deep structure of history and society ([1887] 1990: 61–73); de Saussure uncovered the fundamental sign-based communication structure of language ([1916] 2011: 65–70); Propp distilled from Russian folktale a set of common actions, agents, and outcomes (1968: 3–65). A structuralist approach might, say, apply C. L. Barber's germinal investigation of celebratory traditions in what he dubbed Shakespeare's 'festive comedies' (1959) to contrast the day-to-day and the holiday in the loose Bollywood adaptation of *Much Ado*, *Dil Chahta Hai* (2001), which stages climactic scenes on the beaches of Goa. It might encourage us to consider the 'calumniated lady' plot – in this case, the slandering of Hero – as a motif borrowed by Shakespeare (Sexton 1978) but also taken from his works for both feminist and anti-feminist purposes, as in the portrayal of the sophisticated divorcée Tara in *Dil Chahta Hai* (2001) or the 'slut-shaming' of Hero (Desmet 2019) in the Candle Wasters' streaming video series in vlog (video log) form, *Nothing Much To Do* (2014). Structuralist strategies can also give us innovative teaching methods, particularly 'gamification', such as the '*Much Ado* Connect Four' game (2021) that encourages students to 'match' quotations, characters and actions.

In the second half of the twentieth century, however, post-structuralist critics such as Roland Barthes ([1967] 1977), Michel Foucault ([1969] 1977), Jacques Lacan ([1973] 2018), Julia Kristeva ([1980] 1982), Jacques Derrida ([1967] 2013), Luce Irigaray ([1977] 1985), and Gayatri Spivak (1988) began to critique the field of structuralism for its idea of the Enlightenment subject – imagined as white, male, Western, heterosexual, educated and cisgender – and for its ambition to explain all human activity through fixed sets of rigid structures. Post-structuralist, feminist, anti-racist, post-colonial, and cultural materialist critics continued to move beyond structuralism by considering the experiences of those excluded from or marginalized by the 'deep structure' – women, immigrants, prisoners, poor people, colonial subjects ('subalterns', in Spivak's now-classic formulation) and members of subcultures.

Most of these models foreground language as a site for potential resistance and (one could say, borrowing yet again a biological metaphor) adaptation or resilience. If in a Freudian psychoanalytic model the language that we use is important mostly as an indication of our unconscious feelings 'beneath', for Lacan, famously, 'the unconscious is structured like a language': we cannot separate base and superstructure, the personal and the institutional ([1973] 2018: 20 and *passim*). If within so-called vulgar Marxism human relationships and attitudes are subordinate to the movement of capital, labour movements in the era of post-structuralism have fragmented into local or identity-based protest movements, often centred around highly mediatized performance (Lavender 2019). Kenny Leon's acclaimed production of *Much Ado* (2019), which set the play among Atlanta's distinctive upper-middle-class Black community during the Black Lives Matter protests, crystallized these expanding ideas surrounding identity. The men returned not from war but from a demonstration, bearing placards; the actors delivered Shakespearean words with the recognizable intonations and timbre of twenty-first-century African American Language; and the play opened and concluded with a performance of 'Lift Every Voice', the so-called Black National Anthem, challenging received notions of Shakespeare as 'white property' (Little 2016: 88) through these interventions.

Master-narratives and superstructures can push marginalized persons and perspectives even further out of view; poststructuralists therefore suggest that we 'deconstruct', in Derrida's terms, the seeming binary opposition between base and superstructure, by acknowledging the implicit hierarchy that structuralism sets up and by reaffirming the importance of the details that a reductive structuralism can ignore as 'just' or merely superstructure. If for de Saussure semiotics, or the study of signs, allowed us to identify the deep structure of the sign in language – in which sounds and scratches on a page become language once one knows the particular code that lets us interpret them – for post-structural linguistics, the very idea of discrete 'languages' can be broken down into individual 'idiolects' or personal languages, and political coalitions, conversely, can be built through language. Playwright and politician Dev Virahsawmy, writes Roshni Mooneram (2009), deliberately 'under-translates' Shakespeare into Kreol Morisien (Mauritian Creole) his *Enn ta Senn dan Vid* [*Much Ado About Nothing*] (1995); Asheesh Besoondial suggests that this partial translation participates in Virahsawmy's ongoing project 'to valorize the language and to give it the status of a national language, at par with the colonial languages' (2018: 12).

And if Propp's morphology gave us Joseph Campbell's *Hero with a Thousand Faces* (1949) and present-day screenwriting software, post-structuralist folklore and narrative studies investigate the consequences of 'superstructural' variations and audience responses that in turn fundamentally change our understandings of the 'base'. Our 'hero' today can just as easily be a heroine, and our hero's quests can include peaceful or negotiated resolutions to conflicts, comedic solutions that don't require marriage, and so on. *Nothing Much to Do* (2014) therefore 'reform[s]' or re-educates Benedick and Claudio as feminists before their unions with Beatrice and Hero can take place (Desmet 2019: 47) and matches 'Pedro' and Balthazar, whose roles are meaningfully elaborated, in a same-sex relationship along with the opposite-sex ones.

Post-structuralism, in short, despite its sometimes arcane or off-putting jargon, brings real people – consumers, readers, viewers, speakers – and their infinite variety back into the conversation. And in the study of Shakespearean adaptation, as we'll see, we have moved from evaluating how 'true' or faithful a given adaptation is to Shakespeare (a structural analysis). Rather, we have moved into what culturally conservative skeptics notoriously call 'the muck of a postmodern swamp' (Welsh 2005: 106) and what its proponents would call feminist 're-vision' (Novy 1990), 'rewriting ourselves' (Erickson 1994), or a racially-empowering 'recreative dialogue' enabled by '[a]daptation's freedom and multiplicity of address' (MacDonald 2020: 6). Scholars of Shakespeare and adaptation consider how an adaptation works aesthetically in itself; how it was produced; how it was received; and what, if anything, it might show us retroactively about Shakespeare's world (a post-structuralist approach), or about imagined theatrical and fictive versions of that world, and how we can use these 'creative collisions' (Holderness 2014) to build new knowledge, ideas, and practices for today (a speculative approach).

Post-structuralism also questions the very existence of original authors for texts – an obvious challenge for Shakespeareans, who were used to thinking of Shakespeare as the poet of human nature, as Samuel Johnson had suggested ([1765] 2009), the exemplar of English poetry, the best-known author in the English canon. What happens to Shakespeare in light of what Barthes called 'The Death of the Author' and, later in the same essay, the 'birth of the reader' ([1967] 1977: 142–8)? Following the insights of post-structuralist linguistics, Barthes asserts: 'Linguistically, the author is never more than the instance writing, just as *I* is nothing other than the instance saying *I*' ([1967] 1977: 145). In other words, the text itself exists independently of the embodied human being who held a pen, tapped a keyboard, or used an eye-tracker or even a computer-brain interface to create that text.[1] Moreover, 'a text's unity lies not in its origin but in its destination', a destination that for Barthes is specifically the reader, or rather the cultural forces and ideas that speak through the reader ([1967] 1977: 145).

For Foucault ([1969] 1977), the author is dead until revived by a punitive state; he imagines a graffito on a wall and asks whether this text has an author, or whether anyone cares, until or unless it wants to condemn the author for vandalism (or, one might add, given the prominence of the artist Basquiat in the later twentieth century and of Banksy in our own Neo-Gilded Age, to profit from him). Jacques Derrida disaggregates the author and the text still further, concluding that the text exists as an entity that refers to itself in language and that creates a world through marks or pixels that refer to each other rather than to a world outside the text. In a famous phrase, he claims 'il n'y a pas de hors-texte': there is no outside-text ('there is nothing outside the text', in the most familiar translation [(1967) 2013: 163]); the world itself is text.

Foucault notes that authors can 'write' things that they never wrote, for example 'Freudian' or 'Marxian' critiques ([1969] 1977), as in my own earlier paragraph. He adds that rather than thinking of the author as a human being, we should imagine the texts attributed to an author as aspects of what he calls an 'author-function' – a set of imagined characteristics that we project on to a set of texts ([1969] 1977). As Denise Albanese has aptly observed (2010), Shakespeare is an exemplar of how this 'author-function' works: when critics talk in adaptation studies about 'Shakespeare', we are talking about the 'Shakespeare-function': the multi-million-dollar publishing, tourism, theatrical, and motion picture industries, the small set of valuable four-hundred-year-old printed books, the classroom recitations and school plays, the metacritical and editorial theories and apparatuses, and millions of Valentine's Day cards, memes, comic strips, memories, T-shirts, salt-shakers, sticky notes, and endless energetic endeavours that circulate around Shakespeare's name (Figure 0.1).

Even if, when we are adapting Shakespeare, we decide that what we understand and what we will adapt are the lines, the texts, the printed books themselves we run into problems. As Stephen Orgel observes ([1988] 2002), perhaps the most famous lines from Shakespeare, Juliet's balcony-scene lament, 'What's in

FIGURE 0.1 *Much Ado About Nothings Shakespeare Sticky Notes.* Screen capture by the author, Amazon.co.uk, 10 July 2021.

a name? That which we call a rose / By any other word would smell as sweet' (*Romeo and Juliet* 2.2.43–4), appear in none of the printed texts but are rather a conflation or combination of the various printed editions created by the great eighteenth-century editor Edmond Malone: there is no 'authentic Shakespeare', concludes Orgel, and what we have is already a process of editorial creation and collaboration. Malone strove, as Margreta de Grazia has written, to recreate 'Shakespeare verbatim' (1991), imagining that he could see beyond printers' confusion, actors' improvisations, and lost manuscripts to what Shakespeare *would have written*, had he been able to (or wished to?) oversee his works through the press as diligently as did his contemporary Ben Jonson. *Much Ado* is a relatively easy text to consider, existing in only two contemporary versions, a quarto (single volume) and the Folio (posthumous, collected edition of Shakespeare's works). Yet an editor, director, or adaptor can decide to retain or excise the 'ghost' character 'Innogen'; to call her Innogen or Imogen; and to have her stand silently beside Leonato, wail or gesticulate, or even, as in Aditi Brennan Kapil's 'feminist hijacking', *Imogen Says Nothing*, manifest as an enchanted bear (2018). Would Shakespeare have wanted the enchanted bear, and does it matter?

Perhaps, then, we can turn to the documents from Shakespeare's own life to access something of an authentic Shakespeare? Alas, here, too, we have no respite: as Samuel Schoenbaum writes in his magisterial biography of biographies, *Shakespeare's Lives* ([1970] 1991), and Gary Taylor extends in *Reinventing Shakespeare* (1989), biographers write their own stories more than they write Shakespeare's. Early printed texts can tell us about contemporary performances and printing-house practices; early legal documents can tell us about contemporary life, inheritance, and property, but nothing can tell us what Shakespeare *meant* or *thought*. Everything we have is, indeed, adapted or modified for particular audiences and readers or, to coin a phrase, reader-function.

You will note that just as Foucault's author-function ([1969] 1977) turns into the author when authorities seek for someone to blame – or to pay – so has the Shakespeare-function of adaptation played out as a game of critique or praise. So-called fidelity criticism, which I investigate in greater detail in Chapters 1, 2 and 3, considered Shakespearean adaptations worthwhile insofar as they were true or faithful to an ideal of what an imaginary author might have wanted, or to that imagined, so-called authentic text that we know doesn't exist. Fidelity critics certainly likewise believed that that imaginary authentic Shakespeare ranked more highly than the debased adaptation; the few contemporary complaints surrounding Kenneth Branagh's highly-acclaimed film of *Much Ado* (1993) centred around the supposed implausibility of the African American Denzel Washington (Don Pedro) and the mixed-race Keanu Reeves (Don John) being brothers and around the deliberately 'international' cast with its mixture of accents (Lehmann 2006; Fabiszak 2015).

Post-structural adaptation studies return to Shakespeare's earliest adaptors and critics, considering these adaptations as works worthy of performance, study, and critique in their own right, considering responses, both from professional critics or actors and from ordinary people, in what is known as 'reception studies'. It engages in what Jeffrey Wilson has called 'historical presentism' (2021): the deeply contextualized study of contemporary approaches to Shakespeare (I am going to call the Shakespeare-function simply 'Shakespeare', without 'scare quotes', for the rest of this book) without privileging a Shakespearean past or original to which we can have no access (and on which we might not report accurately even if we could).

Linda Hutcheon, whose work I discuss in Chapter 1, helpfully locates Shakespearean adaptations on a continuum. Some strive to be 'closer' to the texts that we have; others are what we call 'appropriation' or (following its use in Art History) 'recontextualization', in which the adaptor – or the adapting text – is concerned very little, or not at all, with the idea of an original that it's altering or imitating. In some cases, such appropriation becomes what Christy Desmet calls (extending

Ian Bogost's writing about 'procedural rhetoric' in technology, 2012) the 'Alien Shakespeare' (2017) that I analyze in Chapters 6 and 7: Shakespeare that emerges through fragile or ephemeral clusters of information, minds or objects in a particular space and time, radically idiosyncratic, unrecognizable to those outside the alien pod, as it were. The director of *Dil Chahta Hai* has, for example, disclaimed its relationship to *Much Ado* except as 'coincidence' (Menon and Akhtar 2007: 81), yet insightful analyses of *Much Ado* and the film together have emerged (Menon 2008: 79–93). The ultimate 'adaptor' of Shakespeare is the reader or viewer, whose prismatic and unique set of experiences and memories continually engages and transforms the cultural behemoth called Shakespeare.

Is everything, then, an adaptation? And if everything's an adaptation, is everything, then, potentially Shakespeare? My remaining chapters will continue to investigate both these propositions, through the conceptual metaphors that critics and theorists of Shakespearean adaptation have used.

# Metaphors we adapt by

The metaphors that critics use to describe the process and products of Shakespearean appropriation or adaptation establish what they believe Shakespeare to be, whom they think it's for, and what they imagine is its worth to the world. Aristotle suggested that metaphors worked through analogy, or similarity, and that they worked through estranging us or startling us into seeing something anew through an unpredictable resemblance. I. A. Richards suggested that metaphors contained two parts, a 'vehicle' and a 'tenor', a conveyance for the meaning and the underlying meaning, and that both vehicle and tenor interacted with each other, giving metaphors their power ([1936] 1965). Lakoff and Johnson ([1980] 2003) argue that metaphors aren't restricted to poetic or consciously figured speech, but rather permeate our every utterance (and thought). So-called 'dead' metaphors aren't really dead, they argue, but rather have become embedded in our language to such an extent that they have changed the way we perceive the world (they have become a 'frame' or conceptual metaphor, in other words). We no longer, in many cases, even recognize such concepts as metaphors. Conceptual metaphors include PEOPLE ARE PLANTS ('He's really shot up this year!'), TIME IS MONEY ('You're spending too much time on this!'), LIFE AS A JOURNEY ('I've reached a dead end'), THE MIND IS A CONTAINER ('keep it in mind'), HAPPY IS UP ('I'm feeling down today'), and so on. (In order to avoid the appearance of shouting, I will use Lakoff and Johnson's upper-case styling only in this chapter, turning to italics for later uses.)

Many of the fundamental 'frames' or conceptual metaphors identified by Lakoff and Johnson in *Metaphors We Live By* manifest in the metaphors we use to discuss Shakespearean adaptation. The earliest metaphors are botanical, rooted in the conceptual metaphor that 'people are plants' and that Shakespeare reproduces itself through a process of flowering, fruition, and renewed growth through dispersal. Chapter 1, 'Plants, Off-shoots, Genes: Rhizomes', discusses the vegetal metaphors for Shakespeare's art that go back beyond Samuel Johnson and Samuel Taylor Coleridge as far as the First Folio. Later critics rework this metaphor along lines elaborated by Douglas Lanier (following Deleuze and Guattari) as 'rhizomatic' adaptation (2010, 2014), a subterranean and quasi-independent network. The final section of this chapter, 'Rhizomes: Plantation in Some *Tempest*s', revisits Gonzalo's appropriation of Montaigne's essay *Of the Cannibals* in *The Tempest* in order to consider adaptations of this often-cut scene on 'plantation' (the early modern word for colonization).

Metaphors of appropriation connote theft and property, deploying the conceptual metaphors IDEAS ARE OBJECTS or even BELIEFS ARE POSSESSIONS or TO ACT ON SOMETHING IS TO TRANSFER IT. In Chapter 2 I trace the development of Shakespearean adaptation alongside changes in intellectual property law, media, editorial history, and ongoing debates about cultural appropriation in fields ranging from art history to anthropology. Jean Marsden, who popularized the term 'appropriation' for Shakespeare studies, offers the classic definition of appropriation – she does not distinguish particularly between adaptations and appropriations – as 'theft, or seizure for one's own purposes' (1991: 1). Shakespeareans have argued amongst themselves about the relative advantages and disadvantages the term 'appropriation' or 'adaptation', using both interchangeably (Desmet and Iyengar 2015). Within intellectual property law, however, the difference between adaptation and appropriation remains crucial (Iyengar 2017a). In the second decade of the twenty-first century Shakespeareans additionally began to consider the ongoing ethical considerations of appropriation (Joubin and Rivlin 2014), including so-called cultural appropriation. The final portion of Chapter 2 explores *Othello* adaptations. Focusing not only on artistic works of adaptation but also on the law, I investigate the motif of theft, both personal and cultural, surrounding Desdemona's handkerchief and the social virtues associated with it in world cinema, stage-play, and musical.

We conceive figuratively of our minds as parents and our ideas as children: King Henry IV reproves his prodigal son with the famous phrase, 'Thy wish was father, Harry, to that thought' (*King Henry IV, Part 2*, 4.5.92). Discussions of Shakespearean adaptation are both indebted to and resistant towards the Freudian 'family romance' as outlined by Harold Bloom ([1973] 1997), in which authors strive Oedipally to overthrow their literary fathers. Bloom's patriarchal model, however, inadequately accounts for the responses of feminist, postcolonial, working-class and other adaptors. More recently, critics have suggested nuanced responses based on the work of Homi Bhabha (1984) (discussed later in the book), but also in light of the ethical philosophies of Charles Taylor ([1990] 1994) or Emmanuel Levinas ([1961] 1991), which attempt to escape from the power-driven binary of owner/

property through a renewed focus on humility, mutual recognition, and what Taarini Mookherjee (2020) calls 'neighborhood' relations.

In this communal, human-centred ethos, the ethics of adaptation becomes a rejection of the turbulent family romance in favour of voluntary, considered, and politically nuanced relations. Alongside this focus on ethics comes an editorial push to consider editions of Shakespeare's plays as found or chosen family members rather than blood-kin, as it were, countering the traditional conceptual metaphor of editorial practice that called texts 'good' or 'bad', 'corrupt' or 'clean'. Chapter 3 examines family romances in editions and adaptations of *King Lear* that map the play onto women's bodies and that foreground the relationship between fidelity in marriage and male primogeniture, the inheritance of property by the eldest male heir.

If Shakespeare isn't a material property, might it be information or data? The idea that Shakespeare is raw information that can be transferred from one medium to another without distortion or loss, while scorned in academic circles, is nevertheless rife within popular and scientific contexts. Its longevity is no surprise, given the conceptual congruity of the 'lossless transfer' fantasy with the fundamental 'conduit' metaphors Lakoff and Johnson identify, such as CONTENT TRAVELS TO THE EXPERIENCER and CONTENT IS CONTAINED IN THE STIMULUS. 'Transfer, Remediation, Broadcast: Intermedia', Chapter 4, therefore discusses the theoretical concept of 'intermediality', which complicates and questions the idea of seamless communication or transfer from one medium to another. Intermediality acknowledges that one medium may represent another without naively attempting to recreate that medium, and that media themselves comprise a series of signifying systems. I return in this discussion to our consideration of cultural appropriation and ethical adaptations, 'Channeling *Hamlet*' through a range of audio-only and audio-visual interpretations.

Having identified some of the problems in seeing Shakespeare as transmissible content delivered through a channel, I move in Chapter 5 to considerations of Shakespeare as a network, a dispersed community, McLuhan's 'global village' ([1962] 2011), (to adapt the popular 1990s characterization of the internet). The conceptual metaphors at work here are IDEAS ARE ALIVE and IDEAS MAKE A COMMUNITY. Extending but also critiquing Richard Dawkins's suggestion of the meme – the idea that replicates as a gene does (1976), Gary Bortolotti and Linda Hutcheon (2007) suggest that fundamental narratives within Shakespeare function as memes and that critics, artists, and writers can use the process of their adaptation to study changing ideas and stories over time. Writers such as Susan Blackmore (1999) and Limor Shifman (2013) foreground the meme's balance of replication and alteration in social media adaptations, particularly through its ability to circulate virally, or in Henry Jenkins, Sam Ford, and Joshua Green's phrase, its 'spreadability' (2015).

This spreadable Shakespeare circulates through the related metaphoric complex of the object-oriented assemblage or actor-network, as popularized by Bruno Latour (1996). A focus on the life-of-objects puts authors and readers (of texts) into the background and acknowledges that any scenario, artistic or social, engages a multitude of actors – some human, some not. In Latour's actor-network theory, the focus for meaning becomes not the author/reader/audience complex nor the objects that make up a Shakespearean adaptation, but the ghostly paths – nodes of the networks between objects, texts, performances – in which meaning, however transient, resides. Such assemblages or networks comprise both inanimate memes and the lively fans who engage in the phenomenon that Jenkins identifies as 'participatory culture' (1988) or, later, 'convergence culture' (2008). These amateur fan cultures surround Shakespeare, too (Teague 2011; Fazel and Geddes 2022) and have produced a sub-genre of popular Shakespeare in their own right – both online and in real life at Renaissance Fairs. 'The Gender-Agenda in *Twelfth Night*' concludes Chapter 5 by tracing how changing understandings (or memes) of human sexuality among complex human networks influence representations of gender in Shakespeare's plays in novel, film, and prosumer or fan works.

If some Shakespearean adaptors live in a polity where Shakespeare writes the constitution, others, especially translators, travel from one Shakespeare village to another. Translations, tradaptations, and relocations raise once more questions of purity and fidelity. Are Iraqui, Québécois or other non-European sources still Shakespeare? Who has the authority to perform, translate, and enjoy Shakespeare? In a global context, Alexa Alice Joubin suggests that directors and theatre critics sometimes produce 'boomerang Shakespeare' (2016) where a non-English Shakespeare is judged according to changing but still Euro-centric artistic standards. In North America, Arthur Little has urged us as well to question whether Shakespeare is open only to white people (2016) while Ambereen Dadabhoy has suggested that early modernists need to decentre Shakespeare itself if we are serious about fighting white supremacy (2020).

Mooneeram has written about Creole and multi-lingual forms of Shakespearean transfer in Mauritius, borrowing from Québécois writer Michel Garneau the useful term 'tradaptation', a portmanteau-word combining 'translation' and 'adaptation'. The conceptual metaphors enlivening the critics and adaptors in Chapter 6, 'Relocation, Translation, Hybridization: Tradaptation', are undergirded by the metaphorical frames that CHANGE IS MOTION and the subset CAUSED CHANGE IS FORCED MOTION. At the same time, artists, audiences, and readers engage with the concept that CREATIVITY IS MOVEMENT. The oscillation between the discomfort of *forced motion* and *creative movement* also returns us to our earlier debates about fidelity through the conceptual frame that MORALITY IS PURE OR CLEAN OR UNITARY. My case study of the peregrinations of *Pericles* follows Peter Holland's suggestion (2005) that *Pericles* is a play ideally suited for a promenade production. I explore the multilingual transmission and adaptation of the tale of Apollonius of Tyre and Shakespeare and Wilkins's own dramatic adaptation *Pericles* before discussing travelling and translated productions, adaptations, and novelizations of the play.

I move very far geographically from Shakespeare's origins in Chapter 6; in Chapter 7 I travel forwards and backwards in time and among living, undead and algorithmic Shakespearean bodies. 'Accidents, Remains, Traces: Accommodations' considers the status of unacknowledged, unwitting, inappropriate, absurd or attenuated Shakespearean echoes or footprints: 'accidental' appropriations, especially of *Romeo and Juliet*. Accidental appropriation, as originated by Julian Yates (2006) and developed by Desmet (2017), engages with the fanciful, whimsical, or AI-generated (Artificial Intelligence or Machine-Learning) evocation of Shakespeare in modern media and late capitalist objects.

It seems as though we have now reached the end of Shakespeare, and the end of adaptation, and have disappeared into an endlessly self-reflexive series of hypo- and hypertexts (Genette [1982] 1997). Yet investigating accidental connections can reveal surprising insights into objects more traditionally considered Shakespearean. Shakespeare is process, not product; present, not past; is 'Shakespeare/Not Shakespeare', in the title of a recent collection on this topic (Desmet, Loper, and Casey 2017). I therefore conclude with a synthesis of what Robert McRuer has called 'crip theory' (2006) – itself a combination of queer and disability studies – and fan studies to explore the paradoxical conceptual metaphors that THE BODY IS A CONTAINER FOR THE SELF and that THE MIND IS A BODY. I follow this incarnation of Shakespearean traces into non-normative, fiercely present bodies in versions of *Romeo and Juliet* adapted to popular genre-film, zombie novel, and immersive theatre for and by persons with disabilities. These appropriations demand – and receive – accommodation and an independent existence far from the 'fidelity discourse' of earlier adaptations and far from the medicalized normative body of traditional performance and literature. I thus end with Shakespearean accommodation, one of the earliest metaphors for how humans incorporate creative texts into our minds – and bodies.

# Adaptation as annotation in *Much Ado*

As befits a play focused so much on 'notes, forsooth, and noting' (*Much Ado* 2.3.58), one can investigate early adaptations of *Much Ado* as a series of annotations, since to 'note' is both to observe and to alter or make fit for one's own use or understanding (Dawson 1982). One can also consider the 'front matter' of early printed books – or, for that matter, of books today – as a kind of 'annotation' for the reader. King Charles I annotated the table of contents of his personal Shakespeare Folio with the names of his favourite characters – such as 'Bennedick and Betrice' beside *Much Ado*. Audiences were equally keen. The commendatory epistles – essentially blurbs or reviews at the front of a new or republished book – to the 1640 edition of Shakespeare's sonnets included these words from Leonard Digges: 'Let but *Beatrice* / And *Benedicke* be seene, loe in a trice / The Cockpit Galleries, Boxes, all are full' (*3v and *4r).

Restoration and eighteenth-century playwrights playfully and freely adapted Shakespeare's works, in part because, as Michael Dobson (1992) points out, Shakespeare was not reprinted from the first prohibition by the Long Parliament to the Restoration (1642–1660), and theatres were closed, so that a generation had thus grown up without seeing or perhaps even reading the plays. Both playwright and producer Sir William Davenant ([1662] 1970), who notoriously claimed to be Shakespeare's illegitimate son, and clergyman James Miller (1737) adapted Shakespeare in plays that combined *Much Ado* with other plays, modernized topical references, and removed or rephrased words or sentiments the audience might find offensive, in order to make these 'old plays' more appealing to then-contemporary tastes.

Davenant combined *Much Ado* and *Measure for Measure* in his *The Law Against Lovers* ([1662] 1970) in a way that resembles the 'crossover' of present-day situation comedy or the Marvel Cinematic Universe. Davenant adds the technical sub-plot of *Much Ado* to the main plot of *Measure for Measure*, making Benedick and Angelo into brothers, and Beatrice Angelo's ward; excising the bed-trick, Mariana, and the brothel scenes, along with the more serious soliloquies; and adding a musical younger sister for Beatrice called 'Viola' and 'song, dance, a popular young actress, and novelty' (Scheil 1997: sec. 36). His Viola comprises aspects of several Shakespearean heroines, including her namesake: she flirts with Benedick in the opening scenes (Beatrice) but ends the play resolved to 'run from that foolish Boy [Cupid]' (Isabella); performs as a solo one of the major interpolated songs (Viola); and enters in 4.1 'dancing a saraband awhile with Castanietos' (Davenant [1662] 1970: 304). Davenant also transforms the Duke into 'a quite miraculously chaste and paternal version of Charles II' (Scheil 1997: sec. 36) and clarifies Angelo's motives from the start, evidently thinking that Restoration audiences would find the Duke's claim in Shakespeare's play that Angelo 'had never the purpose to corrupt [Isabella]; only he hath made an assay of her virtue' (*Measure* 3.1.183–5) to be as unconvincing as most readers and audience members do today.

Considering the plot as a mash-up or as crossover allows us likewise to interpret Davenant's dialogue as annotated Shakespeare for its time, akin to today's *No Fear Shakespeare*, *No Sweat Shakespeare*, Shmoop, CourseHero and so on. Such 'student notes' modernize archaic grammar and spelling, simplify sentence-structure, omit or smooth out knotty metaphors, and annotate their own annotations where they are worried about giving offense. Davenant modernizes pronouns – 'Who will believe *you* Isabell?', asks Angelo creepily in 3.1 ([1662] 1970: 292, emphasis mine) – and both updates and simplifies Shakespeare's grammar (adding or removing articles, for example) and metaphor. Beatrice's 'I had rather lie in the woolen' becomes 'in woolen' (*Much Ado* 2.1.27; Davenant ([1662] 1970: 293), Claudio's 'Ay, but to die, and go we know not where' pedantically becomes 'to go we know not whither' (*Measure for Measure* 3.1.133; Davenant ([1662] 1970: 299), and 'myself' routinely becomes 'my self'. More substantively, Isabella's

> Th'impression of keen whips I'd wear as rubies
> And strip myself to death as to a bed
> That longing have been sick for, ere I'd yield
> My body up to shame.
> *MEASURE FOR MEASURE* 2.4.106–11

becomes

> Th'impression of sharp whips I gladly would
> As Rubies wear, and strip my self
> Even for a Grave, as for a Bed, e're I
> Would yield my honour up to shame.
> DAVENANT ([1662] 1970: 291)

Isabella's determined statement of chastity only eroticizes her further to Shakespeare's Angelo, as she evokes her body 'strip[ped]' and adorned on a bed (and some productions play this pair as though united in sado-masochistic desire). Davenant tries to minimize the lines' charge by substituting 'honour' for 'body', by simplifying the grammar, removing Isabella's ambiguous line about 'longing', and by re-lineating so that audiences don't hear Isabella mention 'strip' and 'bed' in the same line (the circumlocution of 'Even for a' rather than 'as' again minimizes Isabella's deathly submissive erotic fantasy). *No Fear Shakespeare*, our twenty-first-century equivalent, is no longer coy about nudity and sexuality, but equally reticent about Isabella's 'longing', summarizing the end of the speech as 'I'd go to my death like going to my bed, before I'd surrender my body to sin' (SparkNotes 2021a).

By the time James Miller is writing, Shakespeare is in print and on stage again, albeit much altered. Miller combines Shakespeare's *Much Ado* with Molière's *Princesse d'Elide* (1664) to create his *The Universal Passion* ([1737] 1969). Again, our front matter, the prefatory material, offers a kind of annotation: actor Colley Cibber reassures us that 'There's nought but what an Anchoret might hear', describing Miller's play as an 'orphan' child of the great 'Father' Shakespeare ([1737] 1969: A4r [vii]), a metaphor to which we'll return in Chapters 3 and 7. Miller's bowdlerizations include the replacement of 'hey nonny nonny' with 'hey down, derry, derry' in the song 'Sigh No More', presumably because 'nonny-nonny' was a euphemism for 'vulva'. SparkNotes leaves the refrain intact, but doesn't explain it, just as it modernizes 'the great Cham' to 'Kublai Khan', a 'translation' likely to be equally opaque to the students reading it (SparkNotes 2021b). Miller, in contrast, updates Benedick's request to be sent on far-fetched quests to exotic monarchs, cutting the references to 'the great Cham' or 'Prester John' that his audience members would not understand ([1737] 1969).

Miller enjoys the crossover effect, too. Although he changes the names of his characters and adds a clown-character called 'Joculo' for no good reason, as an early critic tetchily observes (Nichols 1929), some of the Shakespearean names among his fabricated ones alert audiences to the names' connotations, much as a television tie-in might do. The Don John character is 'Byron', perhaps reminding us of the mordant wit of Shakespeare's Berowne, and the Beatrice-character is 'Liberia' (presumably because of her free speech). Her Benedicke, however, is 'Protheus' (alluding to the faithless hero of Shakespeare's *Two Gentlemen of Verona* and implying that Benedick has betrayed Beatrice in the past, as the text indeed suggests).

Cibber's prologue connects Shakespeare with 'Britannia', 'Albion', and the work of empire, through a conceit identifying the playwright with the sun, adaptations with its rays, and a theatre without him to the benighted Arctic, where his people have long been awaiting his refulgent rise. Cibber's diction anticipates the famous colonial tag, 'The sun never sets on the British empire' and enlists Shakespearean adaptation in its service. I will investigate in Chapter 1 Shakespeare's *Tempest* through another naturalized metaphor for both empire and adaptation: flowers, shoots, roots, seeds, and the most common early modern word for colonization, 'plantation'.

# 1

# Plants, off-shoots, genes: Rhizomes

## Plants

In one of the earliest acknowledged adaptations of Shakespeare, John Dryden uses a sustained arboreal metaphor to describe the relationship of his *The Tempest: or The Enchanted Island* (co-authored with William Davenant; henceforth Dryden 1670) to Shakespeare's *The Tempest*:

> As when a Tree's cut down, the secret Root
> Lives under Ground, and thence new Branches shoot;
> So, from old Shakespear's honour'd Dust, this Day
> Springs up and buds a new reviving Play.
>
> DRYDEN 1670: A4r

In this figure, Shakespeare, a mighty tree, 'cut down' when the theatres were closed, continued to thrive through underground roots that now 'shoot' up 'new reviving Play[s]' (Dryden 1670: A4r). Dryden's conceit continues by imagining Shakespeare's friend, the poet laureate Ben Jonson, growing like a creeper beneath the shade of Shakespeare's tree and John Fletcher, Shakespeare's last collaborator, gathering foliage from the topmost branches of Shakespeare's 'Heights' (Dryden 1670: A4r).

Dryden credits Davenant with the invention of the play's most notorious departures from Shakespeare's play: the inclusion of a sister, Dorinda, for Miranda, a young woman who has never seen a man, and a counterpart for her in Hippolito, a young man who has never seen a woman.

Dryden and Davenant's wildly popular adaptation also added sisters for Ariel, and even Caliban (whose mother Sycorax is now the latter's sibling), and contrasted the 'licentious[]' desire of Hippolito for Dorinda with the 'courtly love' of Ferdinand (Bickey and Stevens 2021: 224–5). In its most frequently performed version, an opera adapted by Thomas Shadwell (1674), *The Enchanted Island* replaced Shakespeare's *Tempest* on the stage until 1838.

History has been less kind, however, to *The Enchanted Island*. Post-Enlightenment critics excoriated it (Keenan 2009), and the editor of the Variorum Shakespeare, Henry Howard Furness, memorably complained: 'no imagination, derived from a mere description, can adequately depict its monstrosity, – to be fully hated it must be fully seen' (1892: viii). Furness extenuated the play only somewhat based on its history: 'DRYDEN'S Version is the fruitage of DRYDEN'S times' (1892: ix). Furness finds himself in the thick of the so-called fidelity discourse, in which Shakespearean off-shoots are most valuable when they appear as flowers from Shakespearean seeds, reproducing an imagined original plant and generating 'true' seeds – and 'fruitage' – in their turn.

The assumption of Shakespeare's inherent superiority was dubbed 'bardolatry,' or 'uncritical Shakespeare-worship' (Caines 2013: 146) by George Bernard Shaw, who himself, somewhat inconsistently, complained bitterly about adaptors who 'mutilated' or 'hacked' Shakespeare's plays (Shaw 1901: xxx–xxxi). Many critics have identified the phenomenon with actor David Garrick's great Shakespeare Jubilee in 1769 (Dobson 1992; Caines 2013), in which the dendroid associations of Bardolatry were almost literally consecrated through the 'Eucharistic adoration' of a goblet made from the wood of a mulberry-tree said to be planted by Shakespeare (Holland 2015:8).

Yet the great lexicographer and essayist, Samuel Johnson, one of Shakespeare's earliest editors, uses arboreous metaphors quite differently. Johnson famously characterized Shakespeare as a poet who created 'just representations of general nature' and then clarified the nature of that 'nature' through a series of sustained contrasts between Shakespeare and his more learned contemporaries ([1765] 2009: 355). For Johnson, Shakespeare's middle-class background and lack of, say, Ben Jonson's deep erudition presented not a bug, but a feature, as programmers like to say today: relying upon his own voracious reading, old tales retold, and creative synthesis of popular tastes, rather than, say, classical sources (although Shakespeare, of course, used those too), Shakespeare fabricated a world that encompassed a stunning variety of styles, settings, characters, and fantasies. Johnson elaborates his argument in a conceit in which Shakespeare is a 'forest' that creates a unique, rich, and biodiverse habitat, as opposed to the human-planned, carefully-plotted 'garden[s]' of other writers:

> The work of a correct and regular writer is a garden accurately formed and diligently planted, varied with shades, and scented with flowers; the composition of Shakespeare is a forest, in which oaks extend their branches, and pines tower in the air, interspersed sometimes with weeds and brambles, and sometimes giving shelter to myrtles and to roses; filling the eye with awful pomp, and gratifying the mind with endless diversity.
>
> JOHNSON [1765] 2009: 372

The phrase 'Shakespeare's composition' refers both to the matter of Shakespearean texts and to the sources and inspirations that enabled the creation of those texts. Not only does Shakespeare, in Johnson's woodland comparison, offer lofty, grandiose, or ancient trees, but those trees in addition 'give shelter' to more delicate, fragranced flowers. Johnson also identifies matter that readers and viewers (the foresters or forest-dwellers in this analogy) will find less useful: the 'weeds and brambles' that contribute to ecological diversity, if not to human comfort, and that add a sense of adventure or fairy-tale to our exploration of Shakespeare.

Johnson's next sentence compares Shakespeare to a 'mine' full of unpolished, raw ore, where occasional gems might glisten but where others will require extraction. I'll return to the figure of extractive exploitation later in this chapter; here both images – the forest and the mine – implicitly assume that, just as Shakespeare freely adapted a wide range of source material, so editors, readers, and viewers will necessarily select what they want from Shakespeare – whether to pull up the weeds or leave them, whether to transplant the myrtles, whether to trim the great oak. For Johnson, Shakespeare is not above criticism, and rather, is often fallible, particularly in the latter's 'lack of interest in providing...a moral' (Caines 2013: 108); emendation, correction, and adaptation are therefore necessary tasks for a critic, producer, or editor. Tree-like or botanical metaphors do not necessarily connote a straightforward or reliable lineage, nor any kind of innate quasi-genetic purity, a more expansive understanding of adaptation that anticipates the work of later critics such as Ruby Cohn (1976) or Linda Hutcheon ([2006] 2013).

Such critics of the fidelity discourse contend that it privileges a mythical originary and superior text and judges adaptations according to their faithfulness to this imagined prior, truth-bearing text. Rather, these critics argue, adaptations should stand alone and can offer new insights into traditional readings of Shakespearean texts or even make up for perceived deficiencies in the prior text, just as Johnson had argued that it was our duty to remedy Shakespeare's perceived amorality (Caines 2013:108). A revival of *Enchanted Island* with a student cast at the University of Hull thus enabled 'a judicious expansion of Miranda's emotional range' (Keenan 2009: 70) and the Metropolitan Opera's 2011 opera of the same name 'foreground[ed] the importance of women's desires and dreams, their power of expression, their glorious moments of transgression, their individuality, and their freedom'

(Scott-Douglass 2013: n.p.). Where nineteenth-century editions and performances enshrined a passive Miranda and Restoration adaptations cast added 'girl characters,' including the so-called breeches parts of Ariel and Hippolito (Williams 2014), these twenty-first-century productions allowed Ariel, Miranda, and their interpolated sisters expressive, lyrical freedom.

# Off-shoots

Cohn (1976), one of the earliest critics to challenge the fidelity discourse, uses the term 'off-shoot' to describe creative works inspired by Shakespeare, language that evokes botany firmly in the service of the so-called fidelity discourse of adaptation. An 'off-shoot' typically connotes a plant that can be rooted by cloning, specifically by placing part of the original plant into a potting medium and giving it sun and water. Examples of plants that can easily be 'rooted' this way include *Chlorophytum comosum* (familiarly known as the spider plant, or 'hen-and-chickens' for the frequency with which it produces off-shoots), and other plant species that can become invasive weeds because they flourish and reproduce so successfully far from their origins.

Cohn, however, considers her term 'the looser and more neutral' equivalent to the often-value-laden epithets of prior critics, such as 'abridgements, alterations, ameliorations, augmentations, conversions, distortions, emendations, interpolations, metamorphoses, modifications, mutilations, revisions, transformations, versions' (1976: 1). She differs from most earlier critics who use botanical metaphors in valuing the transformations over either the emendations or the adaptations. She additionally anticipates later criticism in suggesting not only 'how far' such off-shoots 'grow from the Shakespearean stem' but also that that 'stem' itself includes the complicated textual history of the plays in quarto and folio. Cohn, however, restricts her analysis to dramatic texts, considering novelized *Hamlet*s and essays on *Lear* purely 'for purposes of comparison,' although her understanding of the 'dramatic' extends to the dialogue form and to the dramatic monologue (1976: ix).

Cohn places off-shoots in three categories that she names emendations, adaptations, and transformations. Emendations she considers the province of 'theatre history': the necessary and customary changes made to a script before it is performed on stage. Adaptations alter the language but maintain basic similarities of plot, structure, and character. Finally, transformations transfer Shakespeare's characters or language to partly or entirely new situations, sometimes adding characters and plot twists (Cohn 1976). As a modernist and Beckett scholar, Cohn prizes above all the uses that avant-garde theatrical movements in France, Germany, England, Ireland, and the Caribbean make of Shakespeare. In this model, for example, a comparison of the script used by Greg Doran for his virtual and augmented reality Royal Shakespeare Company *Tempest* in 2016 would exemplify 'emendation' and Davenant and Dryden's *Enchanted Island* an adaptation. Robert Browning's dramatic monologue 'Caliban on Setebos' (1864) and W.H. Auden's poem-series 'The Sea and the Mirror' ([1944] 2005) – both of which Cohn discusses at length – she considers transformations (Cohn 1976: 268–72, 280–91).

Transformative too, as we shall see, is Aimé Césaire's *A Tempest*, a post-colonial Black 'revolution erupting onstage, in the person of Caliban' (Cohn 1976: 199). Cohn quotes Césaire's account of how he wished to '"de-mythify" the tale' (quoted in Cohn 1976: 298), a process that, Cohn argues, 'break[s] everything apart – not only the ship's hierarchy but the racial and cultural hierarchy of European tradition' (1976: 299). *A Tempest's* Ariel, a nonviolent, light-skinned intellectual who dreams of converting Prospero to mercy and establishing a shared realm, argues with the play's darker-skinned Caliban, who thinks Ariel is deluded and Prospero a power-mad 'pulveriser' (Césaire [1969] 2002: 23) about the best methods of rebellion. Césaire's signature-changes to Shakespeare's plot – having Prospero forgive the 'three men of sin' at the very beginning of the play; allowing the Yoruba trickster-god Eshun to interrupt the masque; and having Prospero remain on the island with Caliban after the other Europeans depart – undermine, writes Cohn, the very reasons for which *The Tempest* has been sanctified (sometimes almost literally, as in G. Wilson Knight's Christian reading): 'Prospero's celebrated forgiveness becomes a necessary expedient of white rule' (Cohn 1976: 300).

Hutcheon further extended Cohn's argument that adaptations were worthy of study, even broadening the field to include visual, fictional, cinematic, material, performed, and transmedia phenomena rather than the avant-garde theatre that had above all intrigued Cohn (and, in the twenty-first century, Thomas Cartelli [2019], whose discussions of avant-garde theatre and its use of transmedia we will encounter in Chapter 4). Hutcheon argued in her field-defining book *Adaptation* ([2006] 2013), that adaptations exist on a continuum, from faithful adaptation to political appropriation or radical recontextualization, and that it's perhaps most helpful to consider adaptations in light of the 'modes' they deploy: telling, showing, and interacting. She offers a model for how cultural and literary critics should analyze adaptations, namely by asking ourselves of every adaptation the series of questions investigative journalists pose about current events: What? Who? Why? How? Where? When? Asking such questions can help uncover, Hutcheon writes, an 'ongoing dialogue with the past' ([2006] 2013: 117).

Hutcheon notably diverges from fidelity critics in emphasising the pleasure of adaptation for both adaptor and receiver, a joy that she dubs 'the doubled pleasure of the palimpsest' ([2006] 2013: 117). She takes the image of the palimpsest from the narrative theorist Gérard Genette (1982 [1997]), whom we'll discuss at greater length in Chapter 3. Genette identifies within all texts a 'transtextuality' in which an under-text or hypotext appears beneath an over-text or hypertext just as ancient manuscripts – known as palimpsests – include the traces of prior words written and then erased by writers long before. For both Genette and Hutcheon, the joys of the palimpsest (in Genette's terms, 'literature in the second degree') demonstrate the enjoyment of encountering a familiar text in different contexts, of discussing a well-loved text, even (suggests Genette) of 'literariness' itself ([1982] 1997: 4–5). Like Genette, Hutcheon resists the earlier critical commonplace that adaptation was watered-down comfort food for cowardly consumers afraid to try unfamiliar tastes.

Freud was the first to suggest the delights of repetition – imagining a baby playing peekaboo or 'fort-da' (Here/Gone) over and over again, a psychodrama one replays endlessly as an adult to reassure oneself that one lives and breathes in the world (Freud 1922: 11–16). 'Repetition with a difference', in Hutcheon's phrase, offers refreshment – new settings, new characters, new language, and so on – and comfort, in that readers or viewers familiar with the prior text know some of what's coming next. Such 'repetition with difference' creates the 'formal structure' of adaptation (Hutcheon 2013: 142). Extending the reader-response critics Wolfgang Iser and Stanley Fish, Hutcheon valorizes the role and pleasure of the reader in recognizing an adaptation as an adaptation and in noticing changes among different versions. Iser argued that texts create 'implied reader[s]' and sets of expectations that real readers both meet and confound; real readers question, complete, and customize the implied reader of the text (1980). Fish set limits or a horizon of interpretation around the potentially infinite range of meanings that real readers might bring to texts by positing that meaning emerges through specific, culturally focused and historical 'interpretive communities' (1982). Hutcheon also validates the personal and political motives that can drive adapters to seed new versions in turn.

*Knowing* that something's an adaptation is thus important to Hutcheon's theory; adaptation is 'an extended, deliberate, announced revisitation of a particular work of art,' and she excludes 'short intertextual allusions...or bits of sampled music' ([2006] 2013: 170). Rather, adaptation offers a kind of fidelity continuum that ranges from 'literary translations' and 'transcriptions of orchestral music for piano' through 'condensations and bowdlerizations or censorings in which the changes are obvious, deliberate, and in some way restrictive' to 'retellings' or revisions where stories 'are both reinterpreted and rerelated' before finally landing at 'spin-offs,' including objects only tangentially related to the text to which they purport to be related (Hutcheon [2006] 2013: 171). Working through this continuum, one might identify Victor Hugo's or Boris Pasternak's classic translations of Shakespeare into French and Russian on one end; move through the 'obvious [or] deliberate...restrictive' 'censorings' such as the complete exclusion of Stephano, Trinculo, and their plot against Prospero from Charles and Mary Lamb's version of *The Tempest* ([1807] 1886); argue that Leon Garfield's prose in *Shakespeare Stories* (1994) comprises a 'retelling' that works with Michael Foreman's award-winning illustrations or with the S4C/SoyuzFilm *Animated Tales* to 'reinterpret' *The Tempest* as animated television metadrama (Pennacchia 2017) or to establish Prospero and Miranda as idealized overlords through cinematic technique (Semenza 2008). One could end at 'spin-offs' that include everything from academic writing (5,694 'hits' for 'The Tempest' in the World Shakespeare Bibliography, excluding productions, audio recordings, and film), to ceramic Mirandas (Minton n.d.), 'Prospero's Dark and Stormy' cocktail (Bicks and Ephraim 2015), EasyJet cockpits (Bartlett 2018), Miranda Sea Salt chocolate bars (Sweet Theatre n.d.), Tempest coasters (CafePress n.d.) or Shakespeare Sheep's Milk Brie (Book and Bucket n.d.). And indeed, the way that the cheese, coasters, chocolate and so on announce their derivation so loudly (and wishfully) suggests that commercial entities and college professors alike understand the fort-da pleasure of 'repetition with difference'.

## Genes

Hutcheon further develops her arguments about adaptation in an influential co-authored article (Bortolotti and Hutcheon 2007) that likewise attempts to free Shakespearean adaptation from the fidelity discourse and (indirectly) the botanical figure of the off-shoot, through the insights of post-Darwinian biology. Bortolotti and Hutcheon (2007) recommend a genetic model based not on origins but on lines of descent, punning on the sense of the word 'adaptation' used by geneticists and evolutionary biologists. In this way adaptations resemble not off-shoots that reproduce the plant that seeded them, but plants that have adapted contingently to local environments, with corresponding changes to structure, flourishing, and dispersal through time. Like plants that have accommodated through natural selection to particular biomes, artistic re-workings of Shakespeare's plays and poems should be seen, Bortolotti and Hutcheon argue, as the products of cross-pollination and epigenetics rather than as pure or impure descent. Scholars can trace particular lineages, but some of these adaptations/plants will look quite different from their shoots or supposed origins and will in turn unpredictably transfer or pass on different genes or aspects.

The critic's job, then, is to observe how adaptations work through processes of replication and change. For example, one could imagine Julie Taymor's auteur-driven filmed *Tempest* (2010) with Helen Mirren playing a female Prospero ('Prospera') as a descendant both of Shakespeare's play and of Dryden and Davenant's female-centric adaptation, with a specifically feminist auteur-driven aesthetic (Gilreath 2020) and with Ben Whishaw's androgynous Ariel a sibling of the 'breeches' roles Ariel and Hippolito. Or one could consider the inhuman or posthuman presence of *The Tempest* in the acclaimed science-fiction serial television drama *Westworld* (Wald 2020) and Greg Doran's technologically mediated production at the RSC (2016) not only as reclamations of the Shakespearean metaphor of the 'world as stage' (Winkler

2017) but also as different off-shoots of the long history of science-fiction and speculative fiction *Tempest*s that contrast autocratic, technologically mediated Prosperos to the vulnerable human beings they control.

Aldous Huxley's modernist masterpiece *Brave New World* (1932) bitterly applies Miranda's eulogy to the mindless infantilism of a post-industrial eugenic technocracy – Prospero run rampant – and to the pockets of poverty-stricken, disease-ridden reservations that provide the only spaces for the fundamental human growth experiences of love, birth, suffering, and death. Fred Wilcox's film *Forbidden Planet* (1956) externalizes Ariel as Robby the Robot, the perfect automaton, while showing that the sophisticated power of Morbius (the Prospero-figure) both depends on and cannot suppress the naïve violence of his own 'Monster from the Id' or Caliban. C. Dexter Palmer's steampunk *Dream of Perpetual Motion* (2010) perhaps most explicitly of the three connects technological hubris with men's need to control women's fertility; the novel's Prospero has frozen himself, removed Miranda from the world, and trapped her (and Harold, the failed writer who loves her) on a perpetual-motion-powered airship that he equips with deadly weapons. All attempts to control the sexuality and potential offspring of Miranda and young people like her, suggest these *Tempest* responses, can lead only to the complete destruction of the human family tree.

# Rhizomes: Plantation in some *Tempest*s

Given that the fidelity model imagines a single seed or a tree from which true fruit must spring, how else can one account for the variety of pleasurable off-shoots emerging through Shakespeare? The currently dominant model in adaptation studies, popularized by Lanier (2014), jettisons metaphors of tree, fruit, and seed in favour of the rhizome, using theories from the Frankfurt School critics Gilles Deleuze and Félix Guattari. (The work where they present rhizomatic theory, *A*

*Thousand Plateaus* ([1980] 1997) has given us other terms of art in postmodern literary criticism that we'll encounter later, such as the 'assemblage' and 'de-territorialization'.) In a series of essays on the topic, Lanier (2014) argues against simultaneously the fidelity model and the Marxian idea of appropriation by proffering the rhizome as an organic form with no origin or telos – just nodes that spread laterally, in a non-symmetrical fashion. Rhizomes have no beginning or end; less concretely, they are not even three-dimensional objects, but figured more as points on a plane. The result is an emphasis on becoming and difference that mitigates against any sense of social or aesthetic hierarchy.

At the current moment, the Deleuzian rhizome remains a dominant trope for adaptation studies; its critics have suggested on the one hand that it is too organic to account for the algorithmic production of digital Shakespeares (Desmet 2017) and on the other that it doesn't allow sufficiently for nuance or individual creators' agency (Fazel and Geddes 2022) – in other words, that it is both too human and too inhumane. My later chapters investigate these critiques even as they continue to find the location-specific, subterranean movements of the rhizome an apt figure for the mysterious, flattened appearances of Shakespeare in high and low global cultures. Here, I also use the plant metaphor *diaspora*, a word used to describe a culturally distinct group of people scattered far from their origins – by war, famine, climate change, enslavement, empire, curiosity – that literally means the strewing of people like seeds across the world (Braziel and Mannur 2003: 4). While the rhizome is decentred, non-hierarchical, and unexpected, and thus a rich and nuanced method of investigating Shakespearean adaptations, rhizomes themselves – whether they are tubers, off-shoots, root-systems, bulbs – spread through contiguity, immediate proximity, through touching the same soil. Rhizomes spread through the dirt, piece by piece; seeds cross oceans in sudden dislocations, transported by the wind, on flotsam and jetsam – and by invasive animals, human and non-human. To consider Shakespearean texts as diasporic connotes

Shakespeare's imbrication in colonial education – and its literal embodiment in empire through travelling bodies and early modern plantation.

On the one hand, the idea of diaspora can reify or essentialize complex origins to a single national identity, but on the other, such an imagined point of origin can provide the coherence necessary for political action and mutual support (Rushdie 1992; Gilroy 1993; Hall 1994). Hutcheon adduces Edward Said's inspirational essay on 'Travelling Theory' (1982) to suggest that what she calls 'transcultural' adaptations are undergirded by 'travelling ideas' (Hutcheon [2006] 2013: 146–150). The four travelling ideas that both create and allow us to recognize a transcultural adaptation, suggests Hutcheon, are a set of shared initial circumstances between source and adaptation; the distance that the adaptation has crossed; the conditions of acceptance and resistance, and the transmutation of that idea through its new temporal and geographic setting.

*The Tempest* dramatizes travel across time and space and the process of what the early moderns called 'plantation', the customary term for colonialism in Shakespeare's time. Its transcultural adaptations have ranged from the early postcolonial *Tempest* of Aimé Césaire ([1969] 2002) to the meta-critical discussions about the play within Ethnic Studies (Takaki 1994), Indigenous theory (Byrd 2011) and Black Feminism (Brooks 2017). In addition to the much-discussed character of Caliban, the play includes an explicit interlude in which a Neapolitan fantasizes a benign colonial conquest. Revisiting Gonzalo's wish that he '[H]ad. . .plantation of this isle' (2.1.144–169, frequently interrupted by the cynical Antonio and Sebastian), I will use adaptations of this often-cut scene on 'plantation' to track changing attitudes toward colonialism and settlement.

Critics since the great editor Edward Capell (1780, quoted in Go 2012) have noticed that Shakespeare adapts both the name of his character Caliban and Gonzalo's utopian dreams for the island from Montaigne's essay *Of the Cannibals* ([1580] 1603) and that he freely adduces aspects of Montaigne's argument and specific verbal parallels from John Florio's English translation. Shakespeare's Gonzalo makes Montaigne's 'savages' (whom Montaigne argues are not 'savage' at all) more decorous and peaceable than in Montaigne's original. Montaigne describes a realm free from trade, law-courts, literacy, wealth, poverty, service, contracts, inheritance, borders, agriculture, ironmongery, alcohol, clothing, or monogamy, one that prizes in men military and sexual prowess and in women the skills of brewing non-alcoholic drink and procuring younger wives for their husbands.

Gonzalo carefully elides the importance Montaigne's 'Caniballes' place in going to war (and in having the King stand foremost in the battle) and completely omits their imputed belligerence, nudity, polygamy and the 'threates of future death...with mangling and slicing of their members' with which they 'torment' their prisoners (Montaigne [1580] 1603: K4v–5r). *The Tempest* remembers this psychological intimidation but puts the threats in the mouth of Prospero, not the island's inhabitants. Prospero menaces Ariel with a 'torment' worse than Sycorax's (1.2.289) and Caliban with 'pinch[es]', 'stripes', 'old cramps', and 'aches' (1.2.329, 346, 370, 371). Shakespeare's adaptation of the speech in Gonzalo's mouth thus both highlights 'the good old lord's' benevolent intentions even as it demonstrates his failure to envision a world of unconditional human freedom.

The three appropriations of *The Tempest* I discuss below pick up these omissions in the well-meaning old lord's speech and use them to critique his vision and, by extent, the assumptions of the society that has formed him. Césaire's play *A Tempest* ([1969] 2002) begins with Gonzalo and his idealized description of the island, but where Shakespeare's character sincerely believes in his idealized natives, Césaire's Gonzalo plans to 'irrigate' the island with 'fecal matter' (29) – a graphic metaphor for the colonial project itself. Peter Greenaway's arthouse film *Prospero's Books* (1991) presents Prospero as master creator and enmeshes itself deeply in traditional Renaissance art history even as its realized images of naked natives and suffering women make manifest the cruelty paradoxically underlying the beauty of that art. In contrast, Margaret Atwood's prison novel *Hag-seed* (2016) makes the two men who play Gonzalo in her multi-layered, metatheatrical and metafictional versions of Shakespeare envision more humane forms of incarceration – and finally to imagine a world without any prisons at all.

Césaire's Gonzalo echoes the language of Sir Walter Raleigh in the latter's *Description of Guiana* (1596); where Raleigh famously compared the Americas to a woman's virgin body, ready to be deflowered (conquered) by England (Montrose 1991), Gonzalo enthuses of the island that 'bread hangs from the trees and the apricots are bigger than a woman's breast' (Césaire [1969] 2002: 28). Césaire's Gonzalo imagines the unnamed Caribbean isle as an ever-giving, nourishing mother, a willing partner in her own 'exploitation,' potentially 'richer than Egypt with its Nile' (Césaire [1969] 2002: 29) Like Shakespeare's Gonzalo (at least in the eyes of Antonio and Sebastian), Césaire's character is facetious, arguing that the island is so magical that even if it included poisons, it would also include their antidotes – and rhapsodizes about the fertility of guano, found in caves. Césaire's bitter comedy suggests that the colonial project literally floods other countries with 'shit' (29).

Gonzalo's seeming idealism, his lip-service to avoiding the 'shortcomings ... [of]... civilization' (Césaire [1969] 2002: 29) emerges as selfish, superficial, and subject to the conditions of the church. 'They must stay as they are: savages, noble and good savages, free, without any complexes or complications. Something like a pool granting eternal youth where we periodically come to restore our aging, citified souls,' he opines ([1969] 2002: 229–30). When he encounters Caliban, he first tries to exorcise him. When Caliban bursts into mocking laughter, Gonzalo's supposed compassion dissipates: 'I have tried to save you. . . .I leave you to the secular arm!' ([1969] 2002: 60). Kindness (in both its senses) is conditional; utopias exist only for the obedient; Gonzalo can see Caliban as fully human only if the latter's world can be made over in the colonists' image, with the collusion of the colonized. The play ends, bitterly, with Prospero and Caliban marooned with each other in mutual hatred on the island, calling for the 'protect[ion of] civilization' and for 'FREEDOM' respectively (Césaire [1969] 2002: 65–66). But it is Caliban who has the last word.

Greenaway's gorgeous, experimental film *Prospero's Books* (1991) unashamedly 'flaunt[s]' its 'Eurocentrism' (Zabus 2005), modelling its multiply imaginary sets after famous Renaissance buildings (both real and painted), and fashioning its naked spirits, monsters, and demigods (including Caliban) after Elizabethan paintings of Virginians – 'Prospero's idea of the New World' (Greenaway 1991: 58), its 'effete shipwrecked Neapolitans' after the most baroque of courtly Castilian styles (1991: 108), and its Miranda after an idealized 'Botticelli['s]...Spring...a classical deity not out of place in the forest of Arden' (1991: 90–91).

The film used a then-revolutionary technology, the 'electronic paintbox', to imagine *The Tempest* being written in real time by Sir John Gielgud's Prospero (who also utters nearly all the lines) and to superimpose above Shakespeare's text 'intricate layers of text, image, voice, music, and sound in a series of intertextual overlays of double exposures, transparencies, and multiple framings' (Verrone 2011: 185). The twenty-four fantastical, animated, exquisite, Renaissance books – the books that, Greenaway imagines, comprised the 'library' with which Gonzalo embarked the usurped Duke and his infant daughter – frame and establish visual and thematic motifs, even as other frames (what Greenway calls the 'mirror-image', and are sometimes literal mirrors, held up by spirits) show us the actions Prospero imagines and ventriloquizes.

Prospero voices Gonzalo's speech in a segment framed by the former in his study looking over

> The Book of Utopias [...] A book of ideal societies. With the front cover bound in gold leather and the back bound in black slate, with five hundred pages, six hundred and sixty-

six indexed entries and a preface by Sir Thomas More. The first entry is a consensus description of Heaven and the last is a consensus description of Hell, for there are always some on earth whose ideal world is Hell.

GREENAWAY 1991: 112

Greenaway removes one of Antonio and Sebastian's intrusions in order to keep more of the speech intact, while the camera surveys the indigenous island spirits. These resemble what Greenaway identifies as Elizabethan stereotypes of indigenous Americans, 'brown-skinned, naked', decorated with beads, feathers, and woad, talking, smoking, and dancing. The Camera pulls back as Antonio and Sebastian mockingly 'bow and scrape' to 'his Majesty' Gonzalo, but then gazes once more upon 'the Golden Age personified': '[early modern painter] John White Indians and classical, mythological figures camped on the grass' (114). It seems as though Greenaway is endorsing Gonzalo's ideal and suggesting that Prospero's (and Greenaway's) art can reconcile the beauties of high Western art, indigenous American cultures, and the glorious fecundity of the natural world.

But Gonzalo's speech in Greenaway is bookended, as it is in Shakespeare, with a discussion of the voyage that has brought the courtiers to the island, the marriage of Alonso's daughter Claribel to the King of Tunis. In 'a 1600s fantasy of the Near Eastern Orient' (Greenaway 1991: 110), a 'frightened,' slender, teenaged, 'white' Claribel is dressed for marriage in a court filled with nude or armoured 'Arab, Negro and Egyptian courtiers' before her 'fat, handsome, young black king' fiancé, lolling 'naked on a bed' (Greenaway 1991: 109–10). After Gonzalo's speech, when he and Alonso fall asleep in response to Ariel's music, a second interpolated scene presents, in critic William Babula's words, a 'grotesque' and 'terrible depiction...[a] miserable and sexually abused Claribel...with a bloody pudendum while nude white slave girls attend to the obviously polygamous Tunis' (Babula 2001:19). Both scenes demonstrate the cruelty underlying the creation of Prospero's high European art and historically cohere with the snide comments of Antonio and Sebastian surrounding the marriage, including their voiced stereotypes about Africa, and pernicious early modern beliefs surrounding African male sexuality (Babula 2001: 21–22). The film, then, 'flaunt[s]' its 'Eurocentrism' even as it critiques the institutions that immiserate peoples that, as Chantal Zabus (2005) reminds us, Frantz Fanon called 'the wretched of the earth' (title, [1961] 1963).

Atwood's *Hag-Seed* (2016), richly intertextual, literalizes for its central conceit *The Tempest*'s sustained imagery of imprisonment and identifies incarceration as a present-day form of neo-imperial subjugation that disproportionately affects the people known in the US as BIPOC (Black, Indigenous, and of Colour).[1] Through her protagonist, disgraced erstwhile Shakespeare Festival director Felix, Atwood sets the action of the play in and around a men's prison in Canada at multiple, simultaneous levels:

1. The catalysing action from the novel, in which Shakespeare Festival director Felix, on the verge of producing an avant-garde *Tempest*, is ousted by his former collaborator Tony, after which Felix enters self-imposed exile as a Shakespeare teacher and director in a remote men's prison and plots a revenge when Tony and his now-powerful allies come to visit as governmental observers.
2. The musical production performed and adapted by Felix's actors, shared with the in-house audience through video-relay and prerecording.
3. The immersive, drug-filled, revenge-laden secret re-enactment Felix and his felons impose upon Tony and his allies at the same time as the official performance is being broadcast.
4. The actors' escape from the prison of Shakespeare's text and of chronology itself as they imagine other lives

for its protagonists, whether in cynical mode (Antonio overpowers the disenchanted Prospero on the ship), feminist mode (the three goddesses intervene to restore harmony), or utopian mode (Prospero prevails, and Gonzalo establishes his commonwealth on the island).

5  The nine in-text prisons that Atwood, and her characters, identify within *The Tempest* as more microcosms of the island, culminating with the bare stage itself, and the actor Prospero pleading to be 'set. . .free' from the mental prison of revenge by the audience's applause (*The Tempest* Epilogue, line 20; Atwood 2016: 281–2).

These in-novel adaptations or echoes of *The Tempest* feature three Gonzalos, too: Lonnie, the weak-minded but kind-hearted bureaucrat who provides the ignominiously-fired Felix with an umbrella, his script, his walking-stick, and the outlandish cape Felix designed for Prospero (that is, 'the rotten carcass of a butt' [1.2.146], Prospero's books, his staff, and his magical garment); Bent Pencil, a member of the incarcerated acting troupe who is a dishonest accountant jailed for white-collar crime; and the Gonzalo of Felix's imagination, whose life Bent Pencil (who enacts him) imagines continuing beyond the end of the play. '[O]ld Lonnie' (Atwood 2016: 26) means well and, although content to remain on the Festival board, does so while believing Felix has been cruelly treated. '[Q]uavering' in his kindliness (26), he functions through denial, passing through the metal detector 'as if. . .sorry there has to be such a thing as a security checkpoint, in such a thing as a prison' (212). Trapped in the 1990s display cell with Sal, the Alonso-equivalent, Lonnie hopefully speculates, 'maybe. . .someone. . .[is]. . .trying to help us' (231). But Lonnie's ideals are limited. When Lonnie imagines himself as lord of the prison, and claims he wants to offer more autonomy to its inmates to 'make their own decisions,' the farthest freedom he can imagine for them is '[d]esign[ing] their own menus' (226).

Bent Pencil, Gonzalo's counterpart among the incarcerated actors, is both more flawed and more enlightened than either

Lonnie or Gonzalo. He shares Gonzalo's compassion, clarifying that none of the visiting dignitaries will 'get hurt' before he will agree to participate in Felix's enacted revenge (207). But unlike either Gonzalo or Lonnie, Bent Pencil understands the limits of goodness when it lacks institutional power. He thoughtfully asks of Shakespeare's Gonzalo a question that could equally well have been asked of Lonnie: 'Is extreme goodness always weak?' (267) He characterizes Gonzalo as someone who has not fallen because he is never tempted to sin and imagines an afterlife for Gonzalo in which the latter is tested. Gonzalo returns to the island with a group of fellow-optimists and establishes a true utopia, a 'kingdom-republic...[with] no differences of rank and no hard labor...no immoral sexual behaviour...no wars, no crimes, and no prisons' (269). Such an ideal would need to depend upon 'the better natures of other[s],' along with a 'smile' from 'Bountiful Fortune' (269).

Taken in sequence, Gonzalo's utopia in these *Tempest* adaptations tracks changing beliefs about the shock of imperialism. Gonzalo's speech itself, in context, wryly satirizes the myth of the noble savage even as the play seems to suggest that only magic can counter brutality. Césaire's Gonzalo demonstrates the thin façade of so-called civilization and his desire to make over Caliban (non-Western cultures) in the image of the West. Greenaway's Book of Utopias uses radically innovative digital means to show visually the cruelty of colonialism as well as the elegance of the high Renaissance; the images of the bloodied Claribel and the nymph-like Miranda show extremes of what Gayle Rubin has called 'the traffic in women' in which powerful men consolidate their might through arranged dynastic marriages (1975). Finally, Atwood's multi-layered, meta-fictive novel challenges us to consider that the colonial project persists in the present day, brought home by the racial disparities of the prison-system in both Atwood's native Canada and within the US (Owusu-Bempah, Jung, Sbaï, Wilton, and Kouyoumdjian 2021; Nellis 2016).

My next chapter develops the theme of racial and criminal justice through the metaphor of 'appropriation' as used of adaptations of *Othello*. Is appropriation always 'theft'? If so, what are adaptors 'stealing' from Shakespeare? We'll begin by considering the Marxian origins of both the word 'appropriation' and the phrase 'commodity fetishism' before discussing stolen or missing objects in stage, film, and musical adaptations, including the famous handkerchief.

# 2

# Art, property, theft: Appropriation

Current debates within the study of Shakespearean adaptation often become mired among multiple senses of the word appropriation, which has different meanings in legal, artistic, and, in our current moment, racial and colonial contexts. Contemporary North American English uses 'appropriation' to mean variously: adaptation, or derivative of a prior source; theft, or unauthorized 'seizure...for one's own uses' (Marsden 1991:1); allocation, or rightful set-aside for proper uses; gift, or the legitimate making-over of property. The term's most current use appears in the phrase 'cultural appropriation' – the tendency of dominant groups to adopt the practices, artforms, and even the appearance of minoritized ones for entertainment or profit.

For example, consider the uses of the word 'appropriation' in the following anecdote. An appropriation (adaptation) of a scene from *Othello*, Marc Chagall's 1911 oil painting 'Othello and Desdemona', was appropriated (stolen) in a famous heist from the collectors Ernest and Rose Heller thirty years ago and recovered in 2017 by the US Federal Bureau of Investigation. The collectors were long dead, and since the statute of limitations had long since passed, the thieves could not be prosecuted. Nonetheless, the painting could not be appropriated (gifted) to the FBI, which meticulously tracked down the Hellers' descendants, who planned to sell the work at auction with appropriations (allocations) for the insurance company, the MacDowell Colony, Columbia University, and New York University Medical School (Hsu 2018). Some might consider Chagall's painting, of Othello looming over the sleeping Desdemona as he prepares to murder her, an act of cultural appropriation, although I'll argue later why I don't think such a reading is – appropriate.

This chapter clarifies these various meanings of 'appropriation' and suggests which ones Shakespeareans might find helpful to retain and which ones are less relevant to our enterprise. Throughout, I will examine adaptations of the play arguably the most concerned with theft, value, and – in performance, at least – the practice of cultural appropriation: *Othello*. After summarizing the legal context, I will focus upon Marxian *appropriation* as both unethically-acquired 'surplus value' (such as unscrupulous slum-owners charging exorbitant rents to impoverished tenants) and as the rightful enhancement of daily life through the fruits of one's labour (such as the wages workers can spend not only on mere subsistence but also on 'broaden[ing]...the whole life of the worker' [Marx [1848] 1996:14–17] – 'bread and roses', in the words of the legendary labour slogan and folk song [Ross 2013]). Investigating these Marxian roots of the term *appropriation* gets to the heart of why, despite the confusion, some critics (including me) often prefer to consider the works we study and enjoy as appropriations rather than as adaptations, collaborations, transformations, off-shoots, derivatives, remixes, and so on.

Several of Lakoff's primary metaphors shade our discussion of *Othello*, appropriation, and adaptation. The metaphor of appropriation as theft is underpinned by the conceptual metaphors *properties* (or attributes, both abstract and physical) *are possessions* and that *to lose a property* (these possessions) *is to be harmed*. Othello's own dilemma dramatizes the conceptual metaphor *to no longer believe is no longer to have in possession* along with the patriarchal variation of the concept *loved ones are possessions* into *women are men's possessions*. In addition, the play demonstrates the racialization of the conceptual metaphor *light or white is good; black or dark is evil*. Iago steals Othello's sense of self even as the history of *Othello* in blackface performance (and arguably the text itself) appropriates the histories and bodies of the Black Diaspora – the practice we now call *cultural appropriation*.

The chapter concludes with a more detailed look at Chagall's painting before turning briefly to the motif of theft in four dramatic adaptations: Paula Vogel's *Desdemona, or, A Play About a Handkerchief* ([1994] 1996); Toni Morrison's 'prequel and sequel' to *Othello*, *Desdemona* (2012); Djanet Sears' 'prequel' to *Othello*, *Harlem Duet* (1997) and the Q Brothers' *Othello: The Remix* (premiered in 2012 and published in 2018). In response to the play's history and historiography, one that has prevented Black people – and women – from speaking for themselves on and off stage, these adaptations by queer, Black, and of colour authors banish key characters from the stage in order to allow others to tell and revise their stories. Vogel's and Morrison's plays exile men from the stage, including Othello and Iago. Sears and the Q Brothers elide Desdemona. All four attempt to rework or reframe the fundamental metaphors of possession and darkness underlying the play.

# Art

First, let's clarify what appropriation is *not*, at least for most Shakespeareans, most of the time. In legal terms, adaptations, appropriations, and transformative uses all rely upon or derive from previously copyrighted works, but to different degrees. An adaptation, legally speaking, is derivative from a prior, original work and as such the adaptors owe the creators a share of any profits they might make from that adaptation and perhaps also must pay a fee to license their use of the original work. Shakespeare, Dickens, Austen, and other classics of the Western canon necessarily transcend such requirements because, the authors being long-dead – literally so, rather than in a Barthesian sense – they belong to the public domain. They thus belong to what has been called the 'creative commons', which is also the name of the US non-profit dedicated to making more of the world's intellectual property available open-access while protecting creators' rights through a series of variably restrictive or permissible licenses. Julie Sanders and Reto Winckler call Shakespeare's work an 'open-source' repository (Sanders 2011) or 'source code' (Winckler 2017) for creative endeavours and shared cultural exchange, for similar reasons. What we do to Shakespeare is necessarily transformative, given our distance from it in time, space, language, and context (Iyengar 2017a).

Nonetheless, Shakespeareans can encounter difficulties with copyright law when we quote from Shakespearean adaptations and appropriations. In the digital era, the words printed in Shakespeare's scripts and poems themselves are free in both senses of the word that the French language helpfully delineates: *libre* (free from restrictions) and *gratuit* (free from cost). But the editorial, visual, cinematic, and musical apparatus surrounding the dissemination of those words have been subject to copyright ever since the statute of Anne in 1710 created the figure of the Shakespearean editor, and the market that employed him.

Take Jack Good's critically successful 'Manson murders'-inspired rock musical based on *Othello*, *Catch My Soul* (1968); its 'Swinging Sixties' London incarnation (1969); and its box-office-bomb cinematic adaptation (1974), which was later retitled *Santa Fe Satan* to alert potential viewers to the fact that the film boasted a quite different cast, setting, and musical numbers from the stage musical. Good could and did adapt the text of Shakespeare's *Othello* for his musical without needing permission, but the studio that produced the film version, Metromedia, needed to obtain (and did) permission and rights from Good (Mayer 2013; McQueen 2016; Desmet and Schiller

2017). Or consider the popular teen film *O* (2001), which updated Shakespeare's play to an elite Southern co-educational boarding school where the relationship of working-class striver and football star Odin Jones (nicknamed 'O') and delicately-nurtured Dean's daughter Desi descends into rapine and murder through the machinations of O's envious and duplicitous best friend, Hugo. The filmmakers needed no permission to transform: *Othello*'s acoustic patterns into circular architectural features such as cupolas or mirrors (Os); the imagery drawn from hawking and of animals hunting and eating each other into visual motifs of hawks and doves throughout the film (Critini 2004: 117–20); or Brabantio's allegation that Othello has 'conjured' Desdemona (*Othello* 1.3.106) into an accusation of illegal drug use. The filmmakers must, however, have sought permission to use then-contemporary popular music on the film's soundtrack, and the copyrighted recording of music whose scores might belong to public domain, such as the aria from Verdi's *Otello* that opens the film.

An appropriation will not seek permission and, depending on how litigious the original's owners are, how much of the cultural work is allegedly appropriated, and whether courts find its use sufficiently transformative, can fall in or out of the law – or rather, can be perceived to fall out of law. Appropriators (at least in the US) might argue that their use is transformative: in legal terms, that it changes the meaning of the work and offers substantial critique or commentary. A transformative use, even of a copyrighted work, is considered fair use or fair dealing.

So-called appropriation art relies upon the transformative defence. Appropriation art, its practitioners maintain, removes an artwork from its original setting and recontextualizes it within another context, sometimes with major changes, but other times with little or no difference between the original and the appropriated artwork. The significance of the appropriating artwork, and its new contribution to culture, comes from this recontextualization of a chronologically prior work in an unexpected place, medium, or style. In music, this practice is known as 'sampling' and, as in the art world, has often fuelled long-running copyright disputes.

We could consider the fugitive yet reappearing presence of Shakespeare's *Othello* in Claudia Rankine's *Citizen* (2014) as a kind of sampling or recontextualization. The script for Rankine's video essay *Zidane* (co-authored with John Lucas), included in *Citizen*, incorporates quotations from luminaries of Black and postcolonial literature and theory such as Fanon, James Baldwin, and Bhabha along with lines from Shakespeare and (in the video) translations from the sign-language interpreters at the 2006 World Cup (Rankine 2014: 124–26). *Zidane* recontextualizes a controversy surrounding the French-born, Algerian-and-Berber-descended soccer star Zinadine Zidane in which Zidane responded to a racial slur from Italian player Marco Materazzi with a violent reaction. As I've argued elsewhere, Rankine and Lucas suggest that Zidane is haunted by Othello, sent off the field at what should have been his moment of glory and a celebration of the multiethnic French team. Othello in this reading is the brilliant military commander who seems to have earned full acceptance into an initially hostile society but who learns – when what Evelyn Brooks Higginbotham has called 'the politics of respectability' (1993) fail him – that his acceptance is merely contingent, subject to his continuing to perform a kind of superhuman tolerance for injurious conditions (Iyengar 2016).

Rankine's use of television footage and of copyrighted authors such as Baldwin clearly falls under transformative use, but contemporary literature nonetheless often finds itself mired in legal disputes, especially when it aims (as does Rankine's *Citizen*) to highlight or correct the prejudices or omissions of earlier texts. Margaret Mitchell's estate attempted to prevent publication of Alice Randall's *The Wind Done Gone* (1991), a rewriting of Mitchell's *Gone with the Wind* from the perspective of that novel's enslaved characters, and the Vladimir Nabokov estate successfully delayed worldwide publication of Pia Pera's *Lo's Diary* (1995). *Lo's Diary* transformed *Lolita* (1955),

Nabokov's tale of a middle-aged pedophile who kidnaps a young teenager.

Whereas courts determined Randall's book to be 'parody' and thus transformative (Iyengar 2017a), Pera and the Nabokov estate settled the case. As Martin Garbus, the lawyer who 'argued that Pera's work was transformative in nature, and thus encouraged under the law', observes, however, the settlement failed to resolve 'troublesome questions of free speech and property rights' (1999). Garbus notes that the novel is 'not parody or criticism. . .not a prequel or a sequel'; Rather, he calls it a 'variation on a theme' (Garbus 1999). (Today, one might classify it as 'fan fiction' – Shakespearean responses that I will consider in more detail in Chapters 4 and 5.)

Shakespearean adaptations must necessarily be transformative, it seems, given the longstanding status of these works in the public domain. Yet while Shakespeare is indeed an open-source repository for cultural remixing, as Sanders has suggested, some adaptations of Shakespeare are copyrighted. Sonia Massai has explained why what she calls Pier Paolo Pasolini's 'groundbreaking appropriation' of *Othello*, *Che Cosa Sono Le Nuvole?* (1967), remains unsung and unknown among Shakespeareans: a copyright dispute prevented its release for many years (2005; the film now exists, officially or not, in multiple clips on YouTube and as a recording on Vimeo, as Lauren Shohet observes [2010: 72]). Greenaway's *Prospero's Books*, which I discussed in Chapter 1, languished in a similar limbo for many years.

Frustrating though such delays and disputes are for teachers, viewers, and artists, the fact that one cannot freely share, reuse, and remix artistic works that appropriate Shakespeare to make new creative works (unless we seek permission or unless the works are shared under a Creative Commons licence) provides further evidence that readers, writers, and Shakespeare 'users' (Fazel and Geddes 2011) consider adaptations – including adaptations of Shakespeare and other kinds of classical literature – to be works in their own right, not merely derivatives. A market-driven society measures creativity by profit. Even seemingly 'free' downloads or shares on websites or social media sites come with a price, overt or covert. As the contemporary proverb has it, when something on the internet is free, you are not the customer; you (that is, your data, your attention, and even your emotions) are the product.

One might counter with the example of Creative Commons and user-generated content, such as uploaded film clips and commentary on YouTube, or the fan-sourced and maintained domain fandom.com (a rich repository of original research, factual information, wild speculation, and insider information about almost any contemporary popular television show or film in the US). Some Creative Commons sites are underwritten by user communities who pay (in labour and in cash) to support the creation and maintenance of the site, but also by advertisers who mine viewers' hard drives, desires, and time for profit. And even many non-profit, user-supported, advertising-free fan sites or Creative Commons sites are hosted on Amazon Web Services, a company that again monetizes human data, usually without our knowledge or understanding. In this way even user-generated performances, ideas, and material engage in a complex transactional appropriation, an 'exchange that is two-directional, even if not always equitable to all parties' (Desmet and Iyengar 2015: 13). Even the high-definition platform Vimeo, to which content uploaders and creators pay to upload videos and viewers watch ad-free, has now adopted a few paid subscriptions for content-creators to 'monetize' their videos with advertisements so that companies can appropriate the attention of their viewers.

# Property

For Marx, appropriation enabled capital, the 'self-expanding value. . .[that]. . .is essentially the process of reproducing value and producing new value' (Fine and Saad-Filho 2016: 48). Workers produce labour-power, but need to exchange their labour for cash money to pay for what they need to live.

The capitalist begins with a store of money (the benefit of 'primitive accumulation' or inherited wealth or status) that allows them to pay workers just enough while retaining or appropriating enough surplus value that they can continue to accrue more money capital and more productive capital. 'The social relation that is capital successively assumes and relinquishes the forms of money, productive capital and commodities' – commodities that are then purchased and consumed by workers in the unending 'circuit of industrial capital' (Fine and Saad-Filho 2016: 48). In a late-capitalist economy, capital is a relationship of exchange rather than one of what Marx called 'primitive accumulation' or the acquisition of inherently valuable *stuff*. Workers *produce*; bosses *appropriate*; owners *accumulate*.

For example, this book is being written in the USA and, depending on global politics, may be edited in the UK before being typeset in Chennai and printed in China. The typesetters and printers will be paid a wage that they will exchange for the commodities that they need to live (in Marxian terms, they have been *alienated* from the means of subsistence – divorced from the ability for self-sufficiency). Even subtracting workers' wages, however (and any royalties to which the author might be entitled), will still leave the publisher with a profit from sales. If Bloomsbury were a co-operative, owned by its members, these profits would be ploughed back into the business and distributed equally to its authors, editors, designers, typesetters, and printers worldwide. Since Bloomsbury is a public limited company (plc) – an investor-owned business – profits go not towards workers but to shareholders, who have invested their capital in shares of the company.

But Marx disavows neither appropriation nor property. Rather, he acknowledges the psychic pull of property as something that we appropriate to ourselves as extensions of selfhood. Such 'personal appropriation', writes Marx, and human labour, should not be used merely to perpetuate 'a bare existence', a 'miserable...appropriation through which the worker only lives to increase capital, and only insofar as it suits the interests of the ruling class' (Marx [1848] 1996: 14–17). Rather, any 'accumulated labor' – or surplus value – should be used, he suggests, 'to broaden, to enrich, to promote the whole life of the worker' (Marx [1848] 1996: 14–17). Appropriation encompasses the fruits of our labour and a multi-dimensional exchange with varying levels of equity and empowerment (Desmet and Iyengar 2015: 13); we are thus Shakespeare users or even 'prosumers', producers and consumers (Fuchs 2016: 57).

# Theft

M. J. Kidnie helpfully argues that stage productions are already adaptations and thus infused with critics' and audience members' concerns about their 'legitima[cy]' or what is or isn't 'Shakespeare' (2009). She then extends her argument to suggest that 'Shakespeare's works can, logically, never be made free of their adaptations'; that Shakespearean works themselves contain their own potential undoing or perceived illegitimacy; and that Shakespeare's 'work is pragmatically known through production' (2009: 65). In production, Shakespeare's dark-skinned character Othello was predominantly played by a white actor in skin-darkening make-up, that is, wearing what we now would call blackface. The production history of *Othello* therefore enmeshes both play and character in the tradition of blackface minstrelsy or cultural appropriation.

The phrase *cultural appropriation* was first used in the 1940s to mean 'the unacknowledged or inappropriate adoption of the practices, customs, or aesthetics of one social or ethnic group by members of another (typically dominant) community or society' (*OED*, 'cultural', compounds). A Google Ngram search of word frequency (Figure 2.1) suggests that it was used between 1930–90 mostly to connote another sense of 'appropriation': Congress's allocation of funds to arts organizations. From the 1990s to the 2000s art critics began to

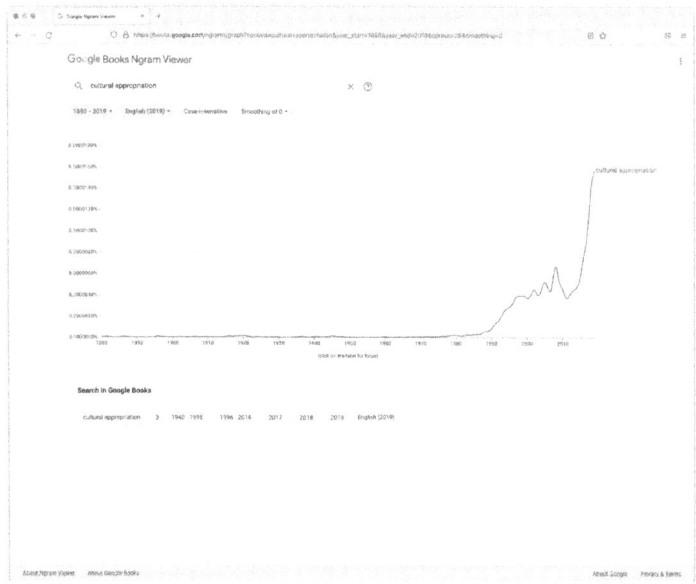

**FIGURE 2.1** *Google Books Ngram search, http://books.google.com/ngrams, 'cultural appropriation'. Screen capture by the author, 1 November 2021.*

use the term to describe the looting of artefacts from Asia and Africa by Western museums. And in 2011 usage of the term dips before suddenly rising exponentially in a true 'hockey stick' curve.

At the time of writing (2021), the phrase connotes an argument that when members of a dominant or more powerful group in a given society try, consciously or unconsciously, to imitate or to claim aspects of the perceived appearance, cultural practices, or ancestry of minoritized groups in that society (through the use of cosmetics, prosthetics, and bodily modifications, subtle or vulgar, to change one's skin-tone, facial features, or hair-style; through fashion, food, and music choices; through speech patterns and vocabulary; through concealing or denying their ancestry in public), such persons are engaging in a kind of psychic theft. Tensions surrounding the phrase stem from the range and scale of activities to which it has been applied, from the openly white supremacist blackface impersonation of the minstrel show (Thompson 2021) to the ambiguously motivated subterfuge of the college instructor born to white parents who 'passes' as Black (Bey 2020) to the ignorant imitation of an admired person (Davis and Smalls 2021) and even to the exercise of professional expertise over cultural contexts (an actor playing a role on stage; an author voicing a character [Sánchez Prado 2021]; a scholar analyzing a literature).

While a few activists argue that one's intentions are moot – what matters is 'impact, not intent' – most of us can recognize and acknowledge differences in motivation and outcome among these activities (Lenard and Balint 2020). Scholars, writers, and readers will continue to extend their minds by engaging with art that is distant from our own time, place, and experience, including through emulation and discussion. Actors will continue to use their voices, bodies, intellects, and imaginations to incarnate characters with which they might share little lived experience. At the same time, the critique of some appropriative activities forces us to acknowledge that the supposed power to ignore these inequities is itself based on privilege available to only relatively few. Blackface performances of *Othello* provide some of the most egregious instances of this kind of unequal or forced collaboration.

Blackface makeup originated in medieval Europe, where actors in mystery plays and Morris dancers blackened their faces to imitate sinful demons or ghouls (Chambers 1933: 1.195–204), embodying the conceptual metaphor good/light; bad/dark. During the age of exploration, early colonialism, and the nascent slave trade, late medieval and early modern performers began to map this ancient tradition on to the newer practice of impersonating parodic or exaggerated versions of the Black and Brown peoples they encountered in the Old and New Worlds (Iyengar 2006: 87). Such actors used many different means to mimic their scripted Moors, Indians, and other characters deemed exotic or racially other.

At the height of the transatlantic slave trade, blackface minstrelsy emerged on both sides of the Atlantic as a mocking, comic form that purported to expose the supposed naïveté, stupidity, vulgarity or other undesirable features of enslaved and freed Black people. Crucially, however, as Ayanna Thompson points out, in both the blackface performance tradition and the blackface minstrel show, white actors used racial prosthetics and the performance of blackness to showcase their supposed virtuosity, even as Black people were thought unable to act as anything other than themselves and their bodies were exploited and displayed for profit (Thompson 2021: 52). Thompson argues that even the purported love or admiration that its blacked-up proponents claim to be demonstrating removes the power of self-realization and self-presentation – even of access to 'authenticity' – from living Black people. It is in this historic and contemporary context that Shakespeare's *Othello*, with its gullible, fallible, blackened hero; its malignant anti-hero named, as Sears reminds us, for the historic Santiago 'Matamoros' or Saint James the Killer of Moors; and the 'ordinary white woman' (Rapetti and Sears 2018: 299, 304) around whose unwilling body men murder each other and themselves has taken on the force of myth.

Returning to the rediscovered painting by Marc Chagall with which I began this chapter can allow us to unpack some of these nuances. Chagall himself was Jewish and lovingly incorporated aspects of Jewish folklore into his art. Having suffered through pogroms during his youth in Imperial Russia, hunger, and poverty in Bolshevik Russia, he narrowly escaped from collaborationist Vichy during the Nazi era. His 'Othello' dates from 1911, an early period of his career, his first stint in Paris. Later, he would paint himself and his beloved wife Bella as an archetype – the young lovers, often floating in the sky – as in his much-later 'Romeo and Juliet' (1964). 'Romeo and Juliet' features other signatures of his vivid style: landmarks (in this case, the Arc de Triomphe and the Paris Opéra, for whose ceiling he painted the original image); bright colours; animals, especially the horse and the goat; floating bunches of flowers; and the childlike humour with which the whole is infused.

'Othello', as befits its subject matter, is quite different, although even its dark palette is lightened with the bright reds and yellows from the off-stage candle that illuminates the reclining Desdemona, and Othello himself wears particoloured (red and black) hose. Desdemona's posture anticipates the pose of the bride in the later paintings, displayed to the viewer, but where Chagall's more typical young wives are cradled, embraced, and beloved by their partners, his Desdemona lies alone. Where Desdemona's features are brightly lit and recognizable, Othello's are shrouded in darkness, his nose an impressionistic grey line. Othello stands behind a curtain that is both the bed-curtain shielding Desdemona and the curtains of the stage. The painting thus exposes to the viewer the structure Vanessa Corredera (2020) has dubbed the 'white racial frame of *Othello*': an active, weaponed, blackened man is – in this case literally – 'framed' or staged as threatening a passive, nude, white woman.[1]

The white racial frame, together with the history of slavery and colonialism, has permeated what Sharon P. Holland calls 'the erotic life of racism' in the West (2012), imbricating sexual and racial violence to such an extent that many women playwrights and adaptors of colour (men and women) find it impossible to represent Othello and Desdemona together. Paula Vogel's alternately farcical and poignant *Desdemona: or, a Play About a Handkerchief* ([1994] 1996) excludes all the men, limiting the cast to three women – the aristocratic lady of leisure Desdemona, the Irish maidservant Emilia, and the Cockney sex-worker Bianca. Without altering the outlines of the plot, Vogel radically alters the characters' language and motivation. These women are more complex than Shakespeare's, if not necessarily more admirable. Vogel's sexually voracious Desdemona hungers for experience, substituting for Bianca in the brothel, and relishes her encounters with dozens of men.

Vogel's embittered Emilia complains about her husband's sexual inadequacy, having married Iago only because she could see no other way to gain a measure of autonomy or power; she seeks his promotion for her own interest as much as for his. Bianca enjoys her independence but, to Desdemona's chagrin, admits to desiring marriage and monogamy with Cassio. Desdemona is a class-conscious snob who exploits Emilia's labour; Emilia is a religious zealot who shuns the sinning Bianca; Bianca joins Emilia in racist jokes at Othello's expense; all three drink to excess. And yet despite these women's complexity, the plot unspools as written: Othello still suspects Desdemona with Cassio, Cassio still gives the handkerchief to Bianca, and Desdemona still dies strangled in her bed. Even without the men on stage, and even with their individuality on full display, Vogel's heroines cannot escape the ritualized marital violence of Shakespeare's play.

Where, like Vogel, Morrison and Traouré chose to exclude Othello from their *Desdemona* (2012), however, Sears and the Q Brothers remove not Othello but Desdemona from the stage. Morrison and Traouré, Sears, and the Q Brothers use the very structure of adaptation – repetition with difference – to remake *Othello* in the Black musical traditions of the griots of Mali (*Desdemona*), the blues (*Harlem Duet*) and hip hop (*Othello: The Remix*). All three address and redress the deep structure of psychic theft identified by Fanon in *Black Skin, White Masks* (2008 [1952]) and further described by Bhabha as 'colonial mimicry' or 'ambivalence' or 'a double articulation; a complex strategy of reform, regulation, and discipline, which "appropriates" the Other as it visualizes power' (1984: 126).

# Appropriation as revisioning: *Othello* without Othello (and Desdemona)

Fanon identified the psychological state of the colonized subject as a process of fundamental self-alienation. With no way to express his identity except through the medium of whiteness, argues Fanon, the colonized subject imitates or takes on aspects of whiteness in order to recreate a lost wholeness or integrity. This 'mimicry', as Bhabha later suggested, can never achieve a union of black skin/white mask, in part because the colonized subject will always be recognized by the dominating group as other or alien through its '*difference that is almost the same, but not quite*' (Bhabha 1984: 126; emphasis original). Yet this appropriation of the dominant culture by the colonized produces a '*menac[ing] mimicry*' that offers a 'double vision' of authority (Bhabha 1984: 129): if the original cannot be imitated successfully, is there an original there at all? What is being appropriated? Are white European men themselves imitators? (Notice the echoes of our earlier discussion of Shakespearean adaptation or appropriation: adapting, and even editing or performing, Shakespeare reminds us that there is no 'authentic' Shakespeare there.)

Fanon invaluably countered the pernicious belief that blackness was inherently pathological by drawing attention to the historical and social conditions of colonialism and slavery that damaged both black and white. His account spoke, however, mostly to 'native elites or those colonised individuals who were educated within, and to some extent invited to be mobile within, the colonial system' (Loomba 2009: 147). Morrison and Traouré pay attention to the groups elided by Fanon – women, and those colonized who do not belong to the educated class. Their incandescent *Desdemona* removes Othello and Iago from the stage in order to foreground the relationships among black and white women of different social classes before and after death. The actress playing Desdemona voices both Othello and Cassio, in dialogue with songs written by Malian lyricist Traouré.

The play foregrounds international, intercultural, and intergenerational connections among women. Desdemona, Emilia, and Barbary, the maidservant (or 'slave', as Morrison's text bluntly points out [2012: 45]) who provided (in Morrison and Traouré's work) the only loving mothering the young Desdemona knew (Carney 2014), meet, converse, and reconcile in an afterlife where, they sing, 'We will never die again' (Morrison and Traouré 2012: 49). Just as Morrison's Desdemona rejects her ill-omened name, so Traouré's young women rewrite an African proverb, 'your bridal veil will be your funeral shroud' (Sellars 2012: 10), about the 'Dongori' or cloth-of-thorns. Othello's and Desdemona's grieving mothers meet after death, forgive each other, and together follow the custom of Soun, Othello's mother, and her people in 'build[ing]...an altar to the spirits who are waiting to console' them (Morrison and Traouré 2012: 27). *Desdemona*'s Othello, spoken and sung by Desdemona and the musicians, recounts his hairsbreadth 'scapes in the proud 'griot tradition...of...Segou and Timbuktu' (Sellars 2012: 10).

Notably, *Desdemona* minimizes the lost handkerchief or missing token, the 'dirty handkerchief', as Cassio, a 'dissolute' and shallow opportunist, describes it (Morrison and Traouré 2012: 52). Rather, the 'ignorant sin' that Desdemona has committed (*Othello* 4.2.71) is one of omission: she acknowledges that her obliviousness to her race and rank blinded her to the truth about her own life. Faced with Desdemona's angry judgement for her failure to intervene, Emilia accuses Desdemona of treating her as 'someone beneath [her] class which takes devotion for granted', oblivious to the 'desperate...life...[of] the truly orphaned', with which Desdemona concurs, 'I should have been more understanding' (Morrison and Traouré 2012: 42–44). Barbary asks Desdemona to acknowledge her true name (Sa'ran) and her status as slave 'with no rank in [Desdemona's] world' (48) even as the two women acknowledge and value the genuine love and loving kindness with which they treated each other.

Othello blames Desdemona for loving 'the exotic foreigner who kills for the state' and his 'strange story' (50–51) and for her idealized wish for a 'bleached, ultra-civilized soul framed in blood' (51). Morrison and Traouré's absent Othello was conscripted as a child soldier and participated in a horrific rape; it is this crime that binds him and Iago 'for ever' (*Othello* 3.3.482). But as Othello and Desdemona speak frankly after death, they learn that there is still a future for human love, a 'passionate peace' in which 'We will be judged by how well we love' (Morrison and Traouré 2012: 56).

Just as Morrison and Traouré drew from West African traditions, so Sears 'cleansed' the theatre and adopted the First Nations practice of 'smudg[ing]...the space' of the theatre before beginning to rehearse her 'prequel' to *Othello*, *Harlem Duet* (Rapetti and Sears 2018: 310). Just as *Desdemona* moves through or beyond chronological time, so *Harlem Duet* is set in three eras: the 1990s (Harlem, New York, in the present day at the time the play was written), the 1860s (Harlem, Georgia, right around the time of the reading of the Emancipation Proclamation in the United States) and the 1920s (the flourishing of Black life and culture in the Harlem Renaissance). In these three eras, two lovers court, kiss, fight, make up, torture one another, and set the tragic outcome of Shakespeare's play in motion – but these two lovers are Othello/He/Him and Billie/She/Her, Othello's first wife. Desdemona is 'Miss Dessy', the white mistress with whom Othello remains out of misguided loyalty in the 1860s when his wife Billie flees to freedom in Canada, and 'Mona', a white woman in the subsequent decades. Sears herself imagined the play giving voice to the ghost of a forgotten woman, much as Morrison would (Kidnie 2009: 71).

Sears rejects the term *appropriation*, 'because these classical texts are things that are force-fed to us as children whether we like it or not [as]...part of a kind of colonization' (Rapetti and Sears 2018: 300). She deliberately moves out of time, causality, and plot to create 'a single story narrated in pieces in three times' that is also 'three independent sequences of events' (Kidnie 2009: 78). If we call this an appropriation, we do so only in Bhabha's sense of 'menac[ing]...mimicry' (1984: 129). Its structure, Sears has written, 'embraces discernible blues qualities that assert tendencies of "antiphonal structures" (that is, call and response), repetition, syncopation, fragmentation, solos, polyrhythmic improvisation, percussive melodies, hollers, scatting, ring shouts, and cyclicality' (Sears 2018). In other words, its repetition with difference provides space for original expression and interaction within a pre-set structure that at any moment threatens to disintegrate.

Sears' Othello feels that he is owed the right to be treated as a full human being, that essential integrity reft from him by colonialism and racism. In this way, Othello's decisions to remain with Miss Dessy or to abandon Billie for Mona demonstrate Fanon's model of colonized subjectivity (Dickinson 2002). Othello/He/Him is variously an enslaved man, a Black minstrel-show performer, and a university lecturer, in an astringent commentary on the different economic and psychic forms that colonial mimicry can take. This debased identity turns Billie/She/Her into a murderer or a madwoman, 'every living moment of [her] life…eaten up with thinking about [white people]', as her landlady Magi observes (Sears 1997: 103). Recall Thompson's suggestion (2021) that blackface makeup expropriates from people of colour our sense of selfhood or authenticity. 'You're so busy reacting, you don't even know yourself', Magi warns Billie (Sears 1997: 103). Can you represent yourself or only a person as represented through white-dominated media, performance, and culture? Can you escape from a hall of mirrors where all you see are reflections?

Aware of these concerns surrounding Othello's representation, Orson Welles presciently filmed his *Othello* (1951) in black-and-white, wearing minimal make-up as the titular character. The film foregrounds Othello interacting with mirrors at crucial moments where Othello questions his self-knowledge and Desdemona's love for him, most frequently after a conversation with Iago. Othello sees himself darkened in the mirror, both alone and when Iago looks over his shoulder and Othello imagines Desdemona's (in the second Quarto) and his own (in the Folio) 'fresh' name and visage 'begrimed and black / As [his] own face' (*Othello* 3.3. 389–91). Later he glimpses Desdemona's reflection on a staircase in a mirror that also reflects him. Welles darkens the lighting when Desdemona appears as a faint flash of white in the reflected mirror (to such an extent that the image is not legibly reproducible in these pages) to indicate that Othello can no longer see Desdemona as she is, nor himself, only a reflection of a reflection, only through Iago's (and the camera's) distorting lens.

The voices of Magi, Billie's landlady, and her father, Canada, remind us that Black communities can and do live in love and joy – but not Othello/He/Him and Billie/She/Her, nor Othello and Miss Dessy/Mona. Billie nearly shoves a man and a woman she thinks are Othello and Mona underneath a subway train before realizing in horror that '[i]t isn't even [them]' (Sears 1997: 44). Othello internalizes the conservative politics of his white colleagues and blames affirmative action, not racism, for the fact that those colleagues don't listen to him (53), and black women for the anger that, he complains, contaminates even the bedroom (70–71), a discussion that anticipates Jeremy Harris's much-later and highly controversial *Slave Play* (2020), which is arguably haunted by *Othello* without ever mentioning it. *Harlem Duet* ends with Billie in a mental hospital and Othello confiding in his closest colleague – a white man named Chris Yago.

In a very different register from either *Desdemona* or *Harlem Duet*, *Othello: The Remix* makes hip hop not an addendum to Othello's story but fundamental to both its premise and its presentation. Carla Della Gatta deftly explains that 'hip hop is. . .a contested discursive strategy. . .[bearing] the legacies of African folk storytelling, New York DJs. . .[,] graffiti artists of Latinx and Latin descent, urban vernacular and. . .global corporate culture' (2020: 77). Commissioned for the 2012 Globe to Globe Festival, 'the only play in spoken English heard on the Globe stage during the Festival' (Della Gatta 2020: 76), the Q Brothers' adaptation foregrounded the ways gender and race intersect in the US to make women's bodies invisible beyond the racial frame.

*Othello: The Remix* uses varieties of hip hop to characterize its players. Othello is a 'modern day hip hop mogul' who has risen from humble beginnings to build an empire and Desdemona, the daughter of a US Senator, 'a powerful soul singer' whose tenderness modulates Othello's 'hardcore' rap style and who appears only as 'a disembodied voice'. Cassio is an 'entertain[er]' drawn to a more popular sound, Iago a 'hip hop purist' who loathes both Othello's mixed soul-rap sound and Cassio's bubblegum studio sound (Q Brothers 2018: 4). The Q Brothers themselves are biracial, and Othello was played by a Black actor, Postell Pringle. Della Gatta acutely observes that all characters use different versions of African American Language (AAL). Bianca speaks a 'Spanish-accented English' while Othello speaks a subtly different version of AAL from the rest of his crew, even 'needing. . .verbal clarification' at a key moment (Della Gatta 2020: 82). The handkerchief became the heavy gold chain associated with hip hop and rap stars. All embodied female roles, including Emilia, Bianca, and some 'Backup Girl [singers]' were performed in drag, often for comedy (Figure 2.2).

FIGURE 2.2 *Jeffery Quaiyum, Postell Pringle, and Gregory Quaiyum as Female Backup Singers, Othello: The Remix. Image © Steve Reynolds/CultureWorks.*

Despite or perhaps because of the fast, witty, contemporary delivery, direct address, and the expert use of comic timing throughout the show, Desdemona's murder was wrenching. As Othello intermittently punches and squeezes Desdemona's absent body, figured as a white pillow upon an empty bed, the sound – produced by a live DJ on the upper stage – is muffled on every blow, and the entire cast convulses. When Othello pauses, the cast extends their bodies as the sound returns. In this way the musical demonstrates how *Othello* is both a deeply personal and a profoundly social tragedy. The only scene in which Shakespeare's audience sees Othello and Desdemona alone in private is the murder scene (5.2): we never see their love outside society's racial frame – and, ultimately, nor can Othello himself.

I have demonstrated how the metaphor of appropriation connotes both the just and unjust seizure of private and public goods (and 'good'). My next chapter turns to another tragedy – *King Lear* – to investigate metaphors of kinship in adaptation studies. Adaptations of *Lear* can question Lear's own conception of his daughters as property and reimagine familial relationship as driven by ethics and affinity rather than by a logic of blood and soil.

# 3

# Fidelity, families, ethics: Derivatives

While my previous chapter addressed adaptation as theft and property as intellectual capital, I consider here – with *King Lear* as my test-case – more intimate transfers of property through the historical tradition of scholarly editing and through the metaphor of lineal or genetic inheritance. Within editorial theory, scholars have discussed not just the ideal text, nor even just the authorial text, but the idea that texts, including adaptations, are offspring of varying legitimacy, members of shifting and vagrant bibliographic families. Late twentieth-century and contemporary editors often challenge the early modern presentation of certain books as legitimate children and others as 'bastard' offspring, overturning, like *King Lear*'s Edmund, the historical legal and social framework in which the 'legitimate' may be entitled (literally, to property and the ability to pass on a family name; figuratively, to love and personal acceptance into that family) where the 'illegitimate' are not. For instance, Gary Taylor argues pugnaciously that all textual critics and '[e]ditors are...pimps of discourse' who prostitute texts for profit or 'cultural authority' (1997: 7) and, in the case of Shakespearean editions, breeding new texts from jaded old ones with dubious regard for whether those reproductions can trace their antecedents to legitimate or illegitimate (however we understand those terms) origins.

Working within the master-metaphor *ideas are children* and that *ideas are writing*, critics and editors have historically extended the figure to 'children are books' and 'books are children' (with all the caveats that such metaphors present for dramatic literature, conceived for stage rather than page). I will begin this chapter by outlining the Freudian framework (popularized as the 'anxiety of influence' by Harold Bloom, [1973] 1997) and the long editorial history and debates that foreground the relationship among fidelity, marriage, and the inheritance of property before considering Genette's figure of the 'palimpsest' or over-written manuscript and its role in contemporary editorial theory.

The final theoretical section of this chapter brings into discussion the role of ethics in adaptation. What do we 'owe' to Shakespeare, to each other, and to readers and audiences? In recent explorations, the ethics of adaptation becomes a rejection of the turbulent family romance in favour of voluntary, considered, and politically nuanced relations, such as collaboration, in all its senses (Henderson 2006); unconventional marriage (Cloud [Randall McLeod] 1982, tongue-in-cheek); 'corrupt' or 'contaminated' families (Greetham 1995, also tongue-in-cheek); humbled and mutually dependent 'hostages' (Joubin and Rivlin 2014, via Emmanuel Levinas [1961] 1991); or, in Taarini Mookherjee's recent intervention, neighbourhood relations, both circumstantially or externally enforced and locally or personally inhabited (2019). Adaptations I will discuss along the way and in conclusion include Nahum Tate's play ([1681] 1965), which superseded both folio and quarto editions of *Lear* in the eighteenth century; the 1986 Gary Taylor and Stanley Wells Oxford editions, which put two separate texts of *King Lear* in print for the first time since the seventeenth century quarto and folio versions; and Kristian Levring's *The King is Alive* ([2000] 2001), a film that fragments *Lear* in a post-colonial context while attempting to reproduce it.

# Fidelity

Harold Bloom's germinal account of literary influence ([1973] 1997) casts adaptation in Freud's Oedipal model, which Freud called the 'family romance'. Within Freud's fable, the male child, identified with and cathected to his mother, suddenly made aware that his mother lacks male genitalia, fears that his father has 'castrated' his mother and that a similar fate looms ahead for him (the so-called castration complex) – unless he can murder his father first, and keep his mother's attention for himself alone (the so-called Oedipus complex). Feminist and postcolonial critiques of Freud's model appeared from both within and without psychoanalytic criticism (Irigaray [1977] 1985; Fanon [1952] 1967), even as psychoanalytic criticism continued to inspire the vocabulary and analysis of these modes and to dominate film studies in the twentieth century.

Bloom's account of adaptation maps the Freudian family romance on to literary influence: a (paternal) strong precursor invites from (male) literary offspring (dubbed 'ephebes' by Bloom, after youthful Greek warriors) a series of revolts against the powerful father, assaults that range from 'poetic misprision' to 'daemonization or the counter-sublime' ([1973] 1997: 99 and *passim*). Sandra Gilbert and Susan Gubar's influential *The Madwoman in the Attic* (1979) both critiques and extends Bloom's male-centred model of adaptation; rather than an 'anxiety of influence', they suggest, women authors suffer an 'anxiety of authorship' or doubts about their own ability to create a tradition of their own, since history and the male-dominated editorial and literary tradition has limited access to the work of their literary foremothers.

Such critiques fostered only resistance in Bloom, whose later work, and especially his popular book about Shakespeare, dismisses feminist, postcolonial, and new historicist or cultural materialist work as 'School of Resentment criticism' (1998, *passim*). Instead, Bloom enshrines an idealized, universal human subject 'invent[ed]' by none other than Shakespeare and embodied in its most otherworldly form by King Lear – the latter a 'touchstone for the sublime' (1998: 512). 'Resentment' critics all fail, according to Bloom, to appreciate the transcendence of Lear, and in doing so, they have 'abandon[ed] a part of our own capacity for significant emotion' (1998: 513). Many of us similarly resisted, for the most part, Bloom's notion of Shakespeare, divorced as it was from theatre history, and from all readers but Bloom himself (Hawkes 2002; Charnes 2002; O'Dair 2002). Nevertheless, as Desmet points out in her chapter in *Harold Bloom's Shakespeare* (2002), Shakespeareans continue to find appealing the idea of character or personality in Shakespeare and of fidelity to a Shakespearean text and the analysis of what such fidelity might mean or entail (even if 'fidelity' to a concept, to a perception of character, or to a desired audience response might necessitate textual 'infidelity' such as cutting or adaptation). Even Jane Smiley, whose extraordinary retelling of *King Lear* in the novel *A Thousand Acres* (1991) enabled a generation of Shakespeareans completely to rethink our understanding of the play, seemed to retract her own interpretation, albeit with limits (1998).

# Families: *Lear* among the editors

In 2016, British and North American newspapers reported gleefully on a Shakespearean family drama unfolding on Twitter within the abstruse world of scholarly editing. University of Toronto professor Holger Syme, assuming only a handful of people would follow his Twitter feed, live-tweeted his notes towards a review of *éminence grise* Brian Vickers' controversial book *The One King Lear* (2016a), eventually producing more than 500 tweets – and finding himself the unwilling centre of a viral media story. Author and reviewer accused each other of shoddy scholarship and bad faith, often quite amusingly, on Twitter and in the more formal pages of the *LA Review of Books* (Syme 2016a; Vickers 2016b; Syme 2016b). Press coverage expressed astonishment at the heat of the disputation (Reisz 2016), but Shakespeareans instantly recognized the stakes. Samuel Schoenbaum observed in *Shakespeare's Lives* (1991) that anti-Stratfordians (those who believe, mistakenly and despite the documentary record, that William Shakespeare did not write the plays attributed to him in the Folio, or perhaps any plays at all) enact a version of Freud's Oedipal drama.

In a similar manner, battles about textual fidelity and about the universality of Shakespeare, Shakespeare's genius, and so on engender generational wars among critics that come to resemble the bitter feuds and broken family bonds within *King Lear* itself. To make sense of these disputes, we need to venture briefly across the contested territory of Shakespearean textual scholarship, which asks who contributed (as author, publisher, printer, actor) to the early texts that we have and how they came to appear in print. As Lotte Hellinga (to whom my summary below is indebted) writes, until the end of the seventeenth century, 'texts were split up into building blocks to be assembled during production. Books were perceived by their makers as structures in which intellectual content had no more than a secondary part' (2019: 382–3), and the accuracy of early modern printed books depends upon how, by whom, and where the book was printed.

The multi-step early modern printing process took several stages. 'Compositors', consulting their copy-text, took sorts (single pieces of lead type) from an upper and a lower case of type (giving us the terms 'upper-case' and 'lower-case', still in use today) and placed them in a tool known as a composing stick. This process was called 'composing' type; it required the compositor to put individual sorts in the stick upside-down and reversed, so that the text would appear right-side up and read left to right correctly when printed. Then the compositors laid each completed line of type into a 'galley' ready to 'impose' them, that is, to arrange galleys of type into pages ready for printing. Since multiple pages were printed on a single sheet, but printers didn't have an inexhaustible supply of type, they imposed pages out of reading order, so that they could 'distribute' the type and re-use it as needed. Printers had to 'cast off' or anticipate how much space they would need for each page, usually by counting lines and by estimating. (Printing multiple pages on a single sheet also minimized the necessary sewing it would take to bind the book.)

*King Lear* exists in both Quarto (1608) and Folio (1623; henceforth I will refer to the Quarto version as the 'Historie' and the Folio version as the 'Tragedie'). A quarto is a small, unbound booklet made by folding a sheet into quarters, hence the name; eighteen of the plays now attributed to Shakespeare first appeared in this form. Quartos, in general, were rushed out quickly after a play's initial performance – Lucas Erne (2003) suggests that most found their way into print within two years of a play's first production – in order to capitalize upon the play's popularity in the theatre. The Folio is the larger-format, illustrated, bound and expensive volume of Shakespeare's collected works published by Shakespeare's colleagues John Heminges and Henry Condell in 1623. Eighteen of the thirty-six plays in the Folio appear only in that volume. (The first Folio excludes two collaborative plays now considered Shakespearean: *Pericles* and *The Two Noble Kinsmen*, presumably because Heminges and Condell could not find copies they considered accurate enough for the press or because they had difficulties obtaining the rights.)

In itself the fact that *Lear* exists as 'Historie' and 'Tragedie' might not concern us, but for the major differences between the two versions, Quarto and Folio. The change in title might simply reflect changing fashions; 'tragedies' were increasingly popular in the early seventeenth century where 'histories' had become unfashionable. Yet the 'Historie', on the one hand, includes scenes missing from the 'Tragedie', including a poignant scene of Lear's madness, in which he fantasizes that a pair of jointed stools are his daughters and that he is putting them on trial; a moment of humanity where servants risk their lives to bind up Gloucester's bleeding eyes; Kent describing Cordelia in sainted terms; Cordelia bringing a 'Doctor' to aid her father. The 'Tragedie', on the other, includes Cordelia entering with French troops (*sans* Doctor), and several lines that are not present in the 'Historie', cumulatively giving Edgar and Cordelia stronger parts and Albany and Kent weaker ones, while changing Lear's final lines in a way that potentially alters the character's entire trajectory (does Lear die happy, but deluded, believing Cordelia to be alive? Is it more or less upsetting for the audience to have Lear die deceived or to have him die in the full knowledge of his daughters' death? The 'Tragedie' raises such questions). Which text should editors pick? Or should they combine them? The answers depend upon each editor's ethic of editing.

Eighteenth-century Shakespeare editions did not distinguish among quarto texts and folio texts, nor were they especially concerned to reprint what Shakespeare might have written, what might have been presented on stage, nor what an early text might have printed, as Margreta De Grazia has documented (1991). Modern Shakespeare editing, including our concerns about authenticity, accuracy, correctness, objectivity and so on, began with Edmund Malone in 1790, De Grazia suggests, and continued through the nineteenth-century editions of the Cambridge, Oxford, and Arden Shakespeare series. Following the rise of the 'New Bibliography', most closely associated with the illustrious bibliographer W.W. Greg, through the twentieth century, Shakespeareans began to distinguish between 'good' and 'bad' quartos: 'bad' quartos contained texts widely variant from the Folio texts, including differences in speech allocation, characters' names, lineation, and sometimes additional or omitted scenes. New Bibliographers speculated that such texts were compiled by secret short-hand writers in the theatre or former actors' 'memorial reconstruction' and that the printers had failed to obtain a legitimate copy-text; 'in contrast, the 'good' quartos, properly entered in the [*Stationers'*] *Register*, offered 'good' texts based on manuscripts that publishers had legitimately purchased from the acting company that owned them' (Werstine 2010: 114). 'Good' copy came from 'foul papers', 'fair copies', 'scribal copies', or a 'prompt-book'. Greg took the Elizabethan phrase 'foul papers', meaning a draft, to connote a text straight from the hand of the author and intended for use by a printer as copy-text. A 'fair copy' came from the author or from a professional scribe, who might also produce a 'scribal copy'. Contentiously, Greg hypothesized the existence of lost 'prompt-books' from Shakespeare's time, printed or manuscript texts marked up for use by the actors' company, analogous to the late seventeenth-century and eighteenth-century prompt-books that we still have.

Heminges and Condell arguably began the critical tendency to devalue quartos when they addressed 'the great variety of readers' in the Folio and promised to protect them from 'stolen, and surreptitious' or even 'maimed' versions of the plays, a claim that most scholars now believe to have been an advertising ploy for the new book rather than a reflection of the value of the quartos (Heminges and Condell 1623, quoted in Werstine 2010: 114). Shakespeare editing likewise had to contend with both Malone's idealized quest for authenticity, for what he called 'Shakespeare Verbatim', and the nineteenth-century crowning of King Shakespeare, in Thomas Carlyle's paean (Sawyer 2003: 52–3). Carlyle's influential lecture ([1841] 2007) exemplifies the reverence in which some Victorian Bardolaters (Shakespeare-worshippers) held the 'great soul' who 'had...to crush itself' into the Globe (179). Carlyle's Shakespeare is a 'Prophet of God' (181), whose works were worth more than the entire Indian Empire (183; Sawyer 2003: 52) even as King Shakespeare would enable England to rule over an empire of readers worldwide. Such a king, sent by divine fiat to save England, deserved to have his words rescued from the 'temporary, conventional' surroundings forced on his work by the stage (Carlyle [1841] 2007: 179).

Inheriting this bardolatrous tradition, and taking literally Heminges and Condell's claim that Shakespeare 'never blotted a line', the twentieth-century New Bibliographers thus developed a theory that an imagined true or authentic Shakespeare had been obscured by 'hard-to-read handwriting, clumsy compositors, arrogant actors, pesky prompters, and stern scribes' (Iyengar 2014b: 41). These editors wished to recreate what Shakespeare actually wrote, or even what Shakespeare might have wanted to write or meant to have written, in some cases, with more time for revision. Vickers' insistence that there is one, and only one, *King Lear* falls within this tradition: he blames the problem-beset printshop of Nicholas Okes for the textual problems in the Quarto and sets himself to reconstruct the single *Lear* that he believes Shakespeare originally to have written.

The editors of the 1986 Oxford Shakespeare, in contrast to bardolaters who believed that Shakespeare's genius – and a putative complete, lost manuscript for a single *King Lear* – had been compromised by the theatre and the printshop, dismissed 'the belief that Q and F were both defective reproductions of a single lost archetype' and argued instead that Shakespeare revised his work (Wells and Taylor 1986: 529). Striving for a different kind of fidelity – a faithfulness to an idealized performance, even down to correcting Anglicized spelling of French or Italian names – Wells and Taylor dethroned King Shakespeare, and divided up the kingdom of *Lear*, publishing the 'Historie' and the 'Tragedie' as separate texts, rather than the combined text that had dominated the previous half-century or so. In this way they finalized the divorce begun by the influential collection *The Division of the Kingdoms* (Taylor and Warren 1983), which first suggested that there were '*Two Versions of "King Lear"* (subtitle). Wells and Taylor's edition as a whole took the Folio texts – usually shorter – as more likely to be from a prompt-book and thus to be accurate representations of the plays as first performed on stage.

There is, however, little or no evidence for the existence of a prompt-book in the technical sense used by the New Bibliographers and later twentieth-century editors; Werstine argues that the term itself is a known anachronism or back-formation from the practices of the eighteenth-century theatre. Instead, Werstine's study of early playhouse manuscripts (2012) suggests that while each company had a 'theatrical manuscript' along with the 'plot' or 'platt' – a list of characters, entrances and exits for each scene of the play being performed – such theatrical supplements lacked the accuracy ascribed by traditional New Bibliographers to promptbooks. Actors themselves, we have long known, did not have copies of the entire play, only of their own parts with their cue lines. Palfrey and Stern (2007) suggest that playhouse scripts comprised actors' parts, playbills, title-pages, sheets of music, broadsides, handwritten or scribally copied manuscripts such as prologues, epilogues and all kinds of other documents; Werstine (2012) argues that a prompter or bookkeeper with a 'prodigious' memory must have used plots and the manuscript – in whatever condition and in however many pieces – to run the show.

# Ethics and editing

So should an editor try to recreate what Shakespeare might have imagined or written (the Riverside and Arden Second Series)? An idealized early modern performance at the Globe or the Blackfriars (the Oxford Shakespeare, the Cambridge Shakespeare, some Arden Third Series editions)? What an early reader might have encountered (albeit with modernized spelling, punctuation, typeface, and so on (the Folger Library Editions)? Multiple versions (Oxford *Lear*, Arden Third Series *Hamlet*)? Not only every performance, then, is an adaptation, but also every edition, as the essays in Kidnie and Massai's collection *Shakespeare and Textual Studies* (2015) argue. The mischievous 'Marriage of Good and Bad Quartos' (by Randall McLeod, writing under the spell-check-generated pseudonym 'Random Cloud') likewise pleads for texts that are (to use another of Freud's terms) polymorphously perverse rather than demurely constrained by what we think a Shakespeare play ought to look or sound like (Cloud 1982), while David Greetham discusses the pleasures of textual contamination, another illicit erotic transaction (1995). Massai even suggests (2017) that we need to reconsider how we edit Shakespeare – typically by the play, rather than by the part – especially in light of new digital interfaces that might let us remix Shakespeare in both historically accurate and interestingly innovative ways. The play thus becomes a unit of reception, rather than composition, just as, Desmet argues, an adaptation manifests as such when the reader or receiver recognizes it as such rather than because of any ontological qualities that Shakespeare shares with it (2014: 55 and *passim*).

A helpful metaphor that takes us beyond ideas of derivation and anteriority – and beyond the moralizing tone of much early editorial theory – has been used of Shakespearean adaptation and within editorial theory by Sanders, Kidnie, Massai, and others: the figure of the palimpsest, a manuscript on which the traces of former inscriptions are still visible. The figure comes, as we learned in Chapter 1, from narratologist Gérard Genette ([1982] 1997). Genette distinguishes among different degrees or kinds of textual relation, from (following Julia Kristeva [1982]), *intertextuality*, where text A explicitly quotes from or alludes to text B; *paratextuality*, the relationship of the text proper to its print surroundings, such as chapter headings, page numbers, gutters, and so on; *metatextuality*, or scholarly or critical commentary; *architextuality*, or the relationship of a given text to the larger genre to which it belongs; and *transtextuality*, or, he prefers, *hypertextuality*, 'any text uniting a text B...the *hypertext*...to an earlier text...the *hypotext*, upon which it is grafted in a metaphor that is not that of commentary' (1997: 5). We could consider Nahum Tate's adaptation of *Lear* as intertextual; Tate presents his adaptation as a 'Revival...with Alterations' ([1681] 1965: 203) and even apologizes for the fact that he has modernized the language less – 'with less Quaintness of Expression' – than his audience might wish, in order to preserve the 'Author's Style' (204).

Paratextuality, we might argue, works to tremendous effect in book artist Claire van Vliet's exquisite fine press edition of the *Tragedie* (1986), which uses the page layout and the rhythm of the page-turn to present the horrifying image of Gloucester – one eye socket empty, the other still in – as if we are looking down on him and taking his eyes out ourselves. The image appears at a moment of pause where the servant protests: for the moment of the page turn, we, like Cornwall, 'hold [our] hand' – suspended, one moment longer for Gloucester to keep his remaining eye, for the valiant servant to keep his life. But this is the 'Tragedie' – and not only does the servant die over the page, we lack even the comfort of the 'Historie' where his two fellows, influenced by him, resolve to help Gloucester, offering him flax and whites of eggs for his bleeding eyes.

The entire Twitter-storm surrounding Syme's review of Vickers, and the editorial apparatus surrounding *Lear*, exemplifies Genette's metatextuality, while a consideration of *Lear* – whichever version – in light of any of the larger literary structures to which it might belong, whether the early modern stage, tragedy, folk-tale, anti-feminist invective (McLuskie 1985), comments on the plays' architextuality. All these examples, however, could be subsumed under Genette's overarching category of hypertextuality, as could *Lear* itself, considering its own relation to the older *Leir* play (1605) that Shakespeare adapted. But hypertextual relations can include both acknowledged and unacknowledged hypotexts. A hypertextual or palimpsestic view of adaptation – in which all hypertexts offer partially erased and partially legible hypotexts and are themselves hypotexts to new hypertexts – includes adaptations of *Lear* that offer no immediate reference to Shakespeare's play but that comprise what Genette calls literature 'in the second degree'. The relationship between Jocelyn Moorhouse's 1997 film of Smiley's novel *A Thousand Acres* has such a 'second degree' relationship to *King Lear*. Anthony Hopkins' entry as Lear dragging the dead Cordelia behind him in a body bag (2018), quoted from Orson Welles' entry in the 1953 Kinescope broadcast of *King Lear* staged by Peter Brook in the United States (Franco 2021), arguably exists in a second degree from the stage direction in both the 'Historie' and the 'Tragedie': 'Enter Lear with Cordelia in his arms' (5.3.254.1).

The turn to an interpersonal perspective on adaptation, in conjunction with legal battles over cultural appropriation, moves adaptation theory into the academic territory of ethics. Diana Henderson modifies Bloom's Freudian model to suggest that we 'collaborat[e]' with prior authors, with all the caveats that, post-Second World War, 'collaboration' evokes. Dismissing both 'adaptation' and 'appropriation' as useful terms, Henderson suggests that collaboration offers a model that connotes the pleasure we derive from 'the connections among individuals' (2006: 8). Bryan Reynolds posits a 'transversal' framework, adapting from Deleuze and Guattari ideas of subjective *and* social 'becoming-other' that, he and his collaborators argue, disrupts human social organization (which, they argue, inevitable leads to hierarchy, whether such organization is 'horizontal' or 'vertical') (Reynolds 2003: 175; 66–7). The essays in Alexa Joubin and Elizabeth Rivlin's important collection *Shakespeare and the Ethics of Appropriation* (2014) likewise alert us to the human costs and benefits of appropriation and of conceiving the relationship among texts and their creators or users in personal terms.

This strand of adaptation study draws on ethical and political thinkers, such as Canadian philosopher Charles Taylor ([1990] 1994), who calls for a 'politics of recognition' that does not assimilate but respects and addresses the Other. Another important touchstone is Emmanuel Levinas's concept of social intercourse with the other through interpersonal means – most famously, the ethics of seeing the Other face-to-face ([1961] 1991). Levinas, who works from the position that both self and other are hostages, rather than thieves and usurpers, offers an ethics in which we recognize others through humility (Levinas [1961] 1991; Morgan 2011: 81). Here Genette's second-degree textual relationships resonate with Niklas Luhmann's 'second-order observation' (1993), as we shall see in Chapter 7, allowing us to engage with adaptations as we acknowledge our own limited perspective. In these explorations, the ethics of adaptation rejects the turbulent family romance in favour of voluntary, considered, and politically nuanced relations.

We can see this ethics of unpretentiousness in contemporary work on fandom (the term used for the mixed domain of fans, creators, and the mixed category of users, consumers, and producers that the portmanteau-word 'prosumers' includes). As we will discuss again in Chapters 4, 5, and 6, Kristina Busse and Karen Hellekson insist that scholars treat fan creators respectfully as collaborators rather than as objects and that we fully account for the contexts that produce this fan work (2012). Busse's later work acknowledges that many researchers are themselves fans and appreciate both the intellectual scrutiny of others and the documentation of what is often ephemeral work; she suggests that in some circumstances, the importance of documenting such work and the risk of exposing identities deliberately concealed behind pseudonyms might permit scholars to publish even in the absence of express permission from the creator (2017b). Most recently, Mookherjee (2019) has called for us to conceive of the relationship between Shakespearean and adapted text as one of neighbourhood relations, connexions that are both circumstantially or externally enforced and locally or personally inhabited.

I have suggested that battles about textual fidelity and about the universality of Shakespeare, Shakespeare's genius, and so on engender generational wars among critics that come to resemble the bitter feuds and broken family bonds within *King Lear*. Thomas Cartelli and Katherine Rowe (2007) dub these consequences 'the Lear-effect' in Kristian Levring's Dogme95 film *The King is Alive* ([2000] 2001). Defining a dramatic 'function' as 'behaviors that are integral to the working out of a dramatic design' and a dramatic 'effect' as the object, character, or situation that 'suffers or embodies the consequences' of such a function, Cartelli and Rowe define the 'Lear-effect' as 'the dislodging of a patriarchal figure from his established position of control or 'effect' of authority' and the patriarch's subsequent 'feelings of loss and inadequacy' and desire for redemption. The Lear-effect creates in turn 'a Cordelia effect' that 'forgives everything...and...recuperate[s] feminine qualities...degraded by what may be termed Goneril/ Regan functions' (2007: 154); this effect 'thus operates as an attribute...of the Lear-effect' rather than independently and renders the character 'a passive redeemer' and 'fellow victim of her sisters' unrelenting rage' (2007: 154). We can see the Lear-effect at work not only in the ways that so-called fidelity debates play out in editorial and critical debates surrounding the integrity of *King Lear* nor just in the film that Cartelli and Rowe analyze but even in how individual authors respond to their past selves.

Take, for example, Jane Smiley's 'retraction' (1998) of her acclaimed novel *A Thousand Acres* (1991). *A Thousand Acres* reimagines *Lear* from the perspective of Rose (Regan), sexually abused along with her sister Ginny (Goneril) by Larry (Lear) and silent for decades in order to protect her younger sister Caroline (Cordelia). In a speech given to the International Shakespeare Conference, Smiley describes her initial relationship with both Shakespeare and Cordelia as antagonistic, feminist, and informed by the great Icelandic family sagas. Commenting that she appreciated Shakespeare 'as a model' for investigating the world (1996: 47), Smiley compares her torturous process of adaptation to Shakespeare's own in adapting the chronicle play *Leir*, through the figure of 'two mirrors facing each other in the present moment, reflecting infinitely backward into the past and infinitely forward into the future' (1996: 56). In 1998, however, Smiley wrote that it was time, according to the title of her piece in the *Washington Post*, for 'Taking It All Back'. As Rivlin describes, Smiley, no longer understanding *King Lear* 'as a brief for the patriarchy, with the author identifying with Lear himself', argued that 'the tragedy results from a failure of vision – no one in the play, even Cordelia, ever knows what love is or where it comes from' (Smiley 1998; Rivlin 2014: 73). 'It is more your book than mine', Smiley tells her readers, a gesture that Rivlin sensitively identifies as an ethical concession. The 'traumatic' reading that Smiley disavows for herself as a relationship among text, author, and reader is one that she can only disavow for herself, not for others (Rivlin 2014). Having dethroned King Shakespeare (the Lear-effect), Smiley enacts a Cordelia-effect herself, for both Shakespeare and for her readers.

## Derivatives: *Lear*'s progeny

We finally turn to our remaining test-cases – Tate's Restoration adaptation of Shakespeare's *Lear* ([1681] 1965) and Kristian Levring's avant-garde film *The King is Alive* ([2000] 2001). Both adaptations resonate, I will suggest, with Levinas's

> claim[...] that that the human condition, intrinsically a social condition where we live together with an in interaction with other persons, has within it something that is irreducibly other. That other, which Plato thought was the Form of the Good, Plotinus the One, and Descartes the infinite and perfect God, Levinas takes to be the utterly particular other person with whom I stand face to face.
>
> MORGAN 2011: 3

Where Tate's adaptation, however, uses textual cuts and explanatory addenda to encourage audiences to 'admire, but not to identify with' the suffering characters (Massai 2000: 445), Levring's film uses cinematic cuts to challenge our ethical, embodied humanity more radically, by refusing to follow the classical Hollywood framing of the face and by offering us the Levinasian challenge of the irreducible and unreadable body and face of the other.

Tate's *Lear* ([1681] 1965) replaced Shakespeare's from 1681 until 1838 (Marsden 1991; Scott-Douglass 2013; Womack 2002). Tate's adaptation famously cuts the Fool and the King of France, gives Cordelia a sympathetic female companion, Arante, and sends both women out to find Lear on the heath (where Cordelia encounters and recognizes her beloved, Edgar, as the half-naked Tom o' Bedlam), turns Gloucester's blinding into a spur for 'revenge' from 'the pitying Crowd' (3.4.89, 86), brings Edgar back in time to rescue Cordelia from a lustful Edmund, returns Kent, with Cordelia, at the head of an avenging English army, and has Edgar rescue Cordelia and Lear from death before Cordelia and Edgar marry at the end of the play.

In the underlying logic of Tate's adaptation ([1681] 1965), writes Craig Womack, 'an opaque event is recontextualized as a transparent motive' (2002: 99). Cordelia remains silent during the love-test because she is secretly in love with Edgar; Edgar remains in disguise because he is anxious lest his father's heart crack with joy; Kent disappears in order to return with an army; Tate 'smooths out the versification, spells out the ellipses, and reduces (particularly by cutting the Fool) the text's extreme stylistic heterogeneity' (Womack 2002: 97). Tate, well aware of the differences between the 'Historie' and the 'Tragedie', writes Massai (2000), chooses to cut the 'moralizing passages' and the servants' kind intervention in the former (443) yet uses the 'Historie''s description of Cordelia weeping, for example, to demonstrate 'how grief can be turned into art' (445). Even as Tate's characters are more immediately comprehensible on stage, Massai suggests that Tate requires from his audience sympathy, but not fellow-feeling or mutual suffering alongside the characters. For Womack, Tate's changes 'unify' the play, but at the expense of 'silence, opacity, disjunction...transcendence' (2002: 101). Womack's reading of Shakespeare's *Lear* or *Lear*s thus returns us to Bloom's idealized King Lear as a 'touchstone' for Shakespearean 'transcendence' or sublimity (Bloom 1998: 513). Where, however, for Bloom (as for Charles Lamb, whom he quotes) any performance of *Lear* must fail to achieve this inhuman morality, for Womack (and for many of Bloom's reviewers) it is through performance that both 'disjunction' and 'transcendence' become manifest.

Tate ([1681] 1965) unveils the potential motives of Shakespeare's characters, a revelation that makes comprehension and compassion both easier and more limiting for his audience. *The King is Alive* ([2000] 2001) refuses any such explanatory gesture. The occlusion of human hearts and minds – even in Levinas's imagined, fundamental ethical social situation – demands far more from audiences, viewers, and other people than does explanation. Chloe Patton (2014), critiquing French legislators for using Levinas to ban the burqa and niqab (the full-body and full-face veil of some observant Muslim women), argues that such lawmakers fundamentally misunderstand Levinas's notion of what we owe to each other, face to face. She suggests that the mystery that a veiled face presents – its irreducibility, its blankness, its speaking or silent presence – precisely sets the ethical challenge to us: how can we relate to other human beings without seeing them as objects? How can we relate to faceless or veiled persons or persons with facial deformities without treating them as objects? If we cannot do so, Patten continues, that is our failing as ethically embodied humans, not a failure of Levinas nor of the veiled one.

Disconcertingly mixing avant-garde or experimental filmic forms with the popular genre of the survival film, *The King is Alive* ([2000] 2001) likewise challenges us to accept its characters' occlusion and opacity, in both plot and form. The film begins with a bus full of tourists – all white Westerners apart from Moses, the Black African driver – mysteriously making its way through the Namibian desert. After a canceled flight, the passengers hope to drive to another airport, but gradually realize that they are hundreds of miles off-track. When their bus runs out of fuel in a long-abandoned colonial outpost where a hermit, Kanana, lives among heaps of ancient cans of carrots, one of them ventures into the desert to seek for help, sternly admonishing the others that they can survive on the carrots – as long as they remain cheerful. As they pass the time waiting for rescue, Henry, a former actor among them – now a Hollywood agent – transcribes *King Lear* from memory, one part at a time (in manuscript scrolls or rolls that, as Cartelli and Rowe [2007] observe, imitate the practice of the early modern theatre) and convinces his fellows to put on the play for themselves in the desert.

Popular reviewers (Ebert 2001) could initially neither understand the function of the *Lear* plot nor identify parallels between the film's characters and the roles they play. Yet multiple Lears are throned and dethroned. Ashley, the first Lear, succumbs to delirium tremens and is replaced by Charles, even as Henry himself is a Lear-like director who is estranged, we learn, from his own daughter and unable to convince the French girl Catherine – most intelligent of all the women, as Henry is of the men – to join his troupe (just as Cordelia denies Lear's love-test). As Martha Nochimson carefully observes (2001), the Cordelia-function is spread between the bitter Catherine and the sexually sophisticated but emotionally naïve Gina, who plays Cordelia when Catherine rejects the role, but these character-functions also split and bifurcate among different persons. Catherine maliciously poisons Gina, as Goneril does Regan in Shakespeare's play. Gina, like the woman she plays, is a 'poor fool' but it is Charles, not Gina, who ultimately hangs himself, seized with remorse after urinating on Gina (and possibly suffocating her) after she reveals her sexual disgust with him. The Fool's wisdom appears only in the non-English narration of Kanana, who opens the film, almost as if the events exist only in his memory (Nochimson 2001: 49). His 'spare' narration cannot answer the questions we have about the characters and the plot (Nochimson 2001: 49).

No more can the cinematography explain these human and natural mysteries. Dogme95 tenets demand what Cartelli and Rowe deftly classify, through *Lear,* as 'unaccommodated' filmmaking: directors are enjoined, among other things, to eschew post-production sound-mixing, extra-diegetic sound, music, illumination, directorial credits, flashy or superficial plot points, black-and-white cinematography or other effects not immediately available on 35mm film, and to adhere to a new version of the classical unities, filming only on location (a unity of space) and at the chronological present (a unity of time). The film's dialogue is therefore sometimes literally muffled, even beyond the difficulty of the Shakespearean language (cruxes thematized within the diegesis as Gina, Liz and others struggle with their lines and as Henry misremembers some of the words that he writes out). The 1980s boom box (portable cassette player) that provides the music to which the players dance dominates the sound in the scenes in which it appears. The stunning backdrop of bleached-out sand dunes, the voice of the wind, the crackling, cataclysmic fire, the suffocating nocturnal darkness and smothering brilliant daylight, in which the characters' faces appear equally mysterious, all occlude our ability to make sense or logic of characters' motives or actions.

Nochimson sensitively identifies the film's and the play's 'ineffability' as 'the social implications of the enigmas that lie at the core of the human heart' – mysteries that, she argues, Levring brings forth through the 'visible surface' of human bodies, in a 'riveting tension between art and immediacy' (Nochimson 2001: 54). Textual, hypotextual, and hypertextual *Lear* demands our ethical attention and our compassion not despite but because of the irreducible, irreconcilable, inconclusive textual and emotional stakes that it projects on to human suffering.

# 4

# Transfer, remediation, broadcast:

# Intermedia

This chapter extends our discussion of fidelity to its technical meaning among audiophiles: the reproduction of sound or signal without distorting 'noise'. It investigates the fantasy that, given the right technology, we can access Shakespeare with what technicians call 'lossless transfer' – in other words, the idea, rife within popular and scientific contexts although scorned by anyone with a smattering of literary history, that Shakespeare is raw information that can be transferred from one medium to another without distortion or loss. Early searchable online editions – such as the MIT Shakespeare – assumed, unaware of the extensive editorial tradition that encompasses adaptation and that is traced in my previous chapter, that Shakespeare existed in a fixed prior state and could be transferred from any codex to the screen. Speeches known by scholars to be misattributed in certain historical Shakespeare editions thus made their way without comment into accessible sites such as the MIT Shakespeare, based on the Moby Shakespeare, itself reportedly based on the 1866 Globe Shakespeare edition (Johnson 2003). In this century, Shakespeare portraits of dubious or at least debatable accuracy verify complex financial transactions (Sawyer 2021: 75–6).

The fantasy of lossless transfer survives in part because conceptually it coheres with another of Lakoff and Johnson's fundamental metaphors, this time, the figure of the conduit or channel ([1980] 2003). Lakoff and Johnson describe the concept underlying this metaphor as *content travels to the experiencer* and *content is contained in the stimulus*, and for everyday uses of this framing metaphor, think of the business-speak that calls for a 'pipeline of ideas' or even the Christian hymn attributed to St. Francis of Assisi, 'Make me a channel of your peace'. So deep-rooted is the notion of Shakespeare's transcendent immutability that, as Alan Galey (2014) and others have observed, Shakespearean words are often used as proof-of-concept for media and technological innovations. Examples from the seventeenth to twentieth centuries include the printing and proof-reading of the First Folio, which advertised itself as containing 'true and faithful copies', in contrast to the earlier quartos; Édouard-Léon Scott de Martinville sampling a French adaptation of *Othello* for his phonautogram (Menke 2019: 4); Alexander Graham Bell reciting snippets of *Hamlet* in his early demonstrations of sound recording (Galey 2014: 160–99), or a British bank using a laser holographic image purporting to be Shakespeare on a physical 'BardCard' (Holderness 2013: 179–91). In this century, geneticists demonstrated DNA's potential for information storage by encoding 154 ASCII text versions of Shakespeare sonnets (Goldman et al. 2013); AI researchers tested their engine called 'Deep-Speare' by assigning it to create 'Shakespearean' sonnets (Lau et al. 2020), as we'll discuss further in Chapter 7; and cryptocurrency traders created bitcoins with images of Shakespeare (Sawyer 2021).

The rest of this chapter outlines twentieth- and twenty-first-century theories of media, in particular, the work of Marshall McLuhan ([1962] 2022) on media transfer, Jay David Bolter and Richard Grusin on remediation (1999), and Irina O. Rajewsky on intermedia (2005), and how critics such as

Richard Burt (2002), Thomas Cartelli (2019), Stephen O'Neill (2014), Laurie Osborne (2011), Daniel Fischlin (2014) and others have extended them to Shakespeare. We will put various theories through their paces using the example of *Hamlet*, a text or set of texts – First and Second Quartos and Folio versions differing significantly from each other – that has long served as a touchstone for Shakespearean authenticity. My final section considers audio-only recordings of *Hamlet* in digital and vinyl format, irreverent *Hamlet*-themed 'podcasts' broadcast and subsequently retrievable via digital radio, and the Seattle Shakespeare Company's bilingual digital audio play of *Hamlet* (2020).

# Transfer

When a Shakespeare play migrates from one technological home to another, its meaning likewise evolves. Initially, fidelity critics took Shakespearean transfers to other media – the 'new' media of film and television in the mid-twentieth-century, of the internet in the late-twentieth, of user-created media environments such as MySpace and YouTube in the early twenty-first-century, and mobile technologies at the present moment – as impoverished substitutes for an imagined original high cultural Shakespearean experience. The collections *Shakespeare, The Movie* (Boose and Burt 1997) and *Shakespeare, The Movie 2* (Boose and Burt 2003), Burt in his encyclopedic *Shakespeares after Shakespeare* (2006), Lanier in *Shakespeare in Modern Popular Culture* (2002), Courtney Lehmann in *Shakespeare Remains,* Laurie Osborne in a series of essays (2002, 2003, 2008, 2011), and many others have, however, demonstrated through the sustained and rigorous attention they have paid to non-print media that filmic, televisual, internet, mobile and other mass media (or, nowadays, niche media) Shakespeares both embody and disembody what we consider a Shakespearean text. Such critics also remind us of the relatively recent rise of so-called Bardolatry or

Shakespeare-worship and that the plays themselves belonged in a sense to a mass medium of their time; Shakespeare has always belonged to both high and low, mass and elite culture (Levine 1988; Bristol 1990, 1996).

Critics of Shakespeare on film, television, and digital media are implicitly or explicitly informed by the work of media theorists such as Marshall McLuhan ([1962] 2001) and Friedrich Kittler ([1985] 1990). Kittler is most often evoked in discussions of 'new media' and 'discourse networks'; he gives us the current critical interest in investigating technological platforms and modalities and in considering how media, genre, and traditional categories of the literary and the humanistic are formed through innovations that are technological and *in*human. Let me offer a brief Kittlerian analysis of a recent digital adaptation of *Hamlet*, its seconds-long representation in an 'NFT' ('non-fungible token') artwork, the Gold Hill Global Shakespeare *Complete Works*, in particular on the technology that enables the production, dissemination, and reception of this digital object. An NFT is 'a cryptographically unique, indivisible, irreplaceable and verifiable token that represents a given asset, be it digital, or physical, on a blockchain' (Valeonti et al. 2021: 3.1). NFTs depend for their cachet on artificial scarcity, generated at tremendous environmental cost and potentially removing lucrative image licensing fees from museums and galleries, which rely on such fees to survive, since anyone can potentially 'mine' cryptocurrency and create an NFT (Valeonti et al. 2021: 6.2).

Currently being auctioned by Gold Hill Global (2021), the *Complete Works* NFT is thus freely available online in its mass-market form, but only the successful bidder will win the one-of-a-kind digitally authenticated video, along with a physical copy of the popular mid-nineteenth-century illustrated three-volume J. O. Halliwell-Phillips *Complete Shakespeare* that the 'digital representation' represents. The NFT artwork itself comprises a streaming video showing a digitally enhanced image of the Halliwell-Phillips volumes and their tables of contents, as if being leafed through by a disembodied reader, before the film depicts a series of objects intended to connote a particular work or genre from the book, for example a golden skull gradually transforming into a realistic, decaying one, for *Hamlet*.

McLuhan gives Shakespeareans our equally important interest in the human beings creating and receiving the media. In the early career *Gutenberg Galaxy*, McLuhan famously identified *King Lear* as a traumatized response to the revolution of print ([1962] 2011: 13–20), a simplistic analysis critiqued by Cohn and others ([1976] 2015: 249) and (in typically flamboyant fashion, as David Linton observes) also argued that one could create an entire textbook on media using only Shakespeare's plays (Linton 1996: 2). Late in his career, writing with his son Eric, McLuhan nuanced his argument to suggest 'four laws' of media (which are more tendencies or poetic inspirations than strict laws): media *enhance*, *reverse*, *return* to, and make *obsolescent* aspects or effects of prior media (McLuhan and McLuhan 1988). The McLuhans represent these four laws in a series of diagrams called 'tetrads'. Let's now take the Gold Hill Global *Complete Works* through the 'Four Laws' [Table 4.1].

The NFT as a media form promises to *enhance* the illustrated edition by offering three-dimensional, animated, full-colour renderings of the black-and-white, cross-hatched engravings within the book. It promises to *retrieve* what Walter Benjamin famously called the 'aura' of original art, the value that accrues to a work that can be traced back to the author's or artist's hand, even in an 'age of mechanical reproduction' and even when the physical book itself is widely available (the three volumes of the same Halliwell-Philips edition are currently [early 2022] widely available at prices ranging from $71 to $375, so the current bidder, at about $3000, is paying for the digital watermark rather than the physical object or the content of the video). NFT art promises to *obsolesce* what André Malraux called 'the museum without walls', the ideal that art could be made available to everyone, not just to the rich patrons who collected it, and open-access or open-source projects such

Table 4.1 *The Four Laws of Media Applied to NFT Artworks*

| RETRIEVES | ENHANCES |
|---|---|
| Aura (*Benjamin: provenance creates value: being able to trace object back to hand of artist*) (*Marx: taking a public good and profiting from it*) | Appropriation (*Desmet, O'Neill: rhetorics of synecdoche*) |
| Exclusivity | Full-color |
| Patronage | Animated |
| Appropriation | Illustrated edition |
| **OBSOLESCES** | **REVERSES** |
| Open Art<br>Open source<br>Open access<br>Museum without Walls (*Malraux*)<br>Creates artificial scarcity | Promise of greatness or quality<br>Promise of financial security: greater risk than even traditional art market<br>All value comes from production<br>Content is negligible |

*Source:* Adapted by the author from Marshall McLuhan and Eric McLuhan, *The Laws of Media* (Toronto: University of Toronto Press, 1988).

as Google Art, in which museums allow patrons digitally to 'walk' through their galleries and see their works on screen. And yet it *reverses* its promises of turning anyone who can code and pay the 'gas fee' (to join the networked computers and mine the tokens) into a financially successful artist. The digital art market is even more fraught with risk than the traditional one, partly because of the difficulty of storing and securing digital items long-term and partly because the 'aura' of NFTs depends upon their means of production and provenance rather than the quality or even popularity of the art itself.

Not only the name of the business touting the Shakespeare NFT – Gold Hill Global – but the gilded digital objects in the video remind viewers and consumers that this art possesses only exchange-value, not use-value, in Marxian terms. To return to our discussion in Chapter 2, we could say that this NFT exemplifies Shakespearean appropriation as an ever-encroaching 'process of reproducing value and producing new value' in the 'circuit of industrial capital' (Fine and Saad-Filho 2016: 48). The NFT thus makes explicit the persistent collective delusion under which we agree that pixels, blockchains, electrons, quipu, paper, precious metals, beads, and grain are all currency, tokens for exchange, independent of any inherent usefulness or beauty. We transfer features of one medium (currency, in this case) to the next, a process classified and described by Jay David Bolter and Richard Grusin as 'remediation'.

# Remediation

Bolter and Grusin's important book *Remediation* (1999) suggests that obsolete characteristics of old media persist in newer ones (the icon of a floppy disk indicating that one has 'saved' a document, decorative bumps on the spines of hardcover books even when there are no cords to cover), in part because of consumers' or users' drive towards what they call *immediacy* (the fantasy of lossless transfer or access) and *hypermediacy* (our continued awareness that there's a medium of some kind in the way). Richard Lanham (2007) calls our movement between hypermediacy and immediacy 'oscillation', a term that evokes early radio in order to theorize the different kinds of attention users bring to diverse media experiences. Bolter and Grusin's study of remediation, particularly its weighing of affordances and constraints that attend on movement of content from one medium to another, provides a context for analyzing what is won and lost in movement from one medium to another, as when silent film gives way to sound or when amateur YouTube productions replicate, with no obvious self-consciousness, the techniques of silent cinema, such as inter-titles, the use of mime, time-lapse photography, and so on (O'Neill 2014; Desmet 2017). We can consider remediation briefly through the 2000 *Hamlet* directed by Michael Almereyda, a film that self-consciously evokes legacy media, as critics have observed (Donaldson 2006; Keyishian 2007): Julia Stiles' Ophelia is a photographer who marks up Polaroids; young Hamlet is a video artist and editor seen watching Laurence Olivier's cinematic Hamlet and other classic performances.

We could also consider the remediation of 'time-lapse' photography on the micro-video sharing site TikTok as part of a genre called '#booktok', or '#booksoftiktok', tiny looping videos expressing affection or hatred for a particular volume, often (as in their YouTube predecessors – O'Neill 2014) to a musical mashup. Micro-videos engender their own genres, with the most popular, such as '#booktok' or '#shakespeare' with creators and viewers in the billions (it made this Shakespearean first sigh, then laugh, to find that '#shakespear' [*sic*] has five million views). Other genres have thousands of creators and viewers, even excluding commercial or institutional videos such as those published by the popular study site SparkNotes or by the Shakespeare Birthplace Trust, such as the tags (or user names) featuring some combination of 'Shakespeare' with the word 'queer' (such as 'shakesqueer') or 'insult' (such as 'shakespeareaninsult'). Micro-videos also grow micro-genres, however, such as the #TimeWarpScan #Hamlet TikTok, with creators in the dozens and viewers in the hundreds, rather than the thousands, at least that I can discover. The table shows the number of views for the most popular hashtags and the number of 'Favourite' tags given to the top two videos including the hashtags #hamlet and #TimeWarpScan [Table 4.2].

Time-lapse TikTok videos (also called 'Time Warp Scan' videos) take advantage of the ease of photographing oneself on a mobile phone to mimic the effects of hand-cranking in early cinema, differences between frame capture speed and playing speed in feature film, or (the way most TikTokers create their

Table 4.2 *Popular* Hamlet-*related hashtags on the micro-video sharing site TikTok*

| Hashtag or Hashtags | Views or 'Favourited' |
| --- | --- |
| #nsBookTok | 35.3 billion views |
| #shakespeare | 261.6 million views |
| #shakespear | 5.0 million views |
| #shakesqueer | 122.1 thousand views |
| #queershakespeare | 2160 views |
| #shakespeareaninsult | 45.7 thousand views |
| #shakespeareaninsults | 6493 views |
| #shakespeare #hamlet #TimeWarpScan #classiclittok #fyp #for you | 45.4 thousand 'Favourited' |
| #TimeWarpScan #hamlet #shakespeare #books #BookTok #theater | 949 'Favourited' |

*Source:* TikTok (20 January 2022).

time-lapse videos) stop-motion animation. Time-lapse videos slow down or, more usually on TikTok, speed up time, and #TimeWarpScan toks typically show TikTok creators holding a closed book which appears to become longer or shorter as they lower the hand that moves the book. The action is meant to demonstrate hypothetical changes in book-length if the book's content were altered. #TimeWarpScan *Hamlet* uses this technique to joke about *Hamlet*'s notoriously delayed action; typically the video will show a book – usually the Folger Shakespeare *Hamlet* – with a caption to the effect of how long or short the play would be if Hamlet had had a firearm, if the Ghost had asked Horatio to kill Claudius, and other scenarios (Figure 4.1).

**FIGURE 4.1** *'Hamlet if Hamlet had a gun', TikTok microvideo, @ivcapvlet. Screen capture by the author, TikTok, 20 January 2022.*

Media Studies have enabled innovative criticism of live Shakespeare performances as well as discussions of so-called new media. Foundational to such studies are Joseph Roach's theory of surrogation ([1996] 2022) and W. B. Worthen's theory of dramatic performativity (2003). Surrogation, as Roach uses the term, connotes performance by a living actor to 'surrogate' or embody the memory of the past, particularly memories of loss and death. We cope with or compensate for death by creating substitutes or 'effigies' to stand in the place of the departed; performance is thus key to a society's survival, even as performance displaces and creates the original; 'an understanding of the text [that] emerges not as the cause, but as the consequence of performance', in Worthen's useful phrase (64: [1996] 2022).

Worthen clarifies that performances are always adaptations and that such adaptations retroactively create the original behind them. What he calls 'dramatic performativity' ([1996] 2002: 3–4) exists in a realm between text and performance.

The dumb-show that introduces 'The Mousetrap' in *Hamlet* exemplifies and comments upon this liminal performative space in its multiple textual iterations and in its production (or omission) in performance. The dumb-show and 'The Mousetrap' in *Hamlet* exist in all three versions of the text that we have. First came 1603's First Quarto or Q1, still called by Shakespeareans a 'bad', 'divergent', 'memorially reconstructed', 'bootleg', 'touring performance', 'unrevised draft' version of the play, because we can't explain its differences in length, quality, and style from the other texts of *Hamlet* that we have (9.82-1–5). Then came 1604's Second Quarto or Q2 (3.2.128.1–11) and the 1623 First Folio or F (3.2.131.1–13). Full versions of all three texts are available in the Arden Third Series, edited by Ann Thompson and Neil Taylor, but here I have conflated all three texts, highlighting only the variants I will discuss, using *italics* to indicate Q1 only, underlining to indicate Q2 only, and **bold** to indicate F only, and I have modernized spelling and punctuation freely.

> **Oboes play**/ Trumpets sound/*Enter in a* dumbshow. Enter a King and a Queen very lovingly; the Queen embracing him, and he her. **She kneels, and makes show of protestation unto him.** He takes her up, and declines his head upon her neck: *He sits down in an arbour*/ **he lyes** / lays him down upon a bank of flowers: she, seeing him asleep, leaves him. Anon comes in *Lucianus with poison in a vial* /a fellow, takes off his crown, kisses it, and pours poison in the King's ears, and exit/ *goes away*. The Queen returns; finds the King dead, and makes passionate action/*Then the queen cometh and finds him dead and goes away with the other*. The Poisoner, with some two or three Mutes/**some three or four,** comes in again, seeming to lament / **condole** with her. The dead body is carried away. The Poisoner woos the Queen with gifts: she seems **loath and unwilling** / harsh awhile, but in the end accepts **his** love.

*Something* is being adapted here, to great ambiguity. Did oboes play or trumpets sound? A brassy flourish is more in keeping with a royal entrance, but gentle woodwind for a love-scene (consider Hamlet's castigations upon the recorder when his erstwhile friends Rosencrantz and Guildenstern try to woo him). How much does the Queen (and by extension, Gertrude) know, and is she 'harsh' by design or genuinely 'loath and unwilling'? Does she 'accept love' out of fear and loneliness, or 'accept his love' because she has complotted with Lucianus? Did audiences have some indication that the 'fellow' was Lucianus, the nephew? To what extent is Lucianus, the nephew, a surrogate for the murdered King?

Theories of surrogation thus uncover the link between text (Kittler, [1985] 1990) and body (McLuhan, [1962] 2011), and locate it dynamically between page and stage. Other critics who have used surrogation, dramatic performativity, or a combination of the two to reconsider text and stage as media and to discuss mechanisms of *Hamlet* adaptations include Sonya Loftis on Heiner Müller's *Hamletmachine* (2013), Maurizio Calbi on the 2006 'experimental low-budget' film *Hamlet* by Alexander Fodor (Calbi 2013: 9), and Cartelli on James Joyce's Shakespearean extravagance in *Ulysses*, silent-film-star Asta Nielsen's revolutionary female Hamlet, and mixed-media performances such as the 'remediation of the 1964 Electronovision *Hamlet*' by the avant-garde theatrical troupe The Wooster Group (Cartelli 2019: 36–46, 185–213). Scholars of Shakespearean adaptation now routinely write about film, television, the internet, games, and objects. The special issue of *Shakespeare Quarterly* called '*#Bard*', edited by Lanier and Gail Kern Paster (2016), for example, included essays on interactive gaming and Ophelia on the web but also on print technologies, experimental mixed-media theatre, and theatre broadcast live into cinemas ('cinecasts'), while the invaluable essay-collection *Shakespeare and the 'Live' Theatre Broadcast Experience* (Aebischer, Greenhalgh, and Osborne 2018) considered liveness, theatricality, and recorded technologies together. In other words, we have decided that Shakespeare adaptations are *intermedia*.

Intermediality further complicates and questions the idea of seamless communication or transfer from one medium to another (Fischlin 2014). Revived from the Fluxus movement of the 1960s, intermediality connotes a range of engagement with media, more than the transmission of content from one medium to another, or even the persistence of those no-longer-functional marks of old media in newer ones. Intermediality extends from merely acknowledging one medium within another all the way to self-conscious commentary about the nature of the old medium within its new media incarnation. It acknowledges that that one medium may represent another without naively attempting to recreate that medium, and that media themselves comprise a series of signifying systems (Rajewsky 2005). Intermediality suggests that media forms are created 'after-the-fact': scrolls become identifiable as forms or formats after the invention of the codex; still photography becomes a genre after the advent of 'moving pictures', and so on, to such an extent that we use a process of differentiation to define media by what they are not. Such media/intermedia have to use metaphors borrowed from other media in order to describe themselves, creating a continuum comparable to the range discussed by Hutcheon ([2006] 2013: 181) and described in my second chapter.

Let us return to our earlier example of *Hamlet* (2000). As Jens Schröter writes in another context, for representations of media within other media to be considered *intermedia*, they 'must…explicitly refer[] to the represented medium' (2012: 27). *Hamlet* (2000) judiciously uses film editing, shot-reverse-shot, and point-of-view to establish legacy and new media as intermedia, by offering wry commentary on the signifying systems within legacy or represented media, such as Ethan Hawke's delivery of the 'To be or not to be' speech in the Action aisle of a Blockbuster video store; Sam Shepard's appearance as the Ghost on closed-circuit television camera; Julia Stiles's tearful Ophelia being 'wired for sound' by her father and the King, and Hamlet's furious discovery of her complicity; and so on.

Calbi and Cartelli offer further examples of intermediality in action in *Hamlet*. Calbi contrasts the presentation of Ophelia in *Hamlet* (2007), in which Ophelia appears both dead and alive and in which her death is presented in contradictory ways at two different points in the plot. Calbi suggests that these films create or recreate a supposed original only to prove that that 'original' itself, like the copy or adaptation, is an 'iteration', '(retrospectively) *produced* as one of the film's intertexts…forced to enter into dialogue with other intertexts' (2013: 101). Adaptation and so-called original haunt and hunt each other, are both active and independent, lacking a fixed ontological presence or state of being (think again of those reduplicated 'Mousetrap' performances, in multiple texts, dumbshows, and reflected in large in the plot of *Hamlet* itself). Cartelli explores in detail the controversial, storied production of *Hamlet* by the experimental theatre troupe the Wooster Group, directed by Ivo Van Hove. This production presented, among other things, actors on a stage voicing and gesturing word-for-word and pause-for-pause a famous earlier *Hamlet*, Richard Burton, in front of a large screen showing his 1964 film. Ironically, as Cartelli notes, the Wooster Group's own work is now itself part of a 'canon' of important theatrical adaptations or interventions for Shakespeareans, and they have revived it many times (2019).

# Broadcast and podcast

Thinking about how we send and receive Shakespeare in the post-internet era and during the time of COVID-19 encourages us to consider how audio Shakespeares such as radio broadcasts work as intermedia when remediated or repeated as streaming or on-demand content such as podcasts. Susanne Greenhalgh has suggested that, because of its limitations and, paradoxically, its aural possibilities, radio was 'arguably the most adaptive' of media because 'the listener subjectively creates the *Hamlet* that she hears' (2011: 134). This section of my chapter briefly discusses a digital recording of Sir John Gielgud playing *Hamlet* in a famous broadcast from 1948, the experience of listening to a later recording of Gielgud's *Hamlet* with the cast of the Old Vic on vinyl LP (1957), some of the *Hamlet* podcasts popular just before and during the COVID-19 pandemic, such as Conor Hanratty's 'The *Hamlet* podcast' and irreverent comedy programs, and the Seattle Shakespeare Company's bilingual digital audio play of *Hamlet* (2020). I am interested in three particular aspects of these *Hamlet*-adjacent audio experiences: 1) the metaphor of the broadcast versus the podcast 2) how these performances understand textual 'fidelity' 3) how they remediate or whether they remediate visual aspects of performance, such as costume, gesture, blocking and so forth using only sound, and to what extent the new medium comments upon or critiques its prior medium (the process known as intermediality). I'll return to the dumbshow and to the general questions actors and directors need to address about this interlude, such as: why does Claudius ignore the dumbshow? When and why is Claudius's conscience caught?

Unlike analogue radio, the digital podcast is not a true mass medium: niche audiences subscribe to various streams and listen when they want, where they want, and usually on their own; any mass or collective response comes after-the-fact in dispersed, asynchronous comments on social media platforms. The difference is apparent in the names of these media. 'Broadcast' refers to the indiscriminate scattering of seed (think of the New Testament parable of the seed that falls on rocky ground, sand, or fertile earth). OED identifies the earliest use of 'broadcast' as 1767, but this date is somewhat misleading: while the portmanteau word does not appear until then, the phrasal use – to cast something abroad or broadly – appears in print much earlier, figuratively, to mean the transmission of ideas, as in Christine de Pisan's imagined 'scyence & cōnynge. . .cast a brode. . .thrughe all [the] worlde' (1521: n3v) and literally, as instructions on the planting of peas and beans, in John

Fitzherbert's treatise on husbandry: 'Put thy pees in to thy hopper and cast a brode' (1530: C2v). And the term *broadcast* is applied to wireless radio transmissions from the early 1920s, on both sides of the Atlantic: the signal is beamed out at the same time on a certain frequency, traditionally live, regardless of whether anyone has tuned in and is listening to it.

*Podcast* has a much more recent history, appearing in digital fora and in newspapers in 2004 as a back-formation from the proprietary, and now obsolete, MP3 music player, the iPod. *The Guardian* asked at the time about this new medium, 'But what to call it? Audioblogging? Podcasting? GuerillaMedia?' (Hammersley 2004). The word podcast perhaps survived out of those possibilities because we already had the term *broadcast* and the effective metaphor of the casting or scattering of ideas. Both metaphors encode the frame *content is embedded in the stimulus* – there's a seed in the scattering hand, and another in the pod. They moreover combine this frame with the prior, ubiquitous dead metaphor of the channel or, today, the stream – the irrigation necessary to grow ideas. The conceptual frame underpinning the idea that ideas need irrigation from a stream or channel is the concept *minds are fertile*, a very early modern notion, since both the womb and the brain were thought to be nourished by phlegm and productive of offspring (Crane 2001).

But whereas the live broadcast disseminates anywhere and everywhere, and typically aimed to attract a mass audience with an ephemeral event, the podcast is both produced and collected selectively, by and for a niche or coterie, in its initial phase, but can then survive and come to life again with successive small audiences. Greenhalgh (2011) concludes that the post-war BBC radio *Hamlet*s navigated, with limited success, the channel between seemingly authoritative, highbrow, uncut Shakespeare audio performance (as exemplified by Gielgud's 1948 'entirety' *Hamlet* and its regular rebroadcasts) and the often comic, sometimes experimental spin-offs that also thrived in the post-war era.

The podcast as a form allows creators and audiences to avoid this tension. Unless you go looking for irreverent comedy

*Hamlet* podcasts, you are not going to find them in your usual *Hamlet* haunts. Podcast has developed an additional connotation during the COVID-19 era of pandemic podding, moving more towards broadcast as individual pods of listeners, trapped together at home, listened together. The same is true of broadcast television: despite the press coverage given to the streaming service Netflix, Nielsen's updated data showed that most households were watching cable news live for a surprising proportion of the time (Koblin 2021).

## Intermedia: Audio *Hamlet*s

Gielgud's three-and-a-half-hour BBC Third Programme broadcast of *Hamlet* on Boxing Day 1948 'proved so popular that it was repeated by public demand on New Year's Eve', writes Greenhalgh (2011). This production was nicknamed the 'entirety' *Hamlet*, because it proudly displayed its length and fidelity to what textual scholars have called a 'maximal' Shakespeare, a script adapted by M. R. Ridley to use a mostly uncut Q2 (the longest text we have) with few emendations or excisions. Greenhalgh notes that the broadcast, and Gielgud's subsequent Hamlets, opposed their 'entirety' Hamlet to Laurence Olivier's film of the same year, which had shocked critics with its cuts. But what the producers meant by a show that was true or faithful to Shakespeare includes what Michael Jensen correctly identifies as an 'intrusive' narrator (2017). It opens nearly every scene with a description of settings ('Midnight on the royal battlements'), or costumes and even stage position ('a little apart, dressed in black: Hamlet'). This narrator also makes judgements, for example saying explicitly that Hamlet's claim to the throne has been 'over-ridden'. At the same time, the show used sound technology of the time innovatively, creating a sense of space or proximity through distance from the microphone, the sound of footsteps, the hubbub of a crowd, and so on.

Both the 1948 transmission and the 1957 vinyl recording cut the dumb show and move straight to the Prologue; the narrator tells us at the beginning of the scene, 'The whole of the castle is now set out in readiness for the play. The court is not yet assembled, and Hamlet is giving some last-minute instructions to the players'. Each version keeps, however, trumpet flourishes, before and after Hamlet's short speech to Horatio, 'They are coming to the play. I must be idle. Get you a place'. Perhaps most interestingly, both Gielgud recordings offer an implicit explanation for why Claudius seems to ignore or at least tolerate both the dumb-show and the opening of the play only to react so extremely to Lucianus. During 'The Mousetrap' Hamlet's words rise in volume from an intimate whisper to Ophelia until he is shouting the speech, 'He poisons him i'the garden for his estate' (3.2.287). Hamlet says these words loudly enough for the King and all courtiers to hear and possibly to elicit Claudius' sudden departure and call for lights.

Every episode of Irish theatre director Conor Hanratty's 'The *Hamlet* podcast' cues us to listen with a melancholy cello line and a greeting from the host. The podcast close-read *Hamlet*, twenty lines at a time, from November 2017 until the end of June 2021. Discussions encompass wonderful detail, with both directorial and scholarly insights, including a surprising amount of natural history, such as an expansive investigation of Osric/Ostricke and his feathered hat. The podcast takes advantage of audio's ability to record a maximal text – Q2 plus additional passages from the Folio – and of the podcast formula; the speaker can break up the text and take much longer to discuss a speech than to deliver it on stage or even to explicate it in a classroom.

Hanratty interprets the dumbshow as a sign of archaism and compares it to a contemporary intermedium, 'something like a trailer, perhaps' (Hanratty 2017–2021). He reads a conflated, maximal account of the dumbshow. He does not, however, explain why Claudius does not react to the dumbshow, nor what in particular might elicit Claudius's rising at that specific time, nor the mystery of why the prologue, supposed to explain what happens, does not do so, but rather merely urges the audience to pay attention.

In contrast, the comedy podcast 'Fuckbois of Literature' (Edwards 2019–21) pays no attention to the dumbshow. The show spins itself as hosts talking about 'the books we love' and 'heroes we hate'. Each guest on the show is asked to define how she understands a fuckboi – a term that crossed over from prison slang, came to mean a handsome but empty-headed young man and now seems to mean a youthful representative of what the hosts will nearly always define as 'toxic masculinity', that is, a young man who is 'misogynistic', 'entitled,' 'whiny', and 'emo', as Desmet observed of YouTube *Hamlet*s (2018a). The 'Hamlet' episode characterizes Hamlet's grief at his mother's remarriage as inherently pathological – in that sense, the episode hearkens back to mid-century psychoanalytic interpretations such as Ernest Jones's or the performances of Laurence Olivier or Mel Gibson – and his delay as inexplicable, self-indulgent and another way to minimize the tragedy of Ophelia. 'That Pretentious Book Club' ([Wheezy and Spoons] O'Rourke and Shaw 2021) in contrast, is more sympathetic towards Hamlet's distaste for his mother's remarriage, although they agree that our hero is 'emo,' and 'whiny'. Both podcasts interpret 'The Mousetrap' as another mechanism for Hamlet's self-aggrandizing delay.

The digitally distributed audio play offers yet another remediation of the radio broadcast. Director and translator Ana Maria Campoy had originally set the Seattle Shakespeare Company's bilingual *Hamlet* (2020), around a Día de los Muertos festival on Olvera Street in Los Angeles. Supported by the ArtsWest and the National Endowment for the Arts, the production had been scheduled for a full tour, including to schools, when the Covid-19 pandemic hit. With the help of sound editor Rafael Molina, the play moved to an audio-only format, streaming each act as a podcast under the 'SeattleShakes' channel.

The play's bilingualism differs from that of the many bi- or multilingual families who use English to discuss academic or intellectual issues or to occlude complex or tabooed emotional concerns from older – or younger – generations. Rather, as

Campoy says, in this production 'To be bilingual often means that you are always searching for the perfect word or phrase to express yourself or to connect with someone' (2019: 4). The families Campoy imagines in *Hamlet* use both English and Spanish to find the right word for the moment. I therefore found little consistency in when each language was used, but a few endearing patterns emerged. Horatio always calls Hamlet *jefe*, which to my non-Spanish-speaking ear at least seems less formal than 'my lord' or 'good sir'. The instructions to the players delightfully 'jump[] back and forth between rolling...R's in Spanish' trippingly on the tongue, iambic pentameter, and code-switching prose, a process that the director herself says that she 'love[s]' (Campoy 2019: 4).

The only English-only scene I identified on first hearing was the section of 1.3 between Ophelia and Polonius (87–135), although Ophelia and Laertes have been uttering a mixture of Spanish and English together in their previous lines. Ophelia delivers her only potential soliloquy (3.1.149–160) in English, apart from one phrase, 'esperanza y flor', for 'the expectancy/ expectation and rose of the fair state' (151). Ophelia's Spanish is English-accented, and it is unclear whether this is an attribute of actor, character, or both.

This performance upended much of the conventional wisdom about audio performances, and certainly the assumptions of the BBC Third Programme and the producers of, in the US, 'the Battle of Bards' on radio between CBS and NBC in 1937 (Jensen 2018). The US producers – and the BBC's – thought that audiences would need a narrator to set the scene and describe costumes. They thought that too much doubling and more than a few characters in a scene would confuse listeners (Greenhalgh 2011). Yet despite the fact that I have never learned Spanish, I could follow this play, which has no narrator, and, I only discovered afterwards, much doubling – the same player, Anuhea Brown, doubled as Ophelia and Horatio, and, in an update enabled by the audio-only format, the same actor, Adrian Alonso Padilla, played Claudius, Old Hamlet, and the Player King. The actors are highly skilled and the actor who played Hamlet, Beth Pollack, is particularly expressive as a very emotional and very young prince, somewhat like Benedict Cumberbatch's 'toy soldier' Hamlet at the RSC (2015). Immersing myself in audio-only this way, I kept noticing the ways in which characters name each other (in contrast to Viola's namelessness in *Twelfth Night*, discussed in my next chapter) and cue each other to sit, stand, kneel, 'go with me' and so on. A bilingual audio play reminds us of Johannes De Witt and other foreign visitors to early modern London with varying fluency in English, listening for words they knew to help them understand what they were seeing.

In this digital, pandemic context, the careful, crafted soundtrack intermediates the dumb show as a loud mariachi band, followed by a strumming guitar. Loud and self-conscious throat-clearing introduces the 'Murder of Gonzago', which The Players deliver heavily, emphasizing the verse. Both Beth Pollack's Hamlet and Marquicia Dominguez' performed Player Queen are histrionic, but the Player Queen slows down and enunciates her delivery to evoke the play's archaism and her own artifice, where Hamlet seems genuinely anguished. Lucianus, the nephew, cackles with a dastardly laugh that seems to allude to the villains of historical radio serials. The production moves Claudius's response immediately after Lucianus's speech, the one Hamlet has theoretically added. This production cut Hamlet's explanation: – 'he poisons him i'th'garden for his estate', in contrast to the Gielgud production. Where Hamlet's louder declamation of those lines clarifies for Gielgud's listening audience why Claudius responds as he does, in the Campoy production Lucianus emphasizes the word *usurp* (which means 'to appropriate for one's own use or benefit' in both English and Spanish) even more than the Old Vic and radio companies had done.

In the absence of visual cues such as Lucianus pouring the poison in the Duke's ear, or Claudius suddenly paying attention where he had paid none before, I suggest that for those who know the play, audio productions become intermedia: they highlight the presence within 'The Mousetrap' of patterns of language that appear throughout *Hamlet*, conceits that appear so frequently that I will list only a few instances of each: *blighting* (1.1.124, 1.3.13, 1.4.43), *infection* (3.2.280, 3.4.160, 4.579), *sickness* (1.1.8, 3.2.182, 3.3.77), *foul-smelling* (1.2.133, 3.2.280, 3.3.39).

As calls for light recede into the distance, Hamlet calls jubilantly in Spanish for music, reminding us that early modern audiences went not only to see but, equally, to 'hear a play' (*Hamlet* 2.2.561, *Shrew* IND. 2.120). As Bruce R. Smith has argued, even the boundaries among our senses were less clearly defined for such audiences, as we will consider further in Chapter 7 (Smith 1999). The play's dramaturgy thus contains a built-in intermediality, just as, some theorists suggest, all media are 'primal' and contain an inherent or 'ontological intermediality' (Schröter 2012: 28–30). Schröter further suggests that 'clearly separated "monomedia" are the result of purposeful and institutionally caused blockades, incisions, and mechanisms of exclusion' (2012: 30). The Seattle Shakespeare Company's bilingual audio *Hamlet* reminds us that people of all levels of aural literacy and comprehension could access Shakespeare's theatre, and so can we. My next chapter explores other 'monomedia...exclusion[s]' that Shakespearean adaptation is breaking down – barriers between professional and amateur, male and female, straight and gay, trans and cisgender, as we consider adaptations of *Twelfth Night* within fan or user communities that often foreground concerns of gender and sexuality.

# 5

# Memes, networks, fans: Transformations

Extending but also critiquing Richard Dawkins's idea of the meme – the idea that replicates as a gene does – Bortolotti and Hutcheon (2007) suggest that fundamental narratives within Shakespeare function as memes and that we can use the process of their adaptation to study changing ideas and stories over time. In Susan Blackmore's terms, drawn from genetics and evolutionary biology, memes are ideas within culture that take up residence in human brains and that are passed on to others through imitation, mimicking the transmission of genetic lineages although memes are not in themselves biologically inherited (1999). Limor Shifman (2013) adapts the meme as a unit for the ongoing transmission of ideas in social media adaptations, foregrounding the metaphor's balance of replication and alteration, and most important of all, its ability to disseminate in the manner of a virus ('to go viral'), or its 'spreadability' (Jenkins, Ford, and Green 2015). These 'expert metaphors' or, perhaps, in traditional rhetorical terms, *metalepses*, are metaphors inside other metaphors that synthesize multiple domains. Conceptual metaphors underlying this terrain include *the mind is a container for ideas*; *ideas are contagious*; *the mind is a body* (a figure to which we'll return in Chapter 7); *to carry the idea is to spread it*; *remembering is reconstructing*.

Later versions of these metaphors of containment, spread, embodiment and dispersal, locate ideas not within individual minds, bodies, or objects but within the networks or relationships among them. Critics who use Bruno Latour's actor-network theory (ANT) find meaning not within the author/reader/audience complex, nor the objects that make up a Shakespearean adaptation, but along the ghostly paths – nodes of the networks between objects, texts, performances – in which meaning, however, transient, resides (Harris 2010). By extension, in the object-oriented ontology (OOO) or 'vital materialism' of philosopher Jane Bennett, objects themselves do not exist stably and might better be characterized as energy flows or 'intensities' whose boundaries shift according to how they are acting (Bennett 2010; Cohen and Yates 2016). Such metaphors begin with the familiar figure that *the mind is a body* and that *to understand is to grasp or to hold* (the figure of the web, the net) but then suggest with increasing complexity that *ideas are locations*, even as these locations are moving or changing, taking us to the counterintuitive *existence is location out of container*.

To date within Shakespearean studies, the meme as metaphor has received the greatest critical attention, having been incorporated into discussion of Shakespearean adaptations by critics of film and television (Lanier 2002; Reynolds 2006; Denslow 2017). Internet memes have also become actors in networks of Shakespeare adaptation, along with the fan cultures that produce them. The phenomenon that Janice Radway identified as a serious cultural phenomenon in *Reading the Romance* (1984) and that Henry Jenkins dubbed 'participatory culture' among *Star Trek* fans (1988) and Shakespearean 'textual poachers' (1998) culminates in our current 'convergence culture' (2008) in which users, producers, and 'prosumers' (Fuchs 2016: 57) sustain each other through multiple media forms.

These non-professional or semi-professional fan cultures produce a sub-genre of popular Shakespeare in their own right – both online and in real life – at events such as Renaissance

Fairs and in shops (Lees-Jeffries 2013). Fan 're-creations' achieve a 'collaborative authority' between text and user (Fazel and Geddes 2016), are genuine 'transformational' uses (Busse 2017a), and include established genres such as fiction or videos posted online within fan communities and publicly for comment (fanfic, YouTube), and newer micro-fictional or synecdochic genres such as TikTok videos, animated GIFs, or Snapchat filters. In my concluding case study, 'A Gender-Agenda in *Twelfth Night*', I use approaches from Fan Studies to show how changing understandings (or memes) of human sexuality among complex human networks influence representations of gender in adaptations of Shakespeare's plays. On the way we'll look at the memeification of Feste's song in a Victorian sensation novel (Marsh 1849), an Edwardian pacifist hymn (Weir 1913), and Joel Coen's film of *Macbeth* (2021) as well as object-oriented eroticism in the Globe's storied *Twelfth Night* (2013). My final section considers in detail Mary Cowden Clarke's prequel, 'Viola, The Twin' ([1851] 1974); the 'Shakesteen' (Keam 2006) film *She's the Man* (2006), and community transformations on stage, YouTube, and TikTok.

# Memes

Blackmore describes the meme as a unit of imitation, a combination of 'heredity (the form and details of the behaviour are copied), variation (they are copied with errors, embellishments or other variations) and selection (only some behaviors are successfully copied…a true evolutionary process' (Blackmore 1999: 51). She identifies the proliferation of high-fidelity replication technologies, 'meme-copying-machinery' (1999: 204), as key fertilizers for memes, because they enable the meme more easily to fulfil its three primary conditions for replication in our brains: 'high fidelity, fecundity, and longevity' (1999: 119). Unconcerned about the vagueness of the memetic unit, Blackmore compares them once more to genes – also notoriously undefined – adopting the term 'memeplex' to suggest how groups of memes might work together.

At the same time, Blackmore cautions us against adhering too strongly to the metaphor of genetics, distinguishing between imitative processes that 'copy the product' versus those that 'copy the instructions'. Let's imagine two directors who seek to remake Trevor Nunn's film of *Twelfth Night* (1996). One is attempting to 'copy the product' by watching the film multiple times; the other, wanting to 'copy the instructions', consults film, screenplay, shooting script, costume bible, and so on. In practice, such a director would probably engage in all these activities; while genes transmit only via the instructions, through sexual selection, memes replicate through multiple, concurrent processes.

Limor Shifman (2013) takes issue with Blackmore's approach, arguing that it fails to acknowledge the agency of actors within internet or participatory culture to choose whether, how, when, and with whom to share, adapt, and transmit memes. For similar reasons, he objects to the metaphor of virality, which casts memes as contagious diseases over we have little control, and distinguishes between virality (stand-alone shareability), and memetics, 'a collection of texts' (2013: 56). We could consider memetics as intermedia, discussed in Chapter 4, the interaction of multiple sign-systems with each other (Ljungberg 2010) as part of a signification *system* that is created by users through imitation.

Video content that propagates *virally* will be funny, emotional, and clear. It will originate from a well-known or prestigious source, well positioned or 'seeded' by marketers and content creators in venues or networks likely to be receptive, and possibly encourage follow-up action (Shifman 2013: 63–74). Video content that disseminates *memetically* will likewise be amusing and simple to grasp, but the memetic video, in contrast to the viral video, includes: 'ordinary people', rather than prestigious or famous ones, as makers or participants in the video, not just as sharers; 'whimsical content', almost impossible to anticipate; 'repetitive actions', and (intriguingly for *Twelfth Night*), 'flawed masculinity' (Shifman 2013: 63–74).

Shakespeare memes are successful when they borrow the highly abstracted instructions or 'code', such as patterns of narrative, character, and action (Bortolotti and Hutcheon 2007; Denslow 2017), or stage groupings that have been called 'theatregrams' (Clubb 1989). Fran Teague identifies as a 'sticky' meme the sonnet form in *Romeo and Juliet*, which reappears in *Romeo and Juliet* in different textual versions for no other reason that that it 'stuck' in the author's mind (2011). Denslow observes that each 'identifiable narrative unit' will entail 'some degree of change and adaptation to a new symbolic environment' when it becomes a meme (Denslow 2017: 99).

The stickiness of Feste's concluding song from *Twelfth Night* (5.1.382–401) has made it memeable as a lyric. Much anthologized, its sticky, 'spreadable' formal pattern encompasses the ballad form, the opening phrase, 'When that I was and a little tine [tiny] boy' and its refrain, 'with a heigh ho, the wind and the rain...for the rain it raineth every day'. Its 'narrative' recounts the singer's life, from childhood to maturity to old age, punctuated by that inclement weather; Shakespeare himself adapts it for the Fool in *King Lear* as 'He that has and a little tiny wit' (3.2.73). As a meme, the song connotes pathos, childhood, or poverty, often together, as when the 'tiny' girl Kitty sings it in a Victorian sensation novel by Anne Caldwell-Marsh, *Mordaunt Hall, or a September Night* (Marsh 1849). Breaking off mid-chorus, Kitty refuses to complete her song until her Papa agrees to succor the '*poor* boy' out in the hall who implicitly reminds her of the 'tiny boy' in the song (1849: 2: 63).

In the early twentieth century, Stanley Weir radically rewrites Feste's song as a pacifist Unitarian hymn in the Christian Register, 'The Super-Dreadnoughts' (Weir 1913: 445). Weir replaces the Fool's resigned 'heigh ho' with a saccharine series of present participial phrases connoting a sentimentalized, pastoral childhood – 'playing in the waving woods', 'skipping over grassy fields', 'tripping up and down', and so on – in order to contrast peace with the 'super-dreadnoughts' or powerful battleships of the ballad's title. In the twenty-first century, Joel Coen's recent film of Macbeth (2021) includes the entire song and twists its sentimental history. The elastic Kathryn Hunter doubles as all three witches and as the Old Man, who sings Feste's ballad when the former encounters the double agent Ross. Hunter's Old Man secretly saves 'the little…boy' Fleance, we learn later in the film; the Old Man's 'heigh, ho' is philosophical but not, as we might have feared, cynical enough to let Banquo's heir perish.

Feste's lyric functions as a verbal or aural meme, but Viola's identity revealed through the mutual encounter of the twins is a visual meme, persisting through multiple versions of *Twelfth Night* on screen that differ in setting, costuming, and even casting choices. *She's The Man* stages the twins' meeting on a soccer field, in soccer strip; Trevor Nunn's film (1996) in the gardens of a country estate, in uniform; the 1969 television production for the British network ATV at a carnival, using differently-coloured, historically appropriate, costumes for each character, a body double seen from the back, and judicious cutting, in order to cast Joan Plowright as both Viola and Sebastian. We can helpfully characterize the memetic quality of this scene in its various iterations by adopting Bryan Reynolds and Donald Hedrick's coinage 'Shakespace' (2000; Reynolds 2006) to suggest that this *Twelfth Night* meme or theatregram emerges not around a fixed object or even in a fixed location but rather in Shakespace, part of a network that involves high culture, literary history, mass media, gender politics and identities, and even legal and financial institutions.

# Networks

Sociologist Bruno Latour describes the abortive, ambitious French public transport project Aramis, in his eponymous book (1996), as a failure of networks rather than of any one individual or set of individuals. Conceived as a revolutionary, self-contained Personal Rapid Transit system, Aramis comprised a train of 'platooning' or 'flocking' small cars that could break off as single units to take passengers to their ultimate termini, solving the so-called 'last-mile problem' of public transit. Latour recounts its mishaps in a hybrid dramatic, mystery-novel, and documentary form, mixing imaginary dialogue between an idealistic young engineer and his professor, newspaper-style crime reportage about 'Who Killed Aramis?' and an explanation of ANT, the only way to account for the collapse of the project. In ANT, nonhuman and human agents – called actants or actors – act or are attributed action by others. In this sense, as Lanier, Reynolds, and others have noted (2014; 2003), Latour's network resembles Deleuze and Guattari's rhizome, discussed in Chapter 1. A 'material-semiotic' approach, ANT treats actants as objects that stand for themselves but that also substitute symbolically within a given culture's signifying systems and can, in OOO, even seem to 'act' agentially. Shakespearean approaches to OOO tease out the repercussions of reading *things* on stage or within texts, which are themselves *things* – Othello's famous handkerchief, bed, or candle (Harris 2010: 58–74), or oranges in *Much Ado* (Yates 2016).

For a sense of how identities can cohere in networks that include non-human objects and how even discrete gestures or body parts can become nodes within a network, consider the 2012 revival of the storied all-male production of *Twelfth Night* at the Globe Theatre in London, filmed and released on DVD in 2013. The production presented a deliberately stylized, theatrical, Shakespearean world that located femininity not only within dresses and whiteface makeup but also within patterns of gesture and movement. Olivia and Maria glided as if on wheels across the stage, their corseted, slightly breathless delivery contrasting with the freer timbres of Orsino and – in contrast to her timid first appearance as Viola – the uncorseted Cesario.

*Twelfth Night* (2013) uses a simple stone bench during Feste's song 'Come away, death' (2.4.51–66) and in the following scene as Malvolio fantasizes a relationship with Olivia. In both scenes, the bench becomes a node in networks of desire, cohering into an agent of that desire as the energies of the humans sitting on it express themselves. During the song, Orsino and Cesario sit facing opposite directions, as if on a love-seat; Orsino, fronting the audience, glances at Cesario from time to time, finally reaching for him, putting his hand on Cesario's shoulder, then taking his hand. When Orsino makes as if to kiss Cesario's hand, Cesario hurriedly rises and crosses the stage. The melancholy music, played in full, forms another node in the network of languishing desire. The same bench enlivens Malvolio's later musings; still alight with its intensity or energy from Cesario and Orsino, the bench draws Malvolio to imagine 'sitting in [his] state', having 'left Olivia sleeping' (2.5.42–6), the erotic fantasy that draws such ire from Sir Toby. The blocking of the scene might seem routine, but an object-oriented approach lets us focus on the function of the music and the way in which properties such as the bench can 'speak' words of love and on Shakespearean networks within and without the stage.

David Weinberger suggests that both Shakespeare and scholarship are networks, since they can: 'contain and connect' to other nodes 'without practical limits'; grow organically from creators and users in a decentred, unplanned manner; develop multiple nodes, depending on individual interest; avoid boundaries; include every node and connection on the network; link nodes through 'any type of relationship. . .almost always explained in the text, explicitly or implicity'; be 'extremely messy' and 'not highly reliable', because they are unauthorized and augmented by anyone; enable a link one-way, that is, we can link to Shakespeare, but Shakespeare cannot link to us, nor did Shakespeare 'give permission to be linked to' (2015: 401). Weinberger's recommendations for how to manage scholarship (and Shakespeare studies) in such a networked world correspond in interesting ways to the practices of existing fan communities. He recommends that we 'support open access', post work-in-progress and clearly explain the stage at which the posted document exists, link generously and imaginatively to sources that might seem unnecessary to an expert reader but that are essential or enlightening to a beginner; and be brave, unafraid to 'experiment[]' or venture something new.

# Fans

Critics now recognize – especially in our outsourced and underfunded era – the value and interest of Shakespeare enthusiasts beyond the academy or the theatre. Fan work in the twenty-first century overlaps with both scholarship and commerce, as Kathleen McLuskie and Hester Lees-Jeffries have suggested (1999; 2013). Taking issue with Richard Burt's complaint that commercial Shakespeare is but 'trash Shakespeare' trying to seem different, and better, than other 'trash Shakespeare' (Burt 2002: 10), McLuskie argues that Shakespeare is a non-rival good, an inexhaustible resource (1999), an 'open-source repository', in Sanders' phrase (2011), and thus appropriations of Shakespeare both transcend and become affectively enmeshed in capital, as YouTubers and others create value through uncompensated yet pleasurable work. Lees-Jeffries' beautiful analysis of the 'Greater Shakespeare' merchandise designed by Kit Grover for the Royal Shakespeare Company demonstrates how the best souvenirs, tokens, and Shakespeare-adjacent works can be 'playful, imaginative and discursive', characterized by a 'dynamic and quite close relationship to literary texts, in this case Shakespeare's plays' (2013: 195); we could say the same of fanwork. Perhaps the most helpful intervention has been the conceit of the 'Shakespeare user' (Fazel and Geddes 2017) or prosumer, a broad category that, like Hutcheon's model of adaptation, encompasses a range of activities, interests, and motives.

Fanfic has its own 'tropes', as they are called in fandom. We could equally well call them memes or, as Teague does, generic conventions, of which Teague mentions in particular: the 'Mary Sue', the insertion of the fan's own identity into the story as an impossibly idealized version of the author (as wittily discussed by Cindy Aleo, 2013); het/slash (erotic lives for characters beyond the text, whether such lives are heteroerotic or homoerotic and whether the characters' gender identities are binary, trans, or nonbinary); and WAFF (warm and fuzzy feelings). To these categories, we can add the Manic Pixie Dream Girl (or, more recently, Manic Pixie Dream Boyfriend): a secondary character with few or no goals of their own beyond serving as a romanticized fantasy vehicle for the author/protagonist. In this next section I will apply these memes from fandom loosely to Shakespearean criticism and adaptation, although, rather than speculating on the motives, identities, or personalities of individual critics or creators, I identify as Mary Sue narratives those in which readers, not just authors, can insert themselves as idealized protagonists, particularly as we adapt, confront, or replicate one of the 'stickiest' of memes, because of its entanglement in genes and sexual reproduction: binary gender.

# Transformations: A gender-agenda in *Twelfth Night*

Gender falls today, as bodily sex arguably did for Galenic physicians in Shakespeare's time (Laqueur 1990; Schiebinger 1989; Schleiner 2000) along a spectrum of identity between male and female that is expressed through social and cultural practices that change historically. People express gender identities through clothing, hairstyles, cosmetics, body modification or its absence, speech, behaviour and so on. Since the language surrounding gender identity is in a state of fluctuation, I use terms considered acceptable by most Shakespeareans at the time of writing (2021). I therefore use the term cis or cisgender to denote a person whose sense of personal identity coheres with the gender identity attributed to them at birth. I use the words trans or transgender to denote a person whose inner identity does not conform to the gender attributed to them at birth. I use the term nonbinary to refer to a person whose inner sense of identity does not correspond to either pole of the gender spectrum, that is, to the genders of male or female, or whose identity fluctuates along the spectrum. I describe love, sex, and erotic attraction between persons who overlap on the gender spectrum, whether as male or female, with the adjective same-sex or homoerotic, and that between persons who inhabit opposite ends of the spectrum as opposite-sex or heteroerotic.

I sometimes follow the many literary critics who deploy the adjective 'queer' (originally a slur, since recovered by many nonbinary, lesbian, gay, and trans people) to connote sexual identities, activities, and expressions that a given culture (including Shakespeare's) has historically found threatening or unacceptable or that do not conform to expected heterosexual expression or behaviour (Traub 1992; Goldberg 1994; Sanchez 2019), such as same-sex love in Thatcher's Britain; virginity, celibacy, or asexuality in early modern Protestant England (Jankowski 2000; Chess 2018), or eroticism among older people on film (Patricia 2017). Some activists prefer the terms 'assigned male at birth' (AMAB) and 'assigned female at birth' (AFAB) to the nouns man/woman or male/female; others also use the adjectives transmasculine or transmasc to indicate a person who identifies more with the masculine side of the spectrum (whether or not they were assigned female at birth) and transfeminine (vice versa). Since – unless agents or narrators wish to disclose such information within the diegesis or story or in some other way – we cannot know a given character's birth assignation, I continue to use 'male', 'female', 'man', 'woman', and so on in this chapter to refer to socially expressed gender; I will clarify pronouns as I go.

*Twelfth Night* is an obvious candidate for Mary Sue fantasies about both fixed and fluid gender: the leading character Viola, unnamed until recognized by their brother, is arguably only legible as a Mary Sue and Sebastian as a Manic Pixie Dream Girl or Boy. We pick the version of the character – Viola, Viola/Cesario, Cesario – and the ending that gives us the greatest WAFF. In early adaptations or extensions, such as Mary Cowden Clarke's prequel 'Viola: The Twin' (1851] 1974), Viola exemplifies conventional cisgender heteroerotic femininity, embodied, as George Gross observes, in the 'timid, shy, and naïve' nature she retains despite her 'astounding and virtue-threatening' escapades in the early life Clarke invents for her (Gross 1972: 43). Clarke transforms Shakespeare's heroines into girls who learn the meretriciousness of courtesans and the worth of ladies, the fragility of female virtue and the need for constant vigilance to protect it, and the need for valiant male rescuers to extricate girls from dangerously compromising positions (Gross 1972). Gross singles out the sexual naïveté of Clarke's girls as particularly un-Shakespearean, classifying Shakespeare's Viola, in contrast to Clarke's, as a 'full-blooded, passionate...expert on love' (1972: 43). No exception to Clarke's habit, Viola is rescued from a savage dog, an unwanted kiss, and finally from a rake's dastardly designs on her virtue, by her brave brother (Gross 1974: 328, 370, 383–6). Even from infancy, Viola's toddling steps are 'less assured' than those of her brother with his infantine 'superior power' (Clarke [1851] 1974: 317).

In Virginia Woolf's first-wave feminism, which idealized 'androgyny' (understood as equal capabilities and potential within men and women, who should, she argued, be able to display and combine features of masculinity and femininity, regardless of what their bodies looked like), Viola and Sebastian together on stage might represent Shakespeare's 'man-womanly' mind, described in *A Room of One's Own* as 'naturally creative, incandescent and undivided' (Woolf [1928] 1998: 128) and the fact that, as she observed in a review, 'Shakespeare wrote for the body and for the mind simultaneously' (Woolf 1933: 385). Beth Schwartz suggests that Woolf reads Shakespeare as 'Anon' (Woolf 1979), the imagined 'anonymous, androgynous singer' or pre-print balladeer who enabled 'a Shakespeare to come into being' (Schwartz 1991: 726). Thoughtfully identifying these lost, anonymous, androgynous, folkloric, quasi-maternal singers in several of Woolf's novels, including *Orlando*, Schwartz argues that such figures 'demythologize' biological motherhood and sex, but doesn't notice the Shakespearean character who most likely generates this figure for Woolf herself: Viola. Lost to herself and her brother through shipwreck, unnamed on stage until reunited with her brother, ungendered or dual-gendered, as both Viola and Cesario, beyond the end of the play, until Malvolio can be pacified to release the captain who holds the key to her woman's weeds, a talented singer whose skill enables another personation of androgyny or nonbinary gender, that of the 'eunuch' (Elam 1996), Viola is Woolf's Mary Sue; we can only wish that, like Viola, Woolf too could have escaped death by water.

In second-wave characterological feminist readings, Viola incarnates cisgender heteroerotic independence from conventionally ladylike norms, exemplified in her decision to dress as Cesario and the greater freedom of mobility and expression that that disguise offers her to develop a more equitable relationship with Orsino (Dusinberre [1977] 2003) or, in materialist feminist criticism, the boy-actor playing a woman's part personifies the misogyny of early modern institutions such as the stage, the church, and the law, which deem women incapable of representing themselves (Jardine 1983). Such readings dominated the twentieth and early twenty-first century, developing into queer feminist approaches, such as the consideration of the popular 'Shakesteen' film *She's The Man* (2006) I offer below.

*She's The Man* (2006) begins with the premise that Viola Hastings, a talented soccer player, can no longer play her sport because her high school cuts the girls' team and the coach refuses to let the girls play with the boys because the latter are allegedly faster, stronger, and more athletic. When Viola's own boyfriend, soccer star Justin, agrees that girls cannot play at the same level as boys, Viola decides to impersonate her twin brother Sebastian, scheduled to enrol in an elite boys' boarding school but planning to abscond to London with his band instead. Viola's participation in a contact, team sport reflects the power of the second-wave feminist movement in passing the 1972 US Education Amendment called Title IX, which requires schools to offer the same number of athletic opportunities to girls as to boys and which opened many more sports to female participation; prior to the amendment, folk and institutional wisdom claimed that certain sports and competition would hurt women's fertility, femininity, and even brain development (Busch and Thro 2018). Viola's resistance to her mother's pleas that she should 'come out' as a debutante in a white gown with 'ruffles' (which Viola hates) and participate in a charity 'kissing booth' (where boys can buy a ticket to buss beautiful belles for a few minutes at a time) likewise suggest that Viola resists stereotypes of conventional upper-middle-class, white American womanhood.

Helped by her stylish stylist friend Paul, Viola uses various cosmetic and behavioural prostheses to become 'Sebastian' (whom I will henceforth call 'Viola-Sebastian' while continuing to use the feminine pronouns *she/her/hers*) and to try out for the soccer team. The film cleverly suggests that rigid gender binaries harm not only Viola-Sebastian and the movie's girls but also the boys in the film. Viola-Sebastian's handsome, reserved roommate and crush, Duke, suffers because he must hide his sensitivity behind a hypermasculine exterior; his friend Toby feels compelled to conceal his affection for Eunice because she is considered undesirable by the other boys on the team; Sebastian hides his musical ambitions from his parents, who want him to enter a more traditionally bread-winning profession, and so on.

At same time, the film carefully presents Viola as cisgender and heterosexual. From the very beginning, we know she has a boyfriend, and her encounter with Duke in the kissing booth cements their mutual attraction. When a box of tampons falls out of Viola-Sebastian's bag, and Duke, shocked, asks why she has them, she feigns surprise that her teammates have never heard of using tampons to stanch a nosebleed, as she demonstrates. The behaviour goes viral; soon Duke, too, is inserting a tampon in his nostril to stop the flow of blood. As Leo Bersani (1987), Lee Edelman (2004), and Jeff Masten (1997) have suggested, traditional forms of cis heterosexual masculinity, especially since the Renaissance, depend upon the myth of the impenetrable male: where women are impressionable, open, and liquid, men are invulnerable, continent, and firm, a construct that can be found in the Renaissance along with the one-sex model (Paster 1993; King 1998). Viola-Sebastian's and Duke's nose-tampons thus provide a satirical Freudian upward displacement that, in little, indicates how Viola-Sebastian's presence, even in disguise, offers a necessary feminizing corrective to the impractical and often uncomfortable manliness the boys feel they must display.

Users have likewise found the film and the image of the tampon-using manly man enduringly amusing; the website tenor.com, which collects user-generated GIFs, shows many such created from the film that 'meme' this moment, with titles such as 'Manliest Way to Handle a Nosebleed'. Returning to Shifman's criteria for memetic video, we see that this figure indeed includes humour, clarity, creation by an ordinary user rather than a marketer (although it transforms commercial, copyrighted content and features a well-known actress), and a joke at men's expense (figure 5.1). The film is likewise careful to include a character coded as gay in Paul, the stylist, although we never see Paul with a boyfriend, only with Viola's other female friends, putting him firmly into the stereotype of the 'Sassy Gay Friend' popularized by Brian Gallivan of the Second City acting troupe (2010).

Some critics have suggested that, in an era of widespread same-sex marriage, gay identities, expressions, and unions can be *homonormative* and conventional rather than queer and counter-cultural (Stryker 2008). In this sense Paul is homonormative, a character who charms mass audiences while he avoids any display of sexuality – even hand-holding – with another man (which might have threatened the film's

**FIGURE 5.1** *'It absorbs right up!' She's the Man*, DVD, USA: Paramount, 2006. Screen capture by the author.

PG-13 rating). Heterosexual desire likewise brings into conformity Eunice, the 'horny nerd', tortured by spectacles, asthma, buck teeth, and unpopularity, as she finds partnership with Toby by the end of the film. Any suggestion of queer or uncontrollable sexuality is displaced on to Malcolm, the Malvolio character, whose unrequited crush on Olivia encompasses his sleeping with a life-sized image of her imprinted on a pillow. Eunice and Malcolm are alike so outlandish, however, that they are clearly recognizable as fantastic elements of the story rather than as realistic Mary Sue or Manic Pixie Dream Boy characters.

The climax of *She's The Man* involves two exaggerated out-of-shot displays of cisgender normativity: challenged on the soccer field, Sebastian exposes his genitals and Viola-Sebastian her breasts to a cheering crowd. Viola-Sebastian prefaces her demonstration by peeling off her prosthetic sideburns and eyebrows and removing her wig, in what is almost certainly a nod to the earlier *Shakespeare in Love* (1999). In *Shakespeare in Love*, Viola de Lesseps displays her gender when her blonde locks cascade down from under her short brown wig, an on-camera revelation that necessitates some clumsy cutting mid-shot (Iyengar 2001). In *She's The Man*, the wig-removal is more realistic – but Duke observes that boys, too, can wear wigs (he could have added that girls can grow sideburns and bushy eyebrows). It's only when prompted by Duke that Viola-Sebastian lifts her shirt to flash the crowd (and Duke). The film even ends with the reconciliation of Sebastian and Viola's divorced parents, making it what Stanley Cavell has called a 'comedy of remarriage' (1984). Its concluding scenes, however, show Viola playing – as Viola – on the boys' team, holding her own, as if heralding a world where gender can be an erotic choice rather than a socially determining condition.

As Viola/Cesario/Sebastian in third-wave feminist and queer feminist criticism, the networked character personifies polymorphous, fluid desire and desirability (Traub 1992; Rackin 2005; Neely 2016) and the distributed electronic, erotic consciousness of what Kirk Hendershott-Frazer (2018) has called, following Leisha Jones, 'the digital collective subject' (Jones 2011; Hendershott-Frazer 2016). As Jones points out, this distributed, network subject becomes a version of Deleuze and Guattari's 'desiring machine' (Jones 2011: 452; Deleuze and Guattari 1987), the embodied mother-child dyad that sustains its own desire and hungrily appropriates that which is outside itself, extending the bounds of self and body. Like other fanwork, moreover, digitally distributed fan videos made by this digital collective subject enable 'alternative readings of canon...not possible in the original setting, particularly [regarding]...gender, sexuality, race, and disability' (Finn and McCall 2016: 31).

Fan videos 'condense' not only the rhetorics of performance, as Desmet has noted in a series of essays (2009; 2019) but also those of Shakespearean and cultural criticism. TikTok videos compress duration (they are mere seconds long) and information. All on a cellphone screen, viewers are made aware, via a scrolling chyron, of the video's creator, the soundtrack, and its hashtags, while the constantly-updating right-hand menu tallies the number of 'favourite', 'follows', 'shared' and 'comment' responses each video has had. In a TikTok video uploaded by the actor 'your pal al'

@nofearshakesqueer (38,500 followers) in July 2021 called 'When people think Twelfth Night is a straight play', tagged 'everyone in illyria is bi you absolute cowards', and 'favourited' by over 12,000 people, the youthful characters are gender-, sexuality-, and race-fluid. The characters' names are identified by labels.

Sebastian, played by a bespectacled Black woman in torn jeans and canary-yellow T-shirt, her hair in short twists, gazes adoringly at Olivia, a brown-haired, stocky white man in blue denim jacket and dark jeans, while a female Orsino with auburn curls is chucked under the chin by her loving Viola, a busty blonde in a white tank top and large earrings (Figure 5.2). The lovers canoodle to a five-second clip of the

FIGURE 5.2. *'When People Think Twelfth Night is a Straight Play', TikTok microvideo, @nofearshakesqueer. Screen capture by the author, TikTok, 17 January 2022.*

song 'Kiss Me More' (2021), a musical collaboration between the artists DojaCat and SZA, specifically to lyrics referring to the lyric speaker's desired infidelity with the addressee, a friend. The lyric speaker figures her long-term relationship as prison and expresses her desire to leave it, either temporarily on her own recognizance (for a non-exclusive affair), or to end the monogamous romance altogether – in either case, the lyric speaker wants to break out from erotic confinement.

Like many of its YouTube ancestors, this video crosses genres, with elements of the remix, the mashup, the vid, the fan performance, and the theatrical trailer. The remix adapts a prior musical work by altering features of various tracks within the sound (beats, instrumentation, lyrics); a mashup uses at least one other piece of music in order to effect its remix; a vid adds the user's own action to a piece of commercial music, often as parody (Teague 2011; O'Neill 2014). The micro-video (and others by this creator) constitute what O'Neill calls a 'fan performance', a parody that, like O'Neill's examples from YouTube, deploys 'a critical edge' (2014: 58). Whereas O'Neill's examples, however, contrast 'the distance between the Shakespearean texts and contemporary culture in terms of attitudes to gender and sexuality' (2014: 57), @nofearshakesqueer uses their videos to highlight their queer readings of Shakespeare, to suggest that these readings are immanent within the texts, and to demonstrate their talents.

Again, as with many contemporary YouTubers and TikTokers, the lines between professional and amateur, fan and commercial, are blurred to the point of nonexistence: @nofearshakesqueer accepts donations via the peer-to-peer payment site Venmo and links out to a website for their theatrical productions, where viewers can sign up to a mailing list to be informed of upcoming events. And like many fanfic writers, the creator presents a persona on Twitter, Instagram, TikTok, YouTube and so on that has a consistently performed and textualized cross-platform identity, in this case (at the time of writing) as queer and nonbinary, allowing us to identify the collective, fluid subject of this micro-*Twelfth Night* Tok as a distributed, electronic Mary Sue.

The COVID-19 pandemic allowed amateur, fan- and semi-professional productions to flourish on Zoom, YouTube, and, carefully and occasionally, outdoors, even as professional live theatre collapsed [Table 5.1]. Many or most of these non-traditional, community-, fan- or amateur productions described themselves as 'queer' or 'genderqueer' or deliberately described their actors as nonbinary, from Midsommer Flight's 'unabashedly queer' immersive production in Chicago (Boland 2021) to Indecorous Theater's gay and nonbinary outdoor production at Strawberry Mansion for the Philadelphia Fringe (Cristi 2021) to the new Irvington Shakespeare Company's ninety-minute 'genderqueer' outdoor show in the Hudson Valley (Irvington 2021) and a hybrid outdoor and digital performance put on by a student-run troupe, 'Ye Rude Mechanicals', at my university (Smith 2021). In such productions, Viola can continue to engender a fluctuating eroticism even as he demonstrates a pause in what Jack

Table 5.1 *Productions of* Twelfth Night *and* Romeo and Juliet *in 2021, 2020, and 2015*

| Year | Number of Professional Productions | Play |
| --- | --- | --- |
| 2021 | 7 | *Twelfth Night* |
| 2021 | 18 | *Romeo and Juliet* |
| 2020 | 7 | *Twelfth Night* |
| 2020 | 13 | *Romeo and Juliet* |
| 2015 | 40 | *Twelfth Night* |
| 2015 | 50 | *Romeo and Juliet* |

*Source:* World Shakespeare Bibliography (January 2022).

Halberstam has called gender as process (Halberstam 2017) or (to return to our constant companions, Deleuze and Guattari), gender-as-becoming rather than gender-as-being.

The Midsommer Flight immersive transformation and the student-run hybrid show cast actors regardless of any of the usual ways we might 'read' gender: the genders assigned to the actors at birth; performed through social cues off-stage; attributed to them by the text; inferred by viewers based on actors' visible bodily features. The net effect, writes Alisa Boland of the Midsommer show, was to make 'gender – once a crucial part of the script...too difficult to follow', turning the play into a vehicle for 'mistaken identity' (2021). In these transformations, Cesario's embodying one gender or another at the end of the play doesn't mean that he was always a boy (although it might) nor that she was ever or still is a girl (although it might) nor that they were consistently nonbinary; the character's variable gender and trajectory emerges through the assemblage of its performance, including the community that engenders and can parse its meanings. The director of the student production at my university engaged head-on with these difficulties, not only changing the final lines of the play to account for their actors' gender journeys but also unashamedly adducing Tate's *Lear* to support their rewriting for their community (Smith 2021). The resulting confusion for those outside the group and for those unfamiliar with their Shakespeare reflects the sense of non-belonging and confusion experienced by many queer teens and young adults, while it simultaneously introduces and welcomes outsiders to the subculture that created it. My next chapter also takes us into contexts unfamiliar to traditional Shakespeare performances, to translations or 'tradaptations' of Shakespeare through a peripatetic play about peregrination: Shakespeare and George Wilkins' *Pericles*.

# 6

# Relocation, translation, hybridization:

# Tradaptation

Translations, relocations, and tradaptations raise once more the questions of purity and fidelity that I have engaged throughout. Theatre practitioners themselves have transported Shakespeare's plays from England to different geographical settings and cultural contexts, just as Shakespeare created a fictitious coastline for his Bohemia in *The Winter's Tale* and as he and George Wilkins buffeted their hapless hero *Pericles* from one Mediterranean shore to another to such an extent that Peter Holland suggests that the play naturally lends itself to a promenade production in which viewers themselves wander from place to place (2005: 20). (For the sake of brevity and in the tradition of adapters, although most commentators believe *Pericles* to be the work of both Shakespeare and Wilkins, I will use 'Shakespeare' to refer to the joint authorship of *Pericles* and 'Wilkins' to refer to the author of the 1608 novella). The portmanteau word *tradaptation*, usually credited to Québécois (*joual*) playwright Michel Garneau in the 1990s (although Trivedi [2000: 75] attributes the term to Patrice Pavis), implies that translation is adaptation and adaptations are translations, and, as we shall see, adds a post- or neo-colonial bite to acts of translation (Lieblein 2004; Hellot and Garneau 2009; Drouin 2014).

Prior to the post-modern turn in translation and adaptation studies, attitudes both towards translation and towards Shakespeare implied, first, that literary translators should aim for accuracy and fluency, and that an accurate or faithful translation was possible (Nida 2006) and, second, that translations of Shakespeare, lacking the language of the early texts, must necessarily be inferior to those early modern English texts (Kennedy 1993). Translation theory (a vast field towards which I can only gesture in this chapter) joins with contemporary adaptation theory and post-colonial theory to argue that a translation is a creative endeavour, an original work (Venuti 1995), and that to read translated and intercultural Shakespeare as adaptations is useful, necessary, and mutually enlivening for Shakespearean text and its adaptation, or, to use more conventional translators' terms, source and target (Bassnett 2014).

'Source' and 'target' are also, of course, the terms used by Lakoff and Johnson and theorists of cognitive metaphor; ideas migrate through metaphor from a source domain to a target domain. The term *translation*, like the term *metaphor* itself, derives from this sense of movement: *translation* in Middle English and in Latin in its earliest uses connoted not only our modern sense of conversion from one language to another but also the removal of objects, from concrete ones such as items of furniture or saints' relics, to abstractions such as property rights, or even the combination of human bodies and abstract principles in the translation of Parliament (*OED*, translation, n.1.II.8, 9, 11,12). 'Translated' Shakespeare thus encompasses not only Shakespeares performed in or with non-English languages but also what we used to call 'Global' Shakespeare and now – recognizing the ways in which the term *global* both irons out the differences within and between source and target cultures and ignores whole regions and cultures of the world, especially the African continent (Plastow 2013) and indigenous peoples

(Fischlin 2020) – 'intercultural' Shakespeare (Kennedy 1993; Bharucha 2010).

Figuring adaptation as relocation, hybridization, and translation deploys two subsets of the fundamental frame *change is motion*: *creativity is motion* and *caused change is forced motion*. Given the dynamic relationship between source and target domains in metaphor, the reverse is also true: to move something is to change it, for our delight or to our discomfort. Relocations and translations thus return us to 'fidelity' debates as they challenge the concept *morality is pure or clean or unitary* through their movement away from a Shakespearean centre, whether that centre is geographical, historical, linguistic, or nationalist.

Having briefly outlined Shakespeare's adaptation of prior versions of the tale, this chapter will contextualize the overlap between translation theory and adaptation theory through the work of Roman Jakobson [1959] (2006), Lawrence Venuti (1995), Susan Bassnett (2014) and others before considering the ways in which relocated theatrical productions can become 'domesticated' (Venuti 1995), hybridized (Bhabha 1984), 'indigenized' (Trivedi 2000; Hutcheon 2013), or tradapted (Lieblein [2004] 2012; Hellot and Garneau 2009; Mooneram 2009). While all Shakespearean translations (to non-English languages or to other forms of English) and all Shakespearean relocations away from the Anglosphere can fruitfully be considered as adaptations, tradaptations explicitly engage post- or neo-colonialism by placing the Shakespearean text at a double removal. I conclude the chapter with a discussion of three twenty-first-century tradaptations of *Pericles* that overtly respond to the migrant crisis in the West, including performances to and with disaster-struck climate migrants: Toby Gough and the Theatrum Botanicum's production *Children of the Sea* (2005), performed on-site in Sri Lanka and at the Edinburgh Festival Fringe; *Périclès, Prince de Tyr* (2018), directed by Declan Donnellan for the Cheek By Jowl company in France; and Ali Smith's lyrical, biting, and paradoxically hopeful English-language novel *Spring* (2019).

I'll ask the following questions: are all adaptations 'translations', and all translations 'adaptations', and what do we gain or lose by collapsing these categories? Is Shakespeare without English words – such as the multilingual adaptation of *Pericles, Children of the Sea* (2005), or the French *Périclès, Prince de Tyr* (2018) from Cheek by Jowl that I will discuss later – still Shakespeare? Is a Shakespeare influenced by Japanese, Indian, Iraqui, Québécois or other non-European sources – as in the portrayal of Patrice Naiambana's Gower as a West African griot or storyteller in the Globe's *Pericles* (2005) – still Shakespeare? Whose 'property' is Shakespeare?

# Relocation

Boika Sokolova and Katy Stavreva (2020), Ania Loomba (1998), Jyotsna Singh (2019), Poonam Trivedi (2000) and Dennis Bartholomeusz (2005) contribute to ongoing conversation about the possibilities for and limits on intercultural Shakespeare and the power of so-called 'glocal' productions. The great promise of the 'glocal' at the end of the twentieth century was supposedly its ability to mesh the power of global brands with local empowerment to create new hybrid forms. Yet within the context of so-called Asian or pan-Asian Shakespeare, Trivedi (2000) observes that so-called intercultural productions tend to be limited to 'metropolitan areas' and to foreground the concerns of a globalized elite. Rustom Bharucha (2001) incisively anticipates the North American critiques of Thompson (2021), Little (2016), Fischlin (2020) and others as he argues that we need to imagine an 'intra-cultural' Shakespeare as well as an 'intercultural' one, in order to avoid eliding the interests of minoritized groups within a given nation-state or institution.

Singh (2019) offers a more optimistic roadmap, suggesting that postcolonial and intercultural adaptors, artists, and audiences can 'decolonize' or subvert Shakespeare through 'travelling Shakespeares' in local, 'non-metropolitan' sites of knowledge (5). These Shakespeares distance themselves from traditional Shakespeare and Western epistemologies in the languages and methodologies they use and the stories they tell. They identify and appropriate both the Shakespeare of the plays and the Shakespeare of sources and adaptations, and remake them in hyper-local ways. In other words, such adaptations create a Shakespeare that is constant yet malleable, resistant yet resisting, familiar yet strange, foreign yet 'neighborly', as Mookherjee has suggested (2019), a true 'travelling theory'.

'Travelling theories', which I introduced in Chapter 1, emanate from: a 'set of initial circumstances'; cover 'a distance traversed', through both 'time and place' as such ideas 'come into a new prominence'; encounter 'conditions of acceptance or. . .resistances', which 'confront' the idea and its alterity; such resistance and acceptance leads to the final stage, in which the idea is 'accommodated' (a term to which we will return in my next chapter) and 'transformed by its new uses, its new position in a new time and place' (Said [1982] 2014: 115). Resisting the 'overtotalizing' tendency of many theoretical frameworks, Said urges us to look constantly for local and immediate differences, modifications, alternatives, possibilities; it is in such adaptation, he suggests, that human growth and change become possible.

Returning to the texts and tales that Shakespeare explicitly and implicitly used to compose *Pericles*, we learn that the story of Apollonius of Tyre has itself served as a travelling theory of forgiveness, redemption, and human change or renewal throughout the ancient, medieval, and early modern worlds and through multiple languages. Thought to originate from a Greek romance (no longer extant), the tale prior to Shakespeare's version spawned 'more than one hundred' Latin manuscripts (Smyth 1898: 217); an Old English romance; early medieval Scandinavian romances; thirteenth-century Danish ballads and fourteenth-century illuminated Italian manuscripts; the fourteenth-century British poet Gower's long narrative poem *Confessio Amantis* ([1386–90] 2006), and an anonymous, well-known sixteenth-century Anglo-Latin collection of classical stories called the *Gesta Romanorum*

(Smyth 1898: 293–312). The circuitous, multi-national, macaronic path of the sixteenth century English version printed by Wynkyn de Worde is exemplary: Robert Copland translated it 'out of the Frensshe language to our maternal Englysshe tongue' (Steinhöwel 1510: [A1v]), and that French version was an adaptation of Heinrich Steinhöwel's German synthesis of multiple Latin sources, including the Latin *Gesta Romanorum* (Wade 1995).

More immediate influences upon Shakespeare and Wilkins' play include Philip Sidney and Mary Sidney Herbert's *The Countess of Pembroke's Arcadia* (revised, collated, and edited by various hands between 1570 and 1621 and whence, some suggest, Shakespeare might have drawn the name 'Pericles', from the hero *Pyrocles*) and a popular novelization, *The Pattern of Painful Adventures*, by Lawrence Twine, published in several editions between 1576–1607. Shakespeare may also have known a Middle French prose romance in which the hero takes the pseudonym *Perillie* after his shipwreck, to connote the dangers or perils he has passed (Smyth 1898: 269; *Pericles* 1986: 3n); this would support the suggestion that the hero's name refers to the dangers he has passed, from the Latin *periculum*. Wilkins seems later to have capitalized on the popularity of his and Shakespeare's play by issuing his own novelized version, supplemented with additions from Twine's earlier novella (1608).

These translations and retellings maintain several consistent narrative elements, although Shakespeare alters and adapts the characters' names in ways that are sometimes confusing [Table 6.1]. A virtuous young hero of Tyre (King Apollonius in the sources, Jourdain in a French source, Prince Pericles in Shakespeare; I'll henceforth call him Pericles) seeks the hand of Antiochus' beautiful daughter (always unnamed) in marriage only to discover that the girl is being raped by her father; his life threatened by the angry king, the horrified prince flees Antioch only to be shipwrecked on the coast of Pentapolis (in some versions, including Shakespeare's, he rescues the kingdom of Tarsus from famine on the way). The now-destitute prince displays his virtuosity (in ball-playing, jousting, music, or some

Table 6.1 *Selected characters as named in Gower, Steinhöwel, Twine, and Shakespeare*

| Character | Gower | Copland | Twine | Shakespeare |
|---|---|---|---|---|
| Ruler of Tyre | Appolinus | Appolyn | Apollonius | Pericles |
| King of Antioch | | Anthyogus | Antiochus | Antiochus |
| Foster-parents in Tarsus | Strangulio and Dionisie | Tranquylyte and Dyonyse | Stranguilio and Dionisiades | Cleon and Dionysia |
| King of Pentapolis | Artestratus | | Altistrates | Simonides |
| Princess of Pentapolis | | Archycastres (variant spelling of 'Cleopatra' [Wade 1995: 9] | Lucina | Thaisa |
| Midwife | Lychoride | | Lychorida | Lychorida |
| Reviver of Apollonius' wife | Cerymon | Cyromon | Cerimon | Cerimon |
| Apollonius' daughter | Thaisa | Tharcye | Tharsia | Marina |
| Ruler of Mytilene | Atenagoras | Anthygoras | Athanagoras | Lysimachus |
| Diana (goddess) | Diana | Diana | Diana | Diana |

*Sources*: Gower ([1386–90] 2006), Steinhöwel (1510), Twine ([?1594] 1966), and *Pericles* (2020).

other courtly activity) and wins the heart of the kingdom's princess (called variously Archycastres, Cleopatra, Lucina, or, in Shakespeare, Thaisa) who writes him a love-letter, marries him, and bears him a child (called Thaisa, Tarsia, and in Shakespeare, Marina) during the voyage home only to die during the birth at sea and be cast overboard in a sealed casket. The heartbroken prince leaves his young daughter to be fostered at Tarsus, but the foster parents, envious, try to murder the child, and tell Pericles that she has perished.

Pericles grieves for many years before miraculously finding his daughter in a brothel in Mitylene, where she manages to convince a would-be client (Atenagoras, Athanagoras, or, in Shakespeare, Lysimachus), who turns out to be the ruler of Mytilene and who eventually marries her, to help her preserve her virginity and gain her freedom. Rejoicing at the reunion with his daughter, Pericles that night dreams of his dead wife, who calls him to Ephesus. At Ephesus, Pericles and his daughter find the queen, who had not died but was rescued from her watery grave, resuscitated, and settled in Diana's temple until her family should find her again. (In the interests of clarity, I'll use Shakespeare's character-names from now on.)

As editors have documented, Shakespeare's play alters or mystifies these characters' motivation, in part because of the exigencies of drama. In the theatre, a moralizing choric voice such as Gower's is one of many actors in the cast rather than a singular, authoritative focalizer such as Twine's. Shakespeare removes the descriptions in Gower and Twine of Antiochus' unnamed, abused daughter pleading with her father not to rape her and grieving over her fate, instead giving us a Gower with the unforgettably cruel line, 'Bad child, worse father' (1.0.27). Shakespeare condenses the courtship of Pericles and Thaisa, adding an urgency and swiftness to their falling in love, and to heighten that intensity, adds a scene in which Simonides feigns an initial anger at the match, although he is secretly delighted (just as Prospero in *The Tempest* creates false obstacles for Miranda and Ferdinand, 'lest too light winning / Make the prize light' [1.2.451–2]).

Pericles grieves for Thaisa's seeming death less extravagantly in the play than in Twine and objects to the sailors' casting her overboard, perhaps giving room for the actor to suggest that the prince agrees with Cerimon, 'they were too rough / That threw her in the sea' (*Pericles* 3.2.78–9). Shakespeare fleshes out the characters in the brothel, setting scenes there rather than having Marina bought at the auction block by Lysimachus or his agents, and adds a certain ambiguity to the ruler of Mytilene. In Twine, Lysimachus clearly intends to ravish Marina until he learns her parentage and is converted, but in Shakespeare the former remains ignorant of her birth until Pericles lands, and claims retroactively (and somewhat unconvincingly) to have been at the brothel for no 'ill intent' (4.5.114).

Perhaps most interesting is Shakespeare's naming – not of Antiochus' unfortunate daughter, anonymous in all early versions of the tale and in *Pericles* – but of Marina's adopted foster-sister, the daughter of Cleon and Dionyza in Tarsus. Although 'Philoten' has no lines and no entrances, her named existence and the account of her close friendship with Marina (4.0.18–31), like the addition of an unnamed 'companion maid' for Marina (5.1.70) when she revives her father, offers viewers and readers more daughter-figures and a constant female presence companioning Marina throughout the play. This female community contrasts the isolation of Antiochus' daughter, who dare not tell even her nurse about the nightly terror of her father's visits; indeed, Gower writes, she could hardly speak at all, for shame ('For schame couthe unethes speke', Gower [1386–90] 2006: 1.8.324). George Lillo's dramatic adaptation *Marina* (1738) and many twentieth-century stage productions of *Pericles* omitted the disturbing incest-plot altogether (Lillo also makes the story conform to the Neoclassical unities, as Dryden had done earlier with *Antony and Cleopatra* in his *All for Love* [1677]).

In contrast, Mark Haddon's novel *The Porpoise* (2019) relocates the story – not in space or geography, but in time – to foreground and to name this child-victim. Set in three eras – the present, Shakespeare's London, and the ancient world –

*The Porpoise* begins when billionaire businessman Phillipe loses his beloved wife in a plane crash. Raising their daughter Angelica alone, Phillipe sexually abuses her in the solipsistic secrecy of the super-rich until the young, handsome playboy Darius awakens Angelica's interest and Phillippe resolves to hunt him down. Haddon's Angelica fights back with her only weapons: silence and starvation. The novel interweaves with its modern cosmopolitan plot a novelized and altered version of the events of Shakespeare's play and the writing of it, with added characters and a vividly imagined ancient Mediterranean world. George Wilkins appears as a broken-down playwright haunted by Shakespeare's ghost. When Darius finds himself wrecked at sea, he comes back to life as Shakespeare's Pericles.

Where the modern characters perish and its Shakespearean ones suffer, however, its ancient. invented or conflated ones thrive, often rescued by the agency of women. Emilia (Haddon's version of Thaisa) rescues her own daughter from the waves and needs no doctor when she herself is pulled from the sea. When Angelica dies by fire, weakened by her long hunger-strike, the goddess Diana stands ghostly by her side to set her free. In this way Haddon's adaptation foregrounds Shakespeare's silent, unnamed, or 'ghost' female characters: Antiochus' daughter; Philoten; Marina's companion; and the other girls in the brothel, just as, we shall see, the promenade production *Children of the Sea* (2006) and Ali Smith's novel *Spring* (2019) emphasize the resilience and 'living hope' of wandering children (Smith [2019] 2020: 325), adapting the emblem of Shakespeare's Pericles, a withered yet greening branch and the Latin tag 'In hac spe vivo', for the children's own motto.

# Translation

Let's use that Latin motto and emblem to survey debates surrounding modes of translation and/as adaptation. Pericles appears after his shipwreck to joust for Thaisa's hand disguised in his father's rusty armour, fortuitously washed up on the shore of Pentapolis; prior to the tourney, each knight displays his *impresa* (shield and motto) to Thaisa and Simonides, who describe the emblems but do not translate the mottos. We can usefully consider the shield and the knights' display – whether effected through a procession followed by offstage 'tilting' or jousting, as the script suggests [*Pericles* 2.3.SD] or, more whimsically, as a series of erotic dances and backstage farce, as in *Périclès* (2018) – as an example of the transmedia I identified in previous chapters as phenomena identifiable across nations and languages.

As the knights parade before Thaisa, she and her father describe and analyze the images before them, with Pericles appearing last:

THAISA
He seems to be a stranger; but his present is
A withered branch that's only green at top,
The motto, *In hac spe vivo*.
SIMONIDES
      A pretty moral.
From the dejected state wherein he is
He hopes by you his fortunes yet may flourish.
FIRST LORD
He had need mean better than his outward show
Can any way speak in his just commend,
For by his rusty outside he appears
To have practiced more the whipstock than the lance.
SECOND LORD
He well may be a stranger, for he comes
To an honored triumph strangely furnishèd.
THIRD LORD
And on set purpose let his armor rust
Until this day, to scour it in the dust.
SIMONIDES
Opinion's but a fool that makes us scan
The outward habit by the inward man.

2.2.41–59

This section of the play in the Arden Third Series edition includes multiple examples of translation, remediation, adaptation, or whatever else we want to call it, namely: the ekphrastic description of the shield from Thaisa (visual signs to spoken or printed word); the translation and glossing of the Latin *impresa* by the volume's editor, Suzanne Gossett, in the footnotes; the allegorical interpretation offered by Simonides; and even the meta-commentary offered by the First and Second Lords – all types of transfer considered 'translation' by modern theorists.

Eugene Nida argued ([1964] 2006) that translators, knowing that they can provide no exact counterpart in their target language for what they are translating from their source, must choose whether or not to provide a 'gloss translation' or a 'dynamic' one. The first, Nida suggests, tries to recreate in the reader the mind or mindset of the writer, within the source language, relying on a literal translation that maintains the structure and even the syntax of the source, even if explanatory notes are required. Most editors of *Pericles,* including Gossett and the Arden Second Series editor, E. D. Hoeniger (*Pericles* [1963] 1986), translate the Latin motto on Pericles' shield, 'In hac spe vivo' (2.2.43) thus: 'In this hope I live' (2.2n.43). Such translations are literally glosses (in Nida's sense) with footnotes explaining the possible provenance of the Latin tag.

The second kind of translation, says Nida, aims for 'dynamic equivalence', in which the translator strives to match not the pattern but the *effect* of the text in the mind of the reader, and in particular aims for 'complete naturalness of expression' rather than the formal strangeness of the gloss ([1964] 2006: 350). There is no full so-called translation of *Pericles* on the popular study site *No Fear Shakespeare*, but there is a plot summary that includes a more dynamic translation of Pericles' Latin motto: 'His shield says "I live in this hope"' (SparkNotes 2022). We might note that where Gossett's and Hoeniger's literal glosses bring out the heightened lyricism of the scene through the unaccustomed word order of the sentence, the naturalness of the contemporary English student 'translation' might not necessarily equate to an 'equivalent' effect, partly because translating verse or experimental fiction presents even greater challenges than do traditional texts.

Essaying just this problem, the controversial 'Play on!' series, commissioned by the Oregon Shakespeare Festival, aimed to 'translate' Shakespeare's plays into 'modern' verse, with the proviso that each text is a 'script' open to change and adaptation with every performance – in other words, a 'dynamic' translation. Ellen McLaughlin's lines (*Pericles* 2022) stay close to Shakespeare in this selection but alter the word order of Thaisa's gloss to 'green only on top' rather than 'only green on top' and the language and meaning of the motto: 'The motto is just: In you lives my hope' (*Pericles* 2022: 27). The reversal of *green/only* arguably clarifies for listeners that 'on top' modifies 'green', though the point is somewhat strained; in the same spirit, Thaisa translates the Latin herself for the audience, somewhat ambiguously, since 'just' could mean either 'simply' or 'equitable'. (I suspect the former, but I am influenced by having listened to the podcast recording of this scene, in which Pericles is the only native English-speaker among the jousting knights ([2021]). In the audio recording, Thaisa responds actively to Pericles with a languishing sigh – 'ohh'. In that podcast performance, then, Thaisa and Pericles enjoy, paradoxically, an instant connection requiring no translation – 'just' McLaughlin's modernized English verse.

The French used in *Périclès* (2018), adapted from François Pierre Guillaume Guizot's 1821 translation, likewise incorporates both literal and dynamic elements. It adds to the script a French gloss of the Latin motto, voiced by Simonides: 'Dans cet espoir je vive!', 'in this hope I live', yet the language necessitates an unavoidable dynamism. Pericles' branch must be more active in French than in English, 'une branche flétri qui ne verdit qu'à une extremité', a withered branch that *greens* or *grows green* or *flourishes* only at the tip. Each translation creates its own poetry.

Roman Jakobson suggested that, in poetry especially, translation must inevitably become a creative act. He distinguishes among 'three kinds' of translation: 'intralingual translation or *rewording*...[,] an interpretation of verbal signs by means of other signs of the same language'; 'interlingual translation or *translation proper*...[,] an interpretation of verbal signs by means of some other language'; and 'intersemiotic translation or *transmutation*...[,] an interpretation of verbal signs by means of signs of nonverbal sign systems ([1959] 2006: 331). Considering Pericles's disguised appearance once more, we could understand Pericles' shield as subject to two of the three modes Jakobson denominates. The shield itself is a physical object with both image and text upon it; the image offers 'an interpretation of verbal signs...by means of nonverbal sign systems', or transmutation.

Simonides 'translates' Thaisa's description of the withered branch into other words, a *rewording* (one that is, however, in Jakobson's terms nonetheless an 'interpretation'). The Lords likewise translate intersemiotically, rather than offering a translation proper. All three comment on the armour's rust, the First Lord translating the rust into class terms when he suggests that Pericles looks like a drover rather than a knight, the second translating it into a theory of national origin by speculating that he is a 'stranger', and the third ambiguously suggests that the seeming disrespect or ill-preparedness of the candidate is deliberate, 'on purpose', without speculating on what that purpose might be. These translators are, as Walter Benjamin argued, seeking a kind of integrity or wholeness, attempting to create 'in the translator's language that latent structure which can awake an echo of the original' (Benjamin [1968] 2006: 303).

Jakobson's intersemiotic corresponds to what some translators call 'cultural translation', but cultural translation, suggests Lawrence Venuti, can be either 'domesticated' or 'foreignized'. Venuti challenges the long-standing idea that the translator should be 'invisible' and a translation 'natural'. Rather, he argues, a translator, especially in a post- or neo-colonial setting, should 'stage an alien reading experience' (1995: 24). Venuti contrasts 'domestication', a neo-colonial, 'ethnocentric reduction' of the source by the target (1995: 20), to what he argues is the more transparent and ethical practice of foreignization, in which the translator needs to keep some measure of distinctiveness so that the listener/receiver knows that some sort of process has intervened. To foreignize, he writes, is 'to develop a theory and practice of translation that resists dominant target-language cultural values...[to] signify the linguistic and cultural difference of the foreign text' (1995: 23).

In this context, we can comment on the fact that the Latin tag itself remains untranslated except in the footnotes; we have no *translation proper*, in Jakobson's terms, no 'literal translation' or 'gloss' in Nida's. For some members of the watching audience, then, the Latin *impresa* contributes to Venuti's ideal of foreignization. In a sense, Venuti propounds a concept we've encountered earlier: what Lanham calls in *The Economics of Attention* (2007) the value of reading AT rather than reading THROUGH (original styling). The playwrights of *Pericles* ensure that even hearers fluent in Latin cannot read THROUGH Pericles' insignia by having Thaisa, Simonides, and even the Lords comment on Pericles' emblem, motto, and apparel. Note that Simonides, however, has the final word, contrasting 'outward habit' to 'inward man', as if to propound a translation doctrine closer to foreignization than to fluency or equivalence: there is a process intervening between thought and deed, intent and effect, Simonides suggests, and only a new translation process – from image to action, through the joust – will reveal Pericles' true worth to the watchers.

# Hybridization

Where Homi Bhabha comments on the 'ambivalence' of colonial discourse, including translations from English into non-English languages and the use of English by colonized peoples, as a form of mimicry that eventually develops into colonial hybridity (1984), Loomba, Trivedi, and Bharucha have critiqued the concept of hybrid translations or performances. Loomba suggests that even nuanced localisms will perpetuate colonial hierarchies unless such attempts begin by affording equal weight to home-grown theories and history (1998). Trivedi suggests a new paradigm for evaluating Shakespeare as it travels in and around India and beyond the Anglosphere. Later in the twentieth century, she writes, such translations and performances become neither neo-colonial mimicry nor hybridizations but rather 'indigenizations...marked by an artistic scrupulosity towards both the essence of Shakespeare and the folk form...a true interculturalism in which the friction between two opposing performance modes results in a creative cross-fertilization of both' (2000: 77).

Bharucha lays out the problems rigorously. On the one hand, although 'intercultural practice is unavoidably subsumed within the inequities of the global economy...there is an oppositional component within interculturalism that cannot be separated from a larger critique of capital' (2001: 107). On the other hand, 'corporate interculturalism facilitated through transnational capital' (109) creates an 'Other...never...on equal terms...but...ultimately...fit only to be consumed' (122).

The full complexity of such issues arises in *Children of the Sea* (2005). By all accounts a transformative and beautiful production (Love 2006), this adaptation was first performed in Sri Lanka starring child-victims of the tsunami that devastated the country in December 2004 and then brought to the Royal Botanical Garden in Edinburgh as part of the Fringe Festival in 2005. It used the reenactment of childhood bereavement, maritime disaster, and rape as what one reviewer called 'a means for therapy in Sri Lanka' but 'art' in Edinburgh, where the children again retold their real-life stories (Walker 2005). It used both comic and tragic modes to what audience members called 'magical' effect (Scott 2005). Genevieve Love (2006) notes the tendency among reviewers of *Children of the Sea* to collapse distinctively Scottish botanical elements infusing the performance and distinctively Sri Lankan music and choreography.

Yet, as Robert Dawson Scott notes, only a tiny portion of the tsunami's victims had the opportunity to recreate themselves as if through 'magic' (2005). As Bharucha writes, such interventions 'can do nothing to transform the existing inequities of cultural exchange, both within the borders of the state and beyond' (2001: 122). Moreover, the problem with calling everything – every adaptation, every cultural reinvention, every relocation – a translation can reaffirm the domination of Western European languages and of Anglophone, Francophone, and Hispanophone settings (Hamburger 2012; Lieblein [2004] 2012).

A related concern, raised by Bharucha, is that once we call everything a translation or a hybridization, Western- or Western-educated critics (such as myself, despite my ancestral origins outside the Anglosphere) can feel comfortable writing about translated texts and even, as in this chapter, foreign-language productions where we know little to nothing first-hand about the specific, local conditions of production, dissemination, and reception. This ethical dilemma parallels the ones we have discussed in earlier chapters surrounding cross-racial or race-conscious casting around the world (in Chapter 2) and regarding how or whether scholars should document, analyze, and participate in fan- or user communities, including how or whether we comment on adaptations for and with persons with disabilities (as I do in Chapter 7), incarcerated actors, and so on. Key to me seems to be the ability to remain humble and to acknowledge one's own limits as observer or analyst, perhaps through the practice of Niklas Luhmann, 'second-order observation' – attempting not to comment on a culture but rather on the way that that culture observes and comments on itself – in other words, on its self-representations or adaptations. Adaptations that originate from the target culture and self-consciously engage with that culture's own enmeshment in corporate and colonial power-structures are what we call tradaptations.

# Tradaptation: The peregrinations of *Pericles*

Tradaptation connotes the blurred boundaries between 'straight' my translation and 'free' adaptation and acknowledges the ideological underpinning of even the most faithful-seeming of translations. In a North American context, Jennifer Drouin uses tradaptation to uncover how Québécois playwrights have deployed Shakespeare for and against the political cause of Québécois separatism (2014). Roshni Mooneeram (2009) has written about Creole and multi-lingual forms of Shakespearean transfer in Mauritius in terms of tradaptation, arguing that the role of Shakespeare in the school curriculum and Shakespeare's creolization in Mauritius places standard English and Creole adaptations of Shakespeare in dialogue with one another.

Garneau explains the genesis of tradaptation thus:

> When it was time to put on Shakespeare, it seems obvious to me that we needed translations made especially for Québec...A translation is only good for the public it's meant for, and it [was] evident that the French translations weren't meant for us. The French translators are probably the worst translators in the world because they didn't doubt themselves or their knowledge enough and, between two words, they always choose *the most pretentious* [*le plus faiseux*; italics original]...The translated text should function in the target language with delight, not as a stranger there.
>
> HELLOT AND GARNEAU 2009: 84;
> my translation

According to its later exponents, in addition to these 'theatrical and local' aspects (Hellot 2009: 85) tradaptation requires the 'the disfiguring of Shakespeare by a scorned language and the demolition of his transcendence' (Lieblein [2004] 2021: 256), a mocking, often witty slant (Drouin 2014) and, for Susan

Knutson, at least, a sense of cultural exchange (2012); Mooneram (2009) and Asheesh Beesondial (2013) extend this colonial resistance beyond North America, to Mauritius. For all commenters, tradaptation's ultimate political end is to affirm the empowerment and self-determination of colonized peoples, often through a mode of double-translation (from English to French to *joual*) or creolization (English to Mauritian Creole).

Not only the migrations of Apollonius/Pericles as a character and as a story but the self-conscious presentation of Shakespeare's play as a story with a teller make the play peculiarly apt for this kind of tradaptation. Twentieth- and twenty-first century productions of *Pericles* often use tradaptation for the figure of 'ancient Gower', the medieval poet brought on stage as a chorus or narrator, to take us across the space of the Mediterranean and the decades between two stories of sexual coercion. Eve Salisbury argues that what she calls 'Non-Anglo Gowers' 'reconfigure temporality, ethnicity, and cultural difference' (2018). In 1958 Edric Connor played Gower as a Trinidian Calypso singer, in 1969 Emrys Jones played him as a Welsh bard, in 1994 Henry Goodman's Gower danced and sung amid Arab, African, South American and Inuit traditions; in *Children of the Sea* New Zealander Rawiri Paratene presented him to orphaned children in Sri Lanka and then in Edinburgh.[1] In *Périclès, Prince de Tyr* (2018), Gower's narration became the disembodied voice on a radio sounding in the hospital room of a catatonic patient, a news story and interviews describing the refugee crisis and the plight of shipwrecked and destitute migrants. The narrative voices of Ali Smith's *Spring* ([2019] 2020) range from the angry sections of internet abuse quoted in the child-heroine's notebook to expansive, exuberant prose-poems to café conversation, and excerpts from imaginary tele-plays, while its intertexts encompass the films of Charlie Chaplin, the monumental, chalky cloud-art of Tacita Dean, the short stories of Katherine Mansfield, and the poems of Rainer Maria Rilke and Percy Shelley. The novel puts *Pericles* in dialogue with the current refugee crisis, Brexit (Britain's contentious exit from the European Union), internet bullying, hope, resilience, contemporary and twentieth-century art, and flowering.

Paradoxically, perhaps, and yet appropriately, *Children of the Sea*, *Périclès,* and *Spring* use tragicomic modes to highlight the transactional sexuality that their translations – and arguably, the play – critique before demonstrating how their characters can escape from these dehumanizing relations. *Périclès* uses lighting and sound cues, and imaginative, provocative doubling (such as Antiochus' daughter as Marina, Antiochus as Lysimachus, doctors and nurses as Cerimon, Diana, and others) and the tragicomic use of properties and costume to show the life of Pericles' unfolding in his memory as a way of restaging prior trauma. A pillow becomes the infant Marina; clad by hospital staff in a strait-jacket to prevent him from harming himself, Périclès must trust Thaisa to lead their courtship. The gradual loosening of the jacket's ties, and Périclès' dawning expression of wonderment, signify his gradual emergence from traumatized fugue-state to loving and active partner (Figure 6.1).

Both these sequences – Marina as infantine pillow, Pericles as strait-jacketed madman clumsily holding a bouquet of flowers in the crook of his arm – show audience members and characters how tragic and comic models overlap in the work of restitution and forgiveness. Just as *Children of the Sea* used Bollywood-style dance and broad comedy to reduce the exploitative aspects of sexual competition within the play, so *Périclès* cast male pole-dancers as Thaisa's suitors, incorporated a Busby-Berkeley-style set-piece, and included a dance between Thaisa and a finally-unjacketed Pericles so erotically charged that the exclamation of Simonides, Thaisa's father, 'Unclasp, unclasp!' (2.3.103) provoked delighted laughter from the recorded audience.

In tragic mode, the broadcast of actual French radio, narrating the tragedies of migrants washed up ashore, creates, in the words of the production's sound engineer, 'the [bond]

**FIGURE 6.1** *Christophe Grégoire as Périclès, from Périclès, Prince de Tyr (2018). Image ©Patrick Baldwin, photographer.*

between the s[ic]k man in the hospital and Pericles['] adventure' (Trevien 2021). Reading backwards through Ali Smith's novel *Spring* and Mark Haddon's *The Porpoise*, we can see that this Pericles is traumatized by having failed to intercede and rescue Antiochus's daughter. In the words of one of my students, 'the performance and play ultimately argue that the only way for Pericles to transcend his guilt is through emotional vulnerability to women' (Karas 2021).

Smith's lyrical novel recasts *Pericles* more radically, elliptically, and humorously than these earlier versions. Smith's reimagined Marina takes the form of a preternaturally brilliant girl, Florence, a child migrant who has escaped death at sea, a notorious 'sex house' in London (188), a detention centre, and the obscure, menacing, imagined quasi-governmental security firm ('SA4A') that features in Smith's other novels. Her Pericles is television playwright Richard Lease (whose name, in the context of Smith's seasonal tetralogy, makes me at least think of Sonnet 18's 'summer's lease hath all too short a date'), who is grieving the death of his best friend, occasional lover, and lifelong writing partner Patricia Heal (another emblematic name, as working with her when she lived and reading her last letter to him is what has healed and will heal Richard). Like Marina, Florence saves this older man's life, preventing him from leaping in front of a moving train. But Smith's Pericles is also security guard Brittany ('Brit' – 'Britain', or 'Britannia', perhaps), shaken out of her complacent, mechanical dehumanization of the detainees ('deets') in her charge by Florence's clear-eyed brilliance and candor. Mothering or befriending Florence despite herself, Brit is also the revived Thaisa, even though Brit's reincarnation as loving human rather than soulless machine proves temporary.

In lieu of *Pericles'* Gower, Smith gives us imagined storytellers Lease, his appalling boss, and the real-life letters of Katherine Mansfield. But the most important unifying feature in Smith's novel is Pericles' device, the 'leafless tree' (265) boldly greening year after year with the relentless force of Spring, pushing shoots through ice and rock. Pericles' motto appears as the novel's epigraph but also in mysterious, modified form throughout the book as 'spe vivunt' or 'vivunt spe', translated in the novel as 'they live in hope' or 'they are living hope' (171). Florence's mother is reunited with her only to be torn from her moments later, but Richard Lease's new 'lease' on life includes advocacy for migrants like Florence and films about (in the novel's closing words) the endlessly human, renewable, acts of 'hopeless hope' that germinate in 'time's factory' (336).

My final chapter considers the local endpoint and limitations of adaptation as a concept along with the constraints of what we consider human. As many of us continue to reflect upon human frailty in light of the COVID-19 pandemic and the climate crisis, I conclude by discussing the materialized body of adaptation and the human body that accommodates and is accommodated by Shakespeare. My test-case is the play that communicates most richly as a medium in its own right: *Romeo and Juliet*.

# 7

# Accidents, remains, traces: Accommodations

This final phase of my argument explores the paradoxical conceptual metaphors that *the body is a container for the self* AND that *the mind is a body*, metaphors uniting ongoing discussion of what is or isn't an adaptation, where or whether we wish to draw any limits around the term, and whose abilities we understand, respect, and cherish as fully human – fully able to Shakespeare-ify (a term independently coined among online fan communities) and to be Shakespeare-ified, as it were. Such metaphors also go some way to explaining why critics, readers, viewers, and fans adapt Shakespeare (and other authors or materials they love) freely while nonetheless feeling that they are being 'true' to Shakespeare or another source – and that this truthfulness or fidelity is important to them as an index of their own authenticity and integrity (Busse and Hellekson 2012; Fazel and Geddes 2022). Judged in this light, even so-called glancing, accidental, trace, analogical, or 'outgrown' associations to Shakespeare, such as 'the serial Shakespeare aggregate' (the presence of British actors, the clustering of characters around Shakespearean types, repeating language and motif patterns across a series) in prestige serial television (Wald 2020) or 'attenuated' (McCluskie 2015). 'accidental' (Desmet 2017) or 'incidental' (Olive 2013)

Shakespearean references in high and low culture remain worth studying.

Graham Holderness (2005; 2011; 2014), like Mark Fortier (2014), challenges the new generality that not only is there no authentic text, performance, or Shakespeare, there is nothing beyond adaptations. Holderness offers two principal test cases. The first is Descartes's wax, which although it changes from solid to liquid, remains molecularly always the same: ergo, however much you deform or refashion Shakespeare, he remains always Shakespeare (2006). Holderness's newer metaphor, the Large Hadron Collider, considers the possibility that, as in the case of atomic collisions, something new can emerge from the destruction. In other words, what we call Shakespearean is not simply all Shakespeare, nor is it only ever-proliferating adaptations – but rather a creative tension between what is lost and what is new during the process of adaptation (or, as he prefers, 'collision') (2014).

Adaptations that collide with Shakespeare in what might seem like particularly outlandish or distant ways often bring into play (and into the play) human bodies that traditional Shakespeare performance in the twentieth century might have excluded or dismissed as unable 'to Shakespeare' (a term I'm using to mean *able to adapt, read, cite, use, misunderstand, hate, love, programme*, or *do Shakespeare* in any way). The following sections therefore consider adaptations of *Romeo and Juliet* that challenge ideals of integrity or purity with particular respect to ability, health, or able-bodiedness, including the zombie novel *Warm Bodies* (Marion 2011) and its eponymous film adaptation (2013); the martial-arts romance *Romeo Must Die* (2000); the Bollywood favourite *Goliyon Ki Raasleela Ram-leela (A Play of Bullets)* (*Ram-leela*, 2013); and – albeit my reading will necessarily fail to understand the complexity, nuance, and richness of this installation – the documentation and history of *ProTactile 'Romeo and Juliet'* (2018). Textual relics and fragmented bodies in these cultural products remind us that Shakespearean accommodations are processes enacted by and through reading, watching, listening, moving, thinking, feeling, human bodies in conversation with the media technologies (books, stages, buildings, screens, and all manner of what Fluxus founder Dick Higgins called 'life media' [2001: 49]) that extend their reach.

# Accidents

As we also discussed in Chapter 5, Latour's ANT suggests that complex objects form a nexus of associated nodes, working in an 'assemblage' that creates a distributed agency. 'Accidental Shakespeare' uses ANT and OOO to consider how non-human objects within the plays can interact through and with humans to create the 'intensities' or energy flows that we can read as agency (Yates 2006). Accidental appropriation (Desmet 2017) envisions an adaptation so alien to the Shakespearean 'essence' as to be 'merely' accidental – a collection of unpredictable qualities, mysteriously or idiosyncratically attached to Shakespeare. Sarah Olive's 'incidental Shakespeare', by contrast, points to instances in which Shakespeare is mentioned or appears only in passing, often without remark or significance to the user (2013). Winckler (2017) hopes to rehabilitate the activity of adaptation as 'hacking' in order to delineate what constitutes a 'source' domain and a 'target domain' for the study of Shakespearean adaptation and to reinscribe an 'arboreal' model without repeating the inequities and elitism that plagued early adaptation studies and so-called 'fidelity criticism'.

It is almost impossible, however, to enshrine temporal priority without simultaneously claiming ontological superiority for Shakespeare, however we understand that term. As we saw in previous chapters, scholars of Shakespeare and adaptation – and adaptors themselves – are rather moving towards understanding Shakespeare in equal dialogue with contemporary works that might or might not address their Shakespearean analogues or roots or origins or inspirations directly. Fazel and Geddes (2022) identify themselves via Jenkins' phrase, as 'aca-fans', and interpret Shakespeare-adjacent scholarly studies, adapted works, and creative transformations through Bogost's 'procedural rhetoric' (2012), Desmet's 'Alien Shakespeares' (2017) and Donna Haraway's *Cyborg Manifesto* ([1985] 2016). They assert that fan practices enable 'cyborg reading'. In cyborg reading, a 'speculative creator, using historical and contemporary cultural-technological materials to generate new meanings that are formed as part of a humanist practice of world building, contribut[es] to the ever-expanding accretion of any cultural work' (Fazel and Geddes 2022: 13–14). Algorithmically generated yet indubitably human, digital fanworks demonstrate a mode of 'cyborg reading' (Fazel and Geddes 2022: 4–30 and *passim*).

I submit that, if Shakespearean adaptation is like hacking, it's more like biohacking, closer to Fazel and Geddes' 'cyborg Shakespeare' than to Winckler's computer hacking. In comparing the 'hacking' of Shakespeare that underpins its adaptation to the biohacked or technologically mediated human body in the twenty-first century, I suggest that 'Shakespeare' manifests for humans when it activates Shakespeare neurons. Shakespeare lives in your brain, as a way of learning and knowing, an embodied epistemology activated through and by adaptation. We are hacking Shakespeare even as Shakespeare is hacking us.

Let's contrast, for example, the methods of the 'AI poet', Deep-speare, with K. Silem Mohammad's 'Sonnagrams' ([2009] 2022), both of which rely on algorithms. Deep-speare's programmers exposed it to the Project Gutenberg poetry database, trained it to identify iambic pentameter and the sonnets' rhyme scheme from the Project Gutenberg edition of Shakespeare's sonnets, and to use natural-language-processing, a word probability checker, and a rhythm and rhyme checker to generate verse quatrains in iambic pentameter (Lau, Cohn, et al. 2020). Mohammad used an internet anagram generator to create 'fourteen lines of text...quantitatively equivalent to

## Table 7.1 *Humanagrams: K. Silem Mohammad vs. Deep-Speare*

| Mohammad | Deep-Speare |
|---|---|
| Shallow, mascara-hustling cameraman, Does your tyrannosaurus masturbate? (As long as I can get this bitch to scan, I don't care what it says – I'm running late.) | Yet in a circle pallid as it flow by this bright sun, that with his light display roll'd from the sands, and half the buds of snow and calmly on him shall infold away |

*Sources:* K. Silem Mohammad ([2009] 2022), personal communication; Lau, Cohn, et al. (2020).

Shakespeare's poem at the level of the letter' before reordering those letters one by one, using '[a]ll leftover letters. . .to make up a title' (2022). Table 7.1 contrasts the opening of Mohammad's anagrammatical version of Sonnet 18, 'Shall I compare thee to a summer's day?', 'Held, Le Flesh Lengthens; Undertook, Le Flesh Holds; Fed Me, Me, Me, Me, Me, Me, Me, Me, *Me*!' with the ungrammatical Deep-speare sonnet that its programmers juxtapose with the same sonnet.

Deep-Speare's quatrains fooled lay-readers but not experts; it composed doggerel, accurate in rhythm and rhyme, but failed to offer 'readability', coherence, or 'emotional impact', still less to develop a Shakespearean argument in fourteen lines (Lau, Cohn, et al. 2020). Mohammad's, in contrast, have been published to acclaim in *Poetry* and other juried venues; witty, obscene, and poignant, they create arguments even through absurdity, tell stories, and make us laugh, often wryly. Deep-Speare's creators are currently trying to teach it to think more like a human by making it read longer narratives, telling it which words are more emotionally resonant for humans, and giving it a theme or a story around which to compose a poem each time (Lau, Cohen et al. 2020).

Bogost's 'alien phenomenology' defines 'tiny ontology' as 'a dense mass of everything contained entirely – even as it's spread about haphazardly like a mess or organized logically like a network... a singularity, a point where matter reaches infinite density' (2012: 21–2). Humans exist inside such a singularity, writes Bogost, our minds like a black hole that cannot be accessed fully by others except through 'speculation' (Bogost 2012: 22). Where ANT or OOO can leave users feeling helpless or disempowered, tiny ontology requires imagination and foregrounds individual subjectivity even as, in digital networks, writing acknowledges materiality (Desmet 2017). This materiality comprises such items as the literal webs – cables and satellites and radio waves – and the literal power – electricity, however generated – that create the post-human assemblages of objects in which digital subjectivity can emerge.

Cyborg, alien, procedural, and digital Shakespeares are fundamentally post-human models through which to discuss adaptation. They presuppose neither a normative Shakespeare nor a normative 'body of work' nor even a normative human body. In the digital arena, their humanness remains as surplus, traces, something 'extra'; with living human bodies, humanness can be distributed and emerge collectively through other humans and through the objects they encounter.

Just such a collective, post-human identity takes over the ideal of the romantic couple in the martial arts/hip hop film *Romeo Must Die* (2000), which introduced Chinese *wushu* expert and film star Jet Li (as Han/Romeo) to US audiences, to a soundtrack by hip hop artist Aaliyah (Trish/Juliet). Beyond the film's title and set-up (the scions of a Chinese and an African American crime mob fall in love, despite their families' disapproval), Shakespeare's play is referenced directly only once in the dialogue (Hendricks 2006: 202), to the chagrin of reviewers. Critics likewise complained about the macabre technical wizardry used within climactic fights that simulated x-ray photography to show the bones of Han's opponents breaking as he hits them (Ebert 2000; Mitchell 2000; O'Sullivan 2000).

When chivalrous Han refuses to 'hit a girl' (a fierce, Chinese woman warrior) despite Trish's encouragement, Trish opens the car door, sending their opponent flying and giving Han an idea about how to fight without 'hitting a girl'. Han picks up Trish and, with her acquiescence, wields her body as a weapon to slam his enemy into a van. The digitally enabled 'cyborg reading' of this scene appears through 'new meanings' manifest, for example, in the syncretic commentary on sites such as YouTube, Reddit, Buzzfeed and so on. The fact that fans have clipped and uploaded this scene to YouTube and tagged it 'Girls Fight' clarifies that this bizarre interlude reinforces traditional twentieth-century American gender roles; it uses a 'good' woman, literally in her boyfriend's hands, to punish a 'bad' one. Accidental Shakespeare turns our fighting Romeo into a human/technological hybrid, a martial arts assemblage of bones, bodies, and motor vehicles, a fleeting or momentary subjectivity.

Fugitive subjectivities, Bogost suggests, depend upon metaphor for expression, an argument I find most cogent for Shakespearean adaptation and for this book. Alien phenomenology, writes Bogost, 'demands...[that] the character of something is not identical to the *characterization* of that experience by something else' (2012: 63). Bogost counters philosopher Thomas Nagel's famous claim that we should attempt to create 'an objective phenomenology not dependent on empathy or the imagination' in order to understand consciousness (Nagel 1974: 449). Where Nagel suggests that 'loose intermodal analogies...are of little use' in creating such a phenomenology (1974: 449), Bogost argues the opposite: 'Unlike objective phenomenology, alien phenomenology accepts that the subjective character of experiences cannot be fully recuperated objectively, even if it remains wholly real. In a literal sense, *the only way to perform alien phenomenology is by analogy*: the bat, for example, operates like a submarine. The redness hues like fire' (Bogost 2012: 64).

That human beings use a plethora of metaphors to describe Shakespearean adaptation, then, reasserts human subjectivity and individuality through precisely our inability to express the relationships we see *except* through metaphor. The 'dead' metaphors through which we express our relationships to Shakespeare return to life: undead, mechanical, or (like Lanier's rhizomes), deceptively dormant and dry until watered by clement weather, or to climb unseen, even through the air (Gibson 2018), to emerge in unexpected and surprising places. 'Shakespeare Remains', in the title of Courtney Lehmann's influential study (2002).

# Remains

Lehmann's intervention into Shakespearean film (2002) observes that, where Derrida had suggested that there was no outside-text (no *hors-texte*), nothing outside the text (Derrida [1967] 2013: 163), Slavoj Žižek's 'surplus-X' (1989: 82), adapted from Lacanian psychoanalysis, implies that the author remains within a text as a ghostly presence that is 'in the text more than the text'[]...not merely that which eludes interpretation but something that exceeds the narrative frame itself: superfluous *and* vital, it contains the residue of cultural desires, anxieties, and repressions, exerting an affective pull on the reader only to lead to a signifying void' (Lehmann 2002: 2).

This Shakespearean surplus, Lehmann writes, haunts adaptations and is materialized through the technologies and methods of film (the camera and editing, but also point-of-view) and film theory (notably auteur-theory, the attention paid to a film as the creative vision of a director). Lehmann's first example of this exuberant surplus draws from *Romeo and Juliet*. Already, she argues, 'anxi[ous]' about its close relationship to its source (Arthur Brooke's moralistic *Tragical History of Romeus and Juliet* [1562]), Shakespeare's play is therefore filled with explanations and allusions to literacy, from kissing 'by th' book' (*Romeo and Juliet* 1.5.109) to learning 'by rote' (2.3.84) (Lehmann 2002: 18).

The Shakespearean zombie novel and film *Warm Bodies* (Marion 2011; *Warm Bodies* 2013) offer us a darkly witty metaphor for this remaindered revivification through the literal disintegration of bodies. This retelling of *Romeo and Juliet* offers us a narrator, 'R', who is a newly undead zombie – a walking corpse doomed to subsist on living human tissue. R remains human enough to fall in love with 'Julie', whose love eventually brings him back to life, cures the zombie plague, and beats back the 'Boneys' (cruelly marauding skeletons, too zombified to experience even the guilt and remorse of R, his friend M, and the other youngsters at their penchant for human flesh). In addition to the set-pieces or characters we might expect (first-sight lovers, a balcony or casement scene, a sternly disapproving father, a confidant for Juliet/Julie, a plague and so on), the Shakespearean superflux persists through literary and literate remains. All that the deadly deadpan narrator can recall of his human name is the letter 'R'; yet, even when cured, R wants neither his old name back nor a new designation; the letter suffices.

The novel similarly nuances the 'textual compulsion' Lehmann describes. R woos Julie in part through his inadvertent consumption of the brain of Julie's ex-boyfriend, Perry, and the flashbacks to Perry's life that he vicariously recalls. Perry (the novel's Paris-figure), 'want[s] to be a writer', despite the imminent destruction of the book industry with the zombie plague, and Julie, imagining a book as a 'beautiful' way of sharing thoughts, fantasizes about 'tast[ing]' 'a piece of [his] brain' instead (Marion 2011: 96–7). The film (2013) shares with the novel R's wry deadpan narration, and its textual compulsion; it quotes from earlier cinematic versions of the play, notably the balcony scene. One is a traditional balcony or casement scene, quoted from Zeffirelli's film (*Romeo and Juliet*, 1968), in which Julie's friend Nora, inside the house, inadvertently interrupts R's clandestine courtship from outside. The other, set in a swimming-pool, references the lovers' watery encounter in Baz Luhrmann's *William Shakespeare's Romeo + Juliet* [*R+J*] (1996).

The love between living Julie and revived R 'creates a world without the undead', writes Neal Klomp, who contrasts the tale's conclusion to Shakespeare's play, in which, he suggests, Juliet's death demonstrates the continuance of plague and the porous boundaries between dead and undead in a pre-antibiotic era of pandemic disease (Klomp 2016). Katherine Schaap Williams argues, in contrast, that *Romeo and Juliet* uses figures of sickness and debility to conceal and naturalize a tragedy created not by bodily vulnerability but by the society surrounding the lovers (2021). *Warm Bodies*, I would argue, goes further than Shakespeare's play in its bodily critique. Julie and R's love is founded not upon the eradication but the persistence, even necessity, of the undead, through touches of what, following disability theorist Robert McRuer (2006) and other disability activists, we can call touches of the 'cripqueer'.

In *Crip Theory*, McRuer argues that queer theory and disability theory are intermingled in that both resist what he calls 'compulsory able-bodiedness', which, like Adrienne Rich's coinage 'compulsory heterosexuality' (1980), prescribes a normative body that lives, loves, and reproduces in a specific and limited way, namely by labouring for, appropriating or accumulating, and passing on capital within a traditional nuclear family unit anchored by a heterosexual (white) man. This scenario excludes both persons with disabilities and gay people, some of whom have reclaimed two slurs in the portmanteau 'cripqueer' and reclaimed those identities. Cripqueer activists and scholars assert their rights not just to workplace and leisure accommodations (mainstream disability advocacy), nor to raise families within conventional capitalist structures (the gay marriage movement), but to lives that challenge the very notion of what individuality, productivity, and kinship might mean.

Cripqueer identities resist the patriarchal family of early modernity; post-Enlightenment, humanist beliefs that emphasize the physical independence and self-sufficiency of the individual; and late-capitalist ideologies of what it means to be a productive citizen. Popular zombie fiction (including

*Warm Bodies*) presents transgressive, flamboyantly sickened bodies as nonetheless desirable and desiring. First, *Warm Bodies* parodies the heterosexual household when the Boneys match R and his zombie girlfriend with a pair of children and force them into a nuclear family (Marion 2011). Second, readers and viewers learn, along with Julie, that R has come back to life when he starts to bleed from a bullet. Klomp suggests this touch is 'a bit of play upon humoral medicine's practice of phlebotomy' (2016: 49), a reading that would imply that the tale has simultaneously un-cripped and un-queered its lead character by 'curing' him.

To me, however, R's flowing blood recalls not phlebotomy but rather the Renaissance anxieties surrounding male bleeding that Gail Kern Paster (1993) and Ariane Balizet (2005) have outlined so well. Humoral physicians believed women to be 'leaky vessels' tending to dissolution into the watery humor that dominated their composition, and considered blood lost during menstruation a sign of women's inherent pathology. Although such physicians claimed that men shed 'laudable blood' in battle in a demonstration of their superior sanguine temperament and greater physical vigour, they strained logic in their efforts to dissociate laudable from shameful bleeding (Paster 1993). Balizet (2005) traces the early modern myth of male menstruation, thought to afflict Jews and to mark Jewish men as cursed by the devil. In this ugly antisemitic trope, Jewish men and all women are wounded or even undead.

*Warm Bodies* (2013), however, seems to accept debility, disability, and interdependence over independence in the attention it pays to the role of humans in teaching zombies to learn to do activities they want to do again – in other words, it eschews self-sufficiency, purity, and segregation. 'I have zombie fingers', comments R, learning dexterity from the living humans. CGI technology transfigures the irises of both R and Julie to a startling, non-natural gold, as if to show the mutuality of their love. Not Shakespeare's powerful dyad but rather three lovers, dead, living, and undead, Perry, Julie, and R, cure each other; Julie does not simply transfer health or vitality to R, but rather R's body, sustained by Perry's brain, together with Julie's love, renews the community. Perry's brain is what Harris might call 'untimely matter', a temporal hybrid, just as, Harris suggests, Shakespeare is a polychronic body (2009), a palimpsest (Genette [1982] 1997).

The overwhelming popularity of *Romeo and Juliet* and its endless adaptations suggest that we seem to like seeing young people dying (or becoming undead) for love. Fans also received the blatant 'fingore' (fanspeak for bloody hand and finger amputations on film) of *Ram-Leela* (2013) enthusiastically. This wildly popular Bollywood extravaganza transposes *Romeo and Juliet* to two warring organized crime gangs in a fictional Gujarat village whose major industry is fabricating weapons and ammunition. The peaceable, minor thief Ranveer falls in love with the hot-headed Leela, but Leela's mother, Dhankor Baa, the clan leader, has already arranged her marriage to another. Captured by her clan after her runaway wedding to Ranveer but before they have consummated their love, Leela proudly defies her mother and displays her wedding ring. A coldly furious Dhankor Baa amputates Leela's ring finger with a nutcracker at the engagement party Dhankor Baa has arranged for Leela (Figure 7.1); when Ram learns of his

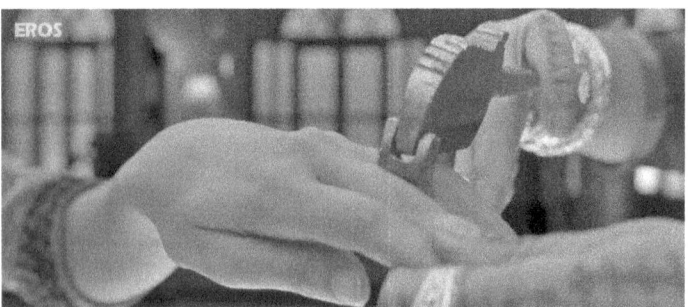

**FIGURE 7.1** *'Dhankor Baa amputates Deepika's finger with a nutcracker', Goliyon Ki Raasleela Ram-leela [Ram-leela], DVD, India: Eros International, 2013. Screen capture by the author.*

lover's disfigurement, he chops off his own finger in a gesture of extravagant love. The film concludes with both lovers becoming leaders of their respective gangs, confessing their undying love, and shooting each other in the head.

Everything about this film is cripqueer, from the death-cult of its gun-forged village industry to its wanton dactylectomies to its repurposing of major festivals (Holi, Dussehra) for mass destruction and even to its controversial title, which the director had to alter following religious protests. And yet it uncovers something new about the play on which it's based, and about the audiences who love that play. Shakespearean traces emerge, submerge, and resurge unpredictably, as flotsam and jetsam, as preserved shipwrecks, as determined survivors, or as life buoys that bear those survivors to shore.

# Traces

Pascale Aebischer (2004) suggests that Shakespeare on stage and screen already foregrounds and magnifies 'violated' and marginalized bodies, such as those of women, racial minorities, persons with disabilities, and other stigmatized categories, in contrast to the Shakespearean text and the critical or metacritical discourses that have historically elided them. Performed adaptations and appropriations turn the Shakespearean traces or footprints of othered bodies into pressing and unruly material presence. We can spot traces that become increasingly bodily, urgent, and irrepressible in the musical *West Side Story* (1957), the acclaimed film version (1961) and its remake (2021).

*West Side Story* (1957 and 1961) avoided Shakespearean dialogue altogether; Tony Kushner reintroduces a Shakespearean trace into *West Side Story* (2021) during the lovers' first meeting at the dance in the gym. That line is Juliet's 'you kiss by th[e] book' (*Romeo and Juliet* 1.5.109), which returns Shakespeare's play as another hypotext and *West Side Story* (2021) into – in a metaphor particularly apt regarding this play already haunted by references to literacy – a palimpsest. The remade film (2021) re-materializes *Romeo and Juliet* and *West Side Story* (1957, 1961) at key points, particularly where the remake addresses contemporary concerns surrounding gender and violence.

Mercutio's and, initially, Romeo's bawdy teasing of the Nurse when she comes to deliver Juliet's message to Romeo in *Romeo and Juliet* (2.4.97–138) becomes in *West Side Story* (1961) a full-fledged attempted assault on Anita in Doc's store. The remake (2021) wrenchingly shows Anita's face during the attack and adds to the 1961 script a warning to Anita from the character Anybodys and frenzied verbal and physical attempts by the Jets' girlfriends to stop the men. Anybodys in 2021 is likewise a more fully materialized trace of another hypotext, a character in the 1961 film. Anybodys in 1961 was, in the language of the day, a tomboy, a girl who wanted to be one of the boys. Screenwriter Tony Kushner, in consultation with the non-binary actor playing this character, rewrote Anybodys as a trans man (Butler 2021). Anybodys, the Jets girls, and Doc's replacement as store owner Valentina (Rita Moreno, who had played Anita in 1961) thus ally to counter the ubiquitous demands of male violence and to offer, in the words of one of the musical's most famous songs, 'somewhere. . .a time and place' (*West Side Story* 1957) for all who will not or cannot heed those demands.

My final example of a Shakespearean 'trace' moving polytemporally through time concerns Bhavabhuti's eighth-century Sanskrit verse drama *Malati and Madhava, or, The stolen marriage* (Wilson [1901] 2007). Romantic-era Orientalist, surgeon, amateur actor, and Indiaphile Horace Hayman Wilson first translated *Malati and Madhava* in 1826, with additional editions appearing in 1835 and 1901. Wilson used blank verse, the Shakespearean phrase 'passing strange' (Wilson [1901] 2007: 7), and pseudo-Shakespearean locutions, such as Madhava's soliloquy on his sudden passion for Malati ('I cease to be / Myself, or conscious of the thing I am', Wilson [1901] 2007: 18), to give this classical drama *gravitas* among his educated colonial audience.

Much later in the century, the Amar Chitra Katha comic book adaptation of *Malati and Madhava* that I cherished as a child described Bhavabhuti's play (on the comic book's front endpaper) as a Romeo-and-Juliet story, and the clever nun who engineers the happy ending as a successful Friar Lawrence (Pai [1967] 1979). The comic book traces Shakespeare in the most distant or attenuated strokes, however. While Bhavabhuti's comedy includes several transmedia elements that we could identify literally or symbolically in Shakespeare's tragedy (parted lovers, misrecognition, a clever cleric-confidant, an attempted suicide, an assayed rescue from a crypt or graveyard), the motif of star-crossed lovers springs equally from folklore (Iyengar 2017b; Engler 2018). Bhavabhuti's play also includes, for example, a cross-dressing bed-trick, a skull-worshipper, a narrowly averted virgin sacrifice, a convoluted sub-plot, fearsome female deities, a tiger, and a flying nun.

These traces and remains of Shakespeare have become 'incidental' (Olive 2013), communicative media in their own right. 'Uncle Pai', as the founder and editor of the Amar Chitra Katha children's comics was affectionately known (Pritchett 1995), presumably added the Shakespearean trace to insert classical Indian texts into the traditional colonial education many of his post-colonial readers (local and global) would still encounter. Shakespeare in my *Malati and Madhava* comic book (Pai [1967] 1979) comes into being as a postcolonial 'trace', in Singh's terms (2019: 4–5) – or maybe the story just fired Pai's Shakespeare neuron.

# Accommodations: *Romeo and Juliet*

Let me introduce, then, yet another metaphor, one of the earliest synonyms for adaptation in Shakespeare's own time. 'Accommodation' first appears in 1566 to connote the application of a Biblical text to something beyond the immediate Biblical context (OED n. 1a, 'accommodation'). In early seventeenth century medical texts, it means the tailoring of a prescription to fit individual disposition (Cotta 1612: G3v) or the general treatment of 'sicke persons' (*Treasurie* 1613: 3S7r); a model letter of 'advice to a friend' in 1613 uses it to refer to the ability of books – 'where the whole wisdom of the earth is daily talking vnto you' (Markham 1613: H1v) – to 'accommodate[e]' malaise. Shakespeare uses the term in both its most common present-day British English sense, to mean 'lodging' (*Othello* 1.3.239) but also to mean, as Laurie Shannon has argued, the requirements of human animals to be sheltered and comforted against the elements and our bodily needs (2013).

Hillary Nunn (2015) helpfully uses Shannon's foundational animal studies text (2013) to connect this early sense of accommodation to its contemporary legal sense in North America (US Department of Labor n.d.), namely how we ensure access to the world to different kinds of bodies, including those that we call disabled. The disguised Vincentio uses the term in something of this sense in *Measure for Measure* as he tells Claudio to 'Be absolute for death'; all the latter's 'accommodations', he warns, will fall away and leave him with only 'baseness' (3.1.14). More recently, Christine Marie Gottlieb (2018) integrates animal studies, disabilities studies, and social justice work to argue that King Lear, newly aware how vulnerable are 'unaccommodated' human beings, realizes the interconnectedness of humans, other animals, and things. Gottlieb suggests that adapting Lennard Davis's concept of 'dismodernism' (2002) – the human being as interdependent rather than autonomous – can help us include *Lear* in an account of disability justice (Gottlieb 2018).

Disability justice demands access not just to workplace accommodations but to full creative, political, and social participation for persons with disabilities in the public sphere. A key tenet of what has been called the strong social model of disability is that people's bodies vary in their capabilities, and that although a medical model of disability considers such variations 'impairments', such impairments or differences only become 'disabilities' when society fails to accommodate them

(T. Shakespeare 2014). Critics within disability studies (including those who experience disabilities themselves) vary in their acknowledgement or tolerance of the idea that some bodily variations even comprise 'impairment' at all, from Tom Shakespeare's impassioned argument that some embodied states are painful and uncomfortable, and 'people are disabled by society *and* by their bodies' (T. Shakespeare 2014: 75) to Peter Coleridge's useful coinage, 'not-yet-disabled', to describe the able-bodied (1993), to Bill Hughes's insistence that all bodily categories are social and political and that there is no essential or ontological body (2007), to the concept of 'Deaf Gain', the belief that persons who culturally identify as Deaf or Hard of Hearing can access 'unique cognitive, creative, and cultural gains manifested through deaf ways of being in the world' (Bauman and Murray 2014: xv). (The upper-case initial and medial letters in DeafBlind, Deaf, and Hard of Hearing [HoH] indicate that these communities identify as politically and culturally Disabled rather than or in addition to experiencing a medical impairment).

The coinage 'disability gain', usually attributed to a keynote speech delivered by renowned disability theorist Rosemarie Garland-Thomson in 2013 (Hobgood 2021: 3), extends the concept of Deaf Gain to argue that persons with all kinds of variations considered within the medical model to be impairments should not be seen predominantly, only, or maybe at all in need of a cure or of normalization. Rather, disability gain suggests, persons with disabilities offer the rest of society invaluable, enriching avenues for human creative and social flourishing – and moreover, deserve to be valued for their embodied qualities, including, controversially, their disability.

ASL and Deaf actors and companies have long existed (Bradbury 2021), but it was only in recent years that Hearing companies began to attend to Disabled audience members with ASL interpretation, wider aisles for wheelchair-users, and other audience accommodations (Amberg 2013). Well-meaning, so-called 'recuperative' Shakespeare performances of or for persons with disabilities have been critiqued by Joubin

(2020) and Sonya Loftis (2021). We are now, however, beginning to see more imaginative practices in mainstream companies who have begun to integrate actors whose disabilities form important and 'desirable components of their personhood' (Hobgood 2021: 3) and their personifying a character.

ASL Shakespeare has likewise evolved. ASL Shakespeare as currently performed today does not attempt to translate English word-for-word but rather 'uses poetics, rhyme, allusion, and extended metaphors' through hand-position, the location of the hands and body, repetition, speed, and 'transformational signs' (Bradbury 2021). Deaf actor Howie Seago at the Oregon Shakespeare festival offers 'not simply literal translations of English into American Sign Language, but lyrical transfigurations of verbal poetry into kinetic poetry' (Cross 2013: 17).

The immersive experimental workshop *ProTactile Romeo and Juliet* (2018) similarly transfigured the experience and understanding of Shakespearean text, through the collective self-determination of its DeafBlind actor-producers-participants. ProTactile (PT), a created language for and by DeafBlind people, enables DeafBlind people to communicate among themselves without the aid of a sighted or hearing interpreter. Moreover, the Seattle-based PT social movement asserts that 'hearing and vision are not necessary for copresence, navigation, interaction, or communication' (Edwards 2018: 273–4). *ProTactile Romeo and Juliet* (2018) was the first Shakespeare performance both by and for DeafBlind people.

Although ProTactile is based on ASL, '[w]hile ASL uses the space around the body, PT uses the body instead' (Bradbury et al. 2019: 82). In a workshop funded by the National Endowment for the Arts, write Bradbury and her collaborators, '[s]ix DeafBlind participants, a sighted Deaf project director, and a sighted hearing theater artist advisor' worked intensively and collaboratively to make a *Romeo and Juliet* that used touch, smell, and taste, and limited visual cues (since some Deaf patrons had 'varying degrees of vision loss', Bradbury et al. 2019: 82, 85). The radically cut script omitted major characters (such as Mercutio), telescoping the action to five abbreviated scenes: the Prologue, the lovers' meeting, the balcony or casement scene, Tybalt's death (in this production, Romeo kills Tybalt after the latter threatens him in a drunken rage), and an epilogue.

The one line that the cast translated word-for-word from standard US English to ProTactile was the final line from the lovers' joint sonnet: Juliet's 'you kiss by the book' (Bradbury et al. 2019; *ProTactile Romeo and Juliet* 2018). It's a beautifully ambiguous line because Juliet is either telling Romeo that he is a good kisser – he's read the right books, he's kissing her just as she would like to be kissed, as she has read about in books – or she's suggesting that he's holding back, being decorous, being proper (the latter interpretation being ultimately what the ProTactile cast preferred [Bradbury et al. 2019: 92]). In either case, Juliet is telling him clearly that she wants more. Tony Kushner retrieved this line in *West Side Story* (2021) in a similar way, as (in another change from *West Side Story* [1961]) it is Juliet who takes the initiative and kisses Romeo.

Tactile elements in *ProTactile Romeo and Juliet* (2018) included historical costuming; the actors lingered in the lobby so that patrons could experience the textures and weight of Elizabethan dress and recognize characters through touch. Spatial innovations included the use of tables arranged with deliberately jutting corners, rather than laid flush, to allow actors to navigate through their performance areas. Patrons were ushered from scene to scene and space to space by a character, initially a 'Townsperson' but later the Nurse or Romeo (Bradbury et al. 2019: 84). Olfactory touches included a signature fragrance for each character, such as peony for Juliet (Bradbury et al. 2019: 90).

My own access to this performance is necessarily faint and distant, not only because I was not present at the workshop and have only a 'second-order' (Luhmann 1993) experience of it through the documentary made about it, but more importantly because my own hearing and sighted body cannot experience the intense tactile, spatial, and olfactory awareness of many DeafBlind people and the PT Seattle community. Luhmann has argued that observing the observers (in this case, watching the film made by participants and reading their reflections), helpfully reduces the complexity of infinitely 'reflexive[e], recursive[e], and self-referen[tial]' (1993: 766) deconstructive systems so that we can continue to analyze phenomena. 'Second-order observers might see less than the observed observers – but they also see differently, and recognize that what appears natural and necessary to first-order observers is contingent on their perspective', explains Nicholas Langlitz, with the goal of 'do[ing] justice to life in pluralist and highly differentiated societies' (2022). While Luhmann suggests that mass media can offer this kind of second-order observation, tiny ontologies, procedural rhetoric, and digital 'distant reading' offer a similar detachment. Across this distance, I realize that other minds and sensoria, even of supposedly able-bodied persons, remain mysterious and ineffable and that Shakespeare-making shows us the interdependence of human beings. It would be hard to imagine a more compelling example of Shakespeare accommodation, nor more insight into the paradoxical metaphors that *the mind is a body* and *the body is a container for the mind*.

I appear to have found myself arguing for Shakespeare as an index to the human, like Harold Bloom (1998), but from opposite premises and to very different conclusions. Where Bloom, as we saw in Chapter 3, argued for that Shakespeare 'invent[ed]' a universal, disembodied, dematerialized human and for subjectivity as a transcendent force (1998), I suggest that Shakespeare manifests itself as human through our inexhaustible, ridiculous, and awe-inspiring capacity to make it part of ourselves. Sometimes we try to incorporate Shakespeare literally, in the case of the chocolate bars or cheese I discussed in Chapter 1, and to excrete it (again, sometimes literally, as with a a 'Milk Shakespeare' toilet-seat cover [Pepycase 2022] and boxes of Shakespeare-themed tissues [Kuso 2022]); and to use technology to do so (as in the many

Google search screens through which I scrolled in order to find these examples).

There can be no reasonable need for a Shakespeare toilet-seat cover nor for a Shakespeare's-head tissue-box holder. Beyond any aesthetic prejudices we might hold against such items, the environmental costs of manufacturing such objects for the Shakespeare industrial-complex are horrifying. Yet we reason not the need. Shakespeare accommodates; capacious, adaptable, extensible, it offers us the possibilities of self-representation. The absurdity of Shakespearean artefacts meant to become or to mop up bodily waste perhaps aptly metaphorizes the inexpressibility, fecundity, and fragility of human beings and of our endless accommodation through, with, and of Shakespeare.

# Glossary of selected terms

## By Philip Gilreath with Sujata Iyengar

**Accidental Shakespeare** Related to Bogost's 'alien phenomenology', in which human perception represents one among multiple ways of relating objects (Ch. 7), 'accidental' Shakespeare plays with the notion of an adaptation that is so alien to the Shakespearean 'essence' as to be 'merely 'accidental – a collection of random qualities, randomly attached to Shakespeare (Introduction; Ch. 7). See **Posthuman Shakespeare**.

**Accommodation** To accommodate is to adapt – to or for an audience. Adaptive texts can accommodate audiences by providing information about their original texts, but also through design features and accessibility options that meet the needs of diverse audiences. Tom Shakespeare notes that accessibility includes information, signage, and emotional warmth as well as physical infrastructure (2018: 69).

**Adaptation** A biological metaphor, derived from film studies, for artistic revision (Ch. 1). Hutcheon defines adaptations as medium specific, 'multilaminated' (2006: 5), and driven by contextual or environmental concerns: they are 'deliberate, announced, and extended revisitations of prior works' (2006: xiv). This definition focuses on creativity, imagination and technological ingenuity. Kilbourne ([1906] 1973) remarked much earlier that 'adaptation' conforms to the taste of the times. Desmet and Iyengar (2015) note that adaptation may still be too rooted in a paradigm of fidelity, cultural selection, and hierarchical, linear relations between individual authors and texts. Adaptation is also increasingly important in terms of accommodation and access, the ability to adapt a medium or performance for a range of audience circumstances.

**Appropriation** A metaphor based in accountancy, resources, ownership, or theft. Whereas *adaptation* relies on a natural metaphor for the exchange of contexts, *appropriation* emphasizes social transactions. For Marx (Ch. 2) appropriation represents the acquisition of ethical as well as unethical surplus values. *Cultural* appropriation refers specifically to the tendency of dominant groups to derive entertainment and profit from the seizure of cultural practices of minoritized groups. Marsden defines it as 'seizure for one's own purpose', thus replacing the artistic/family tree model with one of social or political urgency (1991: 1). Sanders notes that appropriation is more 'decisive' in departing from the 'informing' source (2005: 35). Desmet and Sawyer (1999) suggest that appropriation is two-way (dialogic) rather than deferential: the term relegates more agency to the appropriator than 'adaptation' does. Appropriation also suggests that both objects are altered in this dialogic process; it changes both source and target, much as metaphor does.

**Big-Time Shakespeare** Bristol (1996) coins the term. Big-time Shakespeare connotes institutional, big-budget, and highly publicized adaptations. Desmet (1999) contrasts 'big-time' corporate, conversative, and well-financed Shakespeare adaptations to 'small-time', more individualized acts of revision that can also be aligned with user-produced Shakespeare adaptations, which reach smaller audiences (Ch. 4).

**Cyborg/Algorithmic Shakespeares** 'Shakespeare' manifests for humans when it activates Shakespeare neurons (Ch. 8). Cyborg, procedural, or algorithm-driven Shakespeares might be said to *hack* the human, whom in turn, *makes* the adaptation. Related to Ian Bogost's (2012) alien phenomenology, in which human perception represents one among multiple ways of relating objects (Ch. 4).

**Fandom or Fanfic** 'Fandom' originates from 'fanatical' or 'obsessed' followers of a text, television show, comic, or other pop culture phenomenon. 'Fanfiction' or 'fanfic' is a genre of mostly web-based amateur writing, in which members of a fandom circulate stories that either take place within a preestablished fictional world with recognizable fictional characters, or that create 'crossovers' between preestablished fictional worlds. Such worlds are often seen as niche or nerdy, but Andrew James Hartley and Peter Holland suggest that these subcultures increasingly claim the cultural capital of the 'cool' (2020: 3) (Ch. 5). See also spreadable media and the idea of participatory culture (Ch. 5).

**Feminist Adaptation** Adaptations that critique conventional female roles or misogynistic institutions (Ch.5).

**Fidelity** Related to faithfulness or resemblance to an often inaccessible original. For editors, fidelity might relate to the notion of an ideal authorial text to which to which edited collections, and even adaptations, are descendants of varying legitimacy (Ch. 3). Fidelity is also a technical term in audio recording and equipment, referring to accuracy in the reproduction of sound (Ch. 4).

**Glocal** A blend of global and local. Described by Ana María Fraile Marcos as a 'hybrid oxymoron' (2014: 5), glocal and glocalization emphasize hybridity and fragmentariness (Ch. 6).

**Hypotext/Hypertext** Described by Genette, the hypotext is an antecedent text that provides material to an adaptive text (hypertext) while not necessarily receiving direct mention within the adaptive text. In computation, hypertexts are used for linking and cross-referencing within and between documents (Ch. 3).

**Incidental Shakespeare** Brief appropriations and passing references to Shakespeare that in some cases write back to or resist a monolithic Shakespeare (Ch. 7). Olive suggests that traces and remains of Shakespeare underpin popular television shows to such an extent that they function as cultural shorthand. Incidental Shakespeare may, as Olive suggests, comment or 'write back to' Shakespeare from the point of view of an oppressed or marginalized subjectivity (2013).

**Intermediality** Connected to the 1960s Fluxus Art movement and coined by Dick Higgins. A term in information literacy that evokes new media arising within the spaces between known media; the process by which a medium critiques its predecessors. Defined by Rajewsky (2005) as a term for activity taking place between media; described by Schröter (2012) as synthetic.

Fischlin (2014) emphasizes intermediality's *syncretic* effects (Ch. 4). See also **Remediation**.

**Meme** Coined by Richard Dawkins (1976) in 'Memes: The New Replicators' in *The Selfish Gene* and described as a figure and unit for cultural transmission. Now used most frequently in discussions of social media and web-based iterations on a familiar theme, image, or phrasing. Not just metaphorical, but technical, dynamic structures, like genes, memes prioritize fecundity (spreadability) over longevity. Blackmore describes the meme as a unit of imitation, constituted by repetition, variation, and selection (1999: 51). Can include repeated formal characteristics or 'identifiable narrative unit[s]' (Denslow 2017) that vary despite its stable features. May also be used as a verb, as in *to meme, memeable, memed, memetics, memetic, memeplex* (Ch. 5).

**Off-shoots** An 'inclusive' term for departures, alterations, or updates of Shakespeare, first used by Ruby Cohn (1976). 'Off-shoots' is a looser, more neutral word for "abridgements, adaptations, additions, alterations, ameliorations, amplifications, augmentations, conversions, distortions, emendations, interpolations, metamorphoses, modifications, mutilations, revisions, transformations, versions" (Cohn 1976: 3). Off-shoot suggests travelling, mobility, while also demonstrating how 'far the shoots grow from the Shakespearean stem' (Cohn 1976: 3). The term anticipates later growth-related terms in adaptation (Ch. 1).

**Presentist Shakespeare** A sometimes-pejorative term arising in historical studies that indicates a critic's situatedness in or bias to the present. Terence Hawkes discusses presentism in terms of its ongoing dialogue between past and present: 'The critic's own 'situatedness' does not-cannot-contaminate the past. In effect, it constitutes the only means by which it's possible to see and perhaps comprehend it' (1992: 3). Jeffrey Wilson suggests that performance and adaptation studies engage in 'historical presentism' (2019).

**Postcolonial Adaptation** Focuses on how adaptations from formerly colonized nations can resist, subvert, 'decolonize' or otherwise make Shakespeare their own while nonetheless acknowledging 'alterity, difference, and inequities' beyond 'a politically inflected theoretical approach' (Singh 2019: 4).

**Posthuman Shakespeare** Associated with both the Actor-Network Theory developed by Latour (1996) in which 'assemblages' of

objects and persons, rather than individual humans, become
agents, and with the Object-Oriented-Ontology or 'vital
materialism' of Bennett (2010), in which 'intensity' manifests as
action based on an item's 'entelechy' or inward tendency *and* the
fluctuating energies around that item, posthuman adaptations are
often digitally produced and disseminated; posthuman and
algorithmic; and accidental. Algorithmic Shakespeares (Desmet
2017) and 'cyborg Shakespeares' (Fazel and Geddes 2022)
reproduce through digital networks rather than human
movement or agency. Cyborg, procedural, or algorithm-driven
Shakespeares might be said to *hack* the human, who in turn,
*makes* the adaptation.

**Queer Adaptation** Adaptations that explicitly or implicitly critique
heteronormative institutions, or that feature queer characters and
themes (Ch. 5).

**Race and Adaptation** Adapting Shakespeare's works through the
lives of characters of colour. This form of adaptation often works
to reverse cultural or literary forms of racial erasure. Adaptations
that engage directly with Shakespeare's racialized language and
characterizations. MacDonald argues that 'the site of
Shakespearean adaptation' is 'the place where it can begin to
admit black women into onstage presence' (2020: 4).

**Remediation** Process by which one medium – often a new medium
– represents or refashions another. The term originates with Paul
Levinson (1997), the process by which new media improve prior
media technologies in an 'anthropotrophic' process. Bolter and
Grusin (1999) explain that remediation can either make itself
transparent or make itself hyperpresent in a phenomenon
referred to as 'hypermediacy'. Lanier (2007) suggests that
unfaithful adaptations to Shakespeare's plays can draw greater
awareness to their processes of remediation. In 'William
Shakespeare, Filmmaker' Lanier suggests 'The great virtue of
unfaithful or free adaptations – beside the strengths of individual
films themselves – is that they foreground issues of remediation
and ideological recoding often tacit in many Shakespeare films'
(2007: 69). (Ch. 4).

**Remix** Term from music with special ties to the hip hop genre:
process by which popular songs are extended, repeated,
sequenced, or deconstructed into 'samples' and reassembled.
The remix adapts a prior musical work by altering features of

various tracks within the sound (beats, instrumentation, lyrics). Della Gatta (2020) broadly considers hip hop's discursive strategies in *Othello: The Remix* (Ch. 2, Ch. 5).

**Rhizomatic Shakespeare** The rhizome is a root-structure with an open, distributed, non-hierarchical shape that has become a frequent metaphor for social, artistic, and cultural structures: the rhizome contrasts the top-down, hierarchical structure of the tree or arbor. Deleuze and Guattari first used the term in 1975's *Toward a Minor Literature*, to describe Kafka's work. The rhizome with its numerous lines of escape illustrates Kafka's status as a writer of 'minor literature', that is a literature 'which a minority constructs within a major language' ([1975] 1986: 16). The minor literature, like the rhizome, disrupts and de-territorializes, avoids reinforcing the normative ([1975] 1986: 19). Deleuze and Guattari further explicate the term in 1980's *A Thousand Plateaus* as part of a theory on literature as assemblage that forgoes binary logic. Lanier applies this figure to (Shakespearean) adaptation, preferring it in some instances over 'appropriation', which tends to reify cultural authority. As Lanier explains, a rhizomatic Shakespearean text is 'fundamentally adaptational', and is connected to a network of other adaptations, other texts, performances, scripts, theatres, and other plateaus (2014: 29). Desmet and Iyengar (2015) critique the rhizomatic model of adaptation, however, suggesting that its indeterminacy can diminish the agency of the individual (Ch. 1).

**Shakespeare-Function** Derives from Foucault's author-function, the characteristics projected by readers on to a set of texts. Albanese (2010) describes the Shakespeare function as the sum of Shakespeare's numerous institutional, public, and cultural roles. Under the term 'Shakesperotics', Gary Taylor's describes a similar shifting cultural phenomenon: 'what society does in the name – variously spelled – of Shakespeare' (1991: 6).

**Spreadable Shakespeare** Spreadability is a prominent term in new media studies, marketing, and tech that refers to the ability of audiences, readers, or users to circulate content, whether or not its creators agree (Jenkins, Ford, and Green 2013). '"Spreadability" refers to the technical resources that make it easier to circulate some kinds of content than others, the economic structures that support or restrict circulation the attributes of a media text that might appeal to a community's motivation for sharing material, and the social networks that link people through the exchange of meaningful bytes' (Jenkins, Ford, and Green 2013: 4). Jenkins contrasts spreadability to 'stickiness'. 'Spreadability' has specific relevance to user-generated Shakespeare, but also resists the viral implications of terms such as 'meme', in which a textual bit or artefact circulates through an unwitting transmitter. Spreadability, in contrast, emphasizes agency.

**Social Media Shakespeare** Digitally enabled mass media that deploy Shakespeare as adapted, performed, appropriated, etc. text, that permit conversation about Shakespeare among users, or function as archives or adaptation networks that use each platform's affordances; can encompass text-, image-, and video-sharing sites such as Twitter, YouTube, or TikTok, as well as networked communities such as Facebook groups, group texts, email list-servs, and so on (O'Neill 2014).

**Source** Related to fidelity criticism: source represents the antecedent material drawn on in the production of an adaptation, as in Bullough (1966–69)'s six-volume compilation and Muir (1957)'s catalogue of Shakespeare's sources. Most commonly in law the term has been used in association with copyright and open-access material. Teague offers a critique: '"Source" study suggests that an essentially original source exists like the source of a river, a unique beginning that is fed and increased by other streams. Moreover, there is a sense that finding a source is an action that is somehow complete in itself' (2011: 75). The term raises more questions than it answers: Are sources building blocks? Are they endlessly layered products of intertextuality? Raw material? Dynamic and inconsistent? At stake in this discussion is authorial control: do authors create and control texts, or are authors products of preexisting cultural discourses? The relationship between source and target is dynamic and fluid rather than stable (Ch. 6). Winckler (2017) suggests that Shakespeare is 'source code' that adaptors can 'hack'.

**Surrogation** Term from performance studies for the substitution of a body for a text, one text for another, one author-function for another. Imagines the literary corpus as a human body. Roach ([1996] 2022) defines dramatic performance as a process of surrogation in which a living actor embodies a memory from the past. Loftis uses the term to allude to 'multiple levels of interweaving cultural, literary, and dramatic duplication' (2013: xii). Bodies are surrogates for texts, for other actors' bodies, for cultural memory (Loftis 2013: xii): this process is often violent or violating. Adaptation is thus violently embodied.

**Trace** Related to Derrida's theory of the archive, the trace refers to some sort of linguistic, cultural, or thematic residue, an absence or exile. For Lehmann (2002), Shakespeare's text, absented from cinematic adaptations, nonetheless reappears to 'haunt' film as a ghostly *auteur*. MacDonald argues that the black women in Shakespeare's plays possess this quality: 'almost visible, almost tangible, but not always fully achieved' (2020: 7). Adaptation thus can achieve what, in the plays, is on the verge of legibility.

**Tradaptation** Portmanteau word, usually attributed to Québécois (*joual*) playwright Michel Garneau (Hellot and Garneau 2009), that implies that translation is adaptation and adaptations are translations. It often engages with post- or neo-colonial language forms and adapts them to local, sometimes rebellious, contexts (Lieblein 2004; Hellot 2009; Drouin 2014), perhaps in a similar manner to Deleuze and Guattari's 'minor literature' (1975). Mooneram (2009) evokes the term in Shakespearean scholarship to discuss the dialogue between Shakespeare's place in the core educational curriculum and Shakespeare's creolization in Mauritius (Ch. 6), while Lieblein (2004) and Drouin (2014) connect *joual* Shakespeare to Québec's vexed relationship to both the English and French language.

**Transformation** The transfer of Shakespeare's language or characters to new situations (Cohn 1976). Ranges from Ovidian or Lucretian materialism to (most relevant to modern context) loopholes within copyright law. Associated with adaptation studies as well as the language of copyright law, the transformative principle is an integral part of fair use: to make a claim for fair use, the user must be able to prove that their adaptive work is transformative. Iyengar (2017a) suggests that anything a user does to Shakespeare must be transformative, because each form of use reinvents a source to which no modern user has access.

**Upcycled Shakespeare** Upcycled Shakespeare is a kind of redemptive crafting that takes place when 'crafters transform' Shakespeare's plays 'into other media' not associated with stage or filmed productions (Iyengar 2014a: 12). The term 'upcycling' comes from McDonough and Braungart (2002): 'sources that would otherwise be of little worth are crafted into items of greater financial or environmental value' (Iyengar 2014a: 12). Since Shakespeare is both a 'bearer of high and low culture, printed and bound in...mass-market editions as well as...rare...printings...Shakespearean books [are] a compelling category for book artists' (Iyengar 2014a: 17).

**User** In New Media studies, 'users' replaces students, recipients, or even consumers, who may be 'prosumers', producers of what they themselves use. The user performs as an agent within networks of activity. New media 'users' play a role in breaking down Shakespearean 'text' and 'myth' in unpredictable ways (Fazel and Geddes 2017).

# NOTES

## Introduction

1 Jean-Dominique Bauby composed his best-selling *The Diving Bell and the Butterfly* ([1997] 1998), about his life as a patient with locked-in syndrome, using partner-assisted scanning technology and through blinking his left eyelid. Several patients with severe disabilities have used eye-tracking technology to compose and publish memoirs with independent presses, although I am unaware of any books composed entirely through a computer-brain interface as yet.

## Chapter 1

1 For a discussion of Atwood's novel in the context of programs that teach or perform Shakespeare with incarcerated students, see Cavanagh (2018).

## Chapter 2

1 Forthcoming work by Vanessa Corredera suggests that dramatic interventions by artists of colour, such as Keith Hamilton Cobb's *American Moor* (2020), can break the white racial frame along with the imagined distinction between adaptation and performance, a process that Corredera calls 'adaptive revisioning'. I am grateful to Vanessa for letting me refer to her work.

# Chapter 6

1 References come from Salisbury (2016) and from the invaluable *British Black and Asian Shakespeare Performance Database* (2016–).

# REFERENCES

Aebischer, Pascale (2004), *Shakespeare's Violated Bodies*, Cambridge: Cambridge University Press.

Aebsicher, Pascale, Edward J. Esche, and Nigel Wheale, eds (2003), *Remaking Shakespeare*, Houndmills, UK: Palgrave.

Aebischer, Pascale, Susanne Greenhalgh, and Laurie E. Osborne, eds (2018), *Shakespeare and the 'Live' Theatre Broadcast Experience*, London and New York: Bloomsbury Arden.

Albanese, Denise (2010), *Extramural Shakespeare*, New York: Palgrave Macmillan.

Aleo, Cindy (2013), 'On Writing – and Being – a Mary Sue', in Anne Jamison (ed.), *Fic: How Fanfiction is Taking Over the World*, 207–11, Dallas, TX: BenBella Books.

Allen, Greg (2013), 'Richard Prince's Canal Zone Paintings: Now With 83% Less Infringiness!', *greg.org: the making of*, 25 April. Available online: http://greg.org/archive/2013/04/25/richard_princes_canal_zone_paintings_now_with_83_less_infringiness.html (accessed 15 September 2021).

Amberg, Jim (2013), '"Teach him how to tell my story": Access at the Oregon Shakespeare Festival', *Borrowers and Lenders: The Journal of Shakespeare and Appropriation*, 8 (2). Available online: https://borrowers-ojs-azsu.tdl.org/borrowers/article/view/131/259 (accessed 4 April 2022).

Atwood, Margaret (2016), *Hag-Seed*, London: Hogarth.

Auden, W. H. ([1944] 2005), *The Sea and the Mirror*, ed. Arthur Kirsch, Princeton, NJ: Princeton University Press.

Babula, William (2001), 'Claribel, Tunis, and Greenaway's Prospero's Books', *Journal of the Wooden O Symposium*, 1: 19–25.

Baker, Mona, and Gabriela Saldanha, eds (2008), *Routledge Encyclopedia of Translation Studies*, London: Taylor & Francis Group.

Bakhtin, M. M. (1981), *The Dialogic Imagination*, ed. Michal Holquist, trans. Caryl Emerson and Michael Holquist, Austin: University of Texas Press.

Balizet, Ariane (2005), '"Let Him Pass for a Man:" The Myth of Male Menstruation in Shakespeare's *Merchant of Venice*', in Andrew Shail and Gillian Howie (eds), *Menstruation: A Cultural History*, 200–212, New York: Palgrave.

Balizet, Ariane (2019), *Shakespeare and Girls' Studies*, London and New York: Routledge.

Barber, C. L. (1959), *Shakespeare's Festive Comedy*, Princeton: Princeton University Press.

Barthes, Roland ([1967] 1977), *Image-Music-Text*, trans. Stephen Heath, London: Farrar, Strauss, and Giroux.

Bartlett, Erin (2018), 'The Ten Weirdest Places Shakespeare's Plays Have Been Performed', *Electric Literature*, 14 September. Available online: https://electricliterature.com/the-10-weirdest-places-shakespeare-plays-have-been-performed (accessed 23 March 2022).

Bassnett, Susan (2014), *Translation*, London and New York: Routledge.

Bauby, Jean-Dominique ([1997] 1998), *The Diving Bell and the Butterfly*, trans. Jeremy Leggatt, New York: Vintage.

Bauman, H-Dirksen L., and Joseph J. Murray (2014), 'Introduction', in H-Dirksen L. Bauman and Joseph J. Murray (eds), *Deaf Gain: Raising the Stakes for Human Diversity*, xv–xlii, Minneapolis: University of Minnesota Press.

*BBA [British Black and Asian Shakespeare Performance Database]* (2016–). Available online: https://bbashakespeare.warwick.ac.uk (accessed 1 May 2022).

Beesoondial, Ashish (2013), '"Sa bezsominn Shakespeare la" – The Brave New World of Dev Virahsawmy', in Jane Plastow (ed.), *Shakespeare in and out of Africa*, 98–110, Woodbridge, Suffolk: Currey.

Beesoondial, Ashish (2018), 'Shakespeare's Creolized Voices', *Shakespeare Survey*, 71: 12–17.

Benjamin, Walter ([1968] 2006), 'The Task of the Translator', trans. James Hynd and E. M. Valk, in Daniel Weissbort and Astradur Eysteinsson (eds), *Translation – Theory and Practice: A Historical Reader*, 297–307, Oxford: Oxford University Press.

Bennett, Jane (2010), *Vibrant Matter*, Durham, NC: Duke University Press.

Bennett, Susan, and Christie Carson, eds (2013), *Shakespeare Beyond English: A Global Experiment*, Cambridge: Cambridge University Press.

Bersani, Leo (1987), 'Is the Rectum a Grave?', *October*, 43: 197–222.
Bey, Marquis (2020), 'Incorporeal Blackness: A Theorization in Two Parts – Rachel Dolezal and *Your Face in Mine*', *CR: The New Centennial Review*, 20 (2): 205–241.
Bhabha, Homi (1984), 'Of Mimicry and Man: The Ambivalence of Colonial Discourse', *October*, 28: 125–33.
Bharucha, Rustom (2001), 'Consumed in Singapore: The Intercultural Spectacle of *Lear*', *Theater*, 31 (1): 107–127.
Bharucha, Rustom (2010), 'Foreign Asia/foreign Shakespeare: dissenting notes on New Asian interculturality, postcolony and re-colonization', in Dennis Kennedy and Yong-Li Lan (eds), 253–81, *Shakespeare in Asia: Contemporary Performance*, 253–82, Cambridge: Cambridge University Press.
Bickley, Pamela, and Jenny Stevens (2021), *Studying Shakespeare Adaptation*, London: Arden Shakespeare.
Bicks, Caroline, and Michelle Ephraim (2015), *Shakespeare, Not Stirred*, New York: Penguin Random House.
Blackmore, Susan (1999), *The Meme Machine*, Oxford: Oxford University Press.
Bloom, Harold ([1973] 1997), *The Anxiety of Influence*, Oxford: Oxford University Press.
Bloom, Harold (1998), *Shakespeare and the Invention of the Human*, New York: Riverhead.
Bloomsbury Publishing, Plc (2021), 'Corporate History'. Available online: https://www.bloomsbury-ir.co.uk/about/a_history (accessed 21 September 2021).
Bogost, Ian (2012), *Alien Phenomenology, or What it's Like to Be a Thing*, Minneapolis: University of Minnesota Press.
Boland, Alisa (2021), 'Midsommer Flight's Unabashedly Queer, Choose-Your-Own-Adventure *Twelfth Night* is a Delightful Feat of Whimsy', *Rescripted*, 14 December. Available online: https://rescripted.org/2021/12/14/twelfth-night-midsommer/ (accessed 29 January 2022).
Bolter, Jay David, and Richard Grusin (1999), *Remediation*, Cambridge, MA: MIT Press.
Book and Bucket Cheese Company (n.d.), 'Shakespeare Sheep's Milk Brie'. Available online: https://www.thebookandbucket cheesecompany.co.uk/cheese-selection (accessed 22 July 2021).

Boose, Lynda, and Richard Burt, eds (1997), *Shakespeare, the Movie*, New York: Routledge.
Boose, Lynda, and Richard Burt, eds (2003), *Shakespeare, the Movie, II*, New York: Routledge.
Bortolotti, Gary R., and Linda Hutcheon (2007), 'On the Origin of Adaptations: Rethinking Fidelity Discourse and "Success" – Biologically', *New Literary History*, 38 (3): 443–58.
Bradbury, Jill Marie (2021), [Recording] 'Shakespeare and the Poetics of American Sign Language', University of Georgia, 20 April. Available online: https://kaltura.uga.edu/media/t/1_ieficwf6 (accessed 30 March 2022).
Bradbury, Jill Marie, John Lee Clark, Rachel Grossman, Jason Herbers, Victoria Magliocchino, Jasper Norman, Yashaira Romilus, Robert T. Sirvage, Lisa Van Der Mark (2019), 'ProTactile Shakespeare: Inclusive Theatre by/for the DeafBlind', *Shakespeare Studies*, 47: 81–99.
Braziel Jana Evans, and Anita Mannur (2003), 'Nation, Migration, Globalization: Points of Contention in Diaspora Studies', in Jana Evans Braziel and Anita Mannur (eds), *Theorizing Diaspora: A Reader*, 1–22, Oxford: Blackwell.
Bristol, Michael (1990), *Shakespeare's America, America's Shakespeare*, New York: Routledge.
Bristol, Michael (1996), *Big-Time Shakespeare,* New York and London: Routledge.
Brooks, Kinitra (2017), *Searching for Sycorax*, New Brunswick, NJ: Rutgers University Press.
Browning, Robert (1864), 'Caliban upon Setebos', *Poetry Foundation*. Available online: https://www.poetryfoundation.org/poems/43748/caliban-upon-setebos (accessed 12 July 2021).
Bullough, Geoffrey (1966–69) (ed.), *Narrative and Dramatic Sources of Shakespeare*, 8 vols., New York and London: Columbia University Press/Routledge.
Burnett, Mark Thornton (2012), *Shakespeare and World Cinema*, Cambridge: Cambridge University Press.
Burt, Richard, ed. (2002), *Shakespeare after Mass Media*, 2 vols., Houndmills, UK: Palgrave Macmillan.
Busch, Elizabeth Kaufer, and William E. Thro (2018), *Title IX: The Transformation of Sex Discrimination in Education*, New York; London: Routledge.

Busse, Kristina (2017a), *Framing Fan Fiction*, Iowa City: University of Iowa Press.
Busse, Kristina (2017b), 'The Ethics of Studying Online Fandom', in Melissa A. Click and Suzanne Scott (eds), *The Routledge Companion to Media Fandom*, 9–17, New York: Routledge.
Busse, Kristina, and Karen Hellekson (2012), 'Identity, Ethics, and Fan Privacy', in Katherine Larsen and Lynn Zubernis (eds), *Fan Culture*, 39–56, Newcastle-upon-Tyne: Cambridge Scholars.
Butler, Isaac (2021), 'How *West Side Story*'s Anybodys Went from Tomboy to Trans Character', *Slate*, 15 December. Available online: https://slate.com/culture/2021/12/west-side-story-anybodys-2021-movie-trans.html (accessed 29 March 2022).
Byrd, Jodi (2011), '"This Island's Mine": The Parallax Logics of Caliban's Cacophony', in *The Transit of Empire: Indigenous Critiques of Colonialism*, 39–76, Minneapolis: University of Minnesota Press.
CafePress (n.d.), 'Tempest Tile Coaster'. Available online: https://www.cafepress.co.uk/+the_tempest_tile_coaster,172041386 (accessed 22 July 2021).
Caines, Michael (2013), *Shakespeare and the Eighteenth Century*, New York: Oxford University Press.
Calbi, Maurizio (2013), *Spectral Shakespeares: Media Adaptations in the Twenty-First Century*, New York: Palgrave Macmillan.
Calbi, Maurizio, and Stephen O'Neill, eds (2016), *Shakespeare and Social Media*, special issue of *Borrowers and Lenders: The Journal of Shakespeare and Appropriation*, 10 (1). Available online: https://borrowers-ojs-azsu.tdl.org/borrowers/issue/view/27 (accessed 4 April 2022).
Campbell, Joseph (1949), *The Hero with a Thousand Faces*, New York: Pantheon.
Campoy, Ana María (2019), 'Why Bilingual Shakespeare?', Seattle: Seattle Shakespeare Company. Available online: https://www.seattleshakespeare.org/wp-content/uploads/2017/05/Touring-Study-Guide_Hamlet2020.pdf (accessed 29 July 2021).
Carlson, Brook A. (2020), Review of *The Hurly-Burly Shakespeare Show*, *Borrowers and Lenders: The Journal of Shakespeare and Appropriation*, 13 (2). Available online: https://borrowers-ojs-azsu.tdl.org/borrowers/article/view/96/190 (accessed 4 April 2022).

Carlyle, Thomas ([1841] 2007), *On Heroes, Hero-Worship, and the Heroic in History*, New York: Google Books. Available online: https://www.google.com/books/edition/On_Heroes_Hero_worship_the_Heroic_in_His/Ei1MAAAAcAAJ?hl=en&gbpv=1 (accessed 23 April 2022).

Cartelli, Thomas (1999), *Repositioning Shakespeare: National Formations, Postcolonial Appropriations*, London and New York: Routledge.

Cartelli, Thomas (2019), *Reenacting Shakespeare in the Shakespeare Aftermath*, New York: Palgrave/Springer.

Cartelli, Thomas, and Katherine Rowe (2007), *New Wave Shakespeare on Screen*, New York: Polity.

Cavanagh, Sheila (2018), '"There's My Exchange": The Hogarth Shakespeare', in Marina Gerzic and Aidan Norrie (eds), *From Medievalism to Early Modernism: Adapting the English Past*, 99–116, New York: Routledge.

Cavell, Stanley (1984), *The Pursuits of Happiness*, Cambridge, MA: Harvard University Press.

Césaire, Aimé ([1969] 2002), *A Tempest* [Une Tempête], trans. Richard Miller, 2nd edn, New York: Ubu Repertory Theatre/TCG Translations.

Chambers, E.K. (1903), *The Medieval Stage*, vol. 1, Oxford: Clarendon Press.

Charnes, Linda ([2001] 2002), 'The 2% Solution: What Harold Bloom Forgot', in *Harold Bloom's Shakespeare*, 259–268, New York: Palgrave Macmillan/SpringerLink.

*Che Cosa Sono Le Nuvole* (1967), [Film] Dir. Pier Paolo Pasolini. Italy: Dino De Laurentiis. Available online. https://vimeo.com/145320318 (accessed 29 October 2021).

Chess, Simone (2018), 'Asexuality, Queer Chastity, and Adolescence in Early Modern Literature', in Jennifer Higginbotham, Mark Albert Johnston (eds), *Queering Childhood in Early Modern English Drama and Culture*, 31–55, Cham, Switzerland: Palgrave.

*Children of the Sea* (2005), Dir. Toby Gough, Edinburgh: Edinburgh Fringe Festival.

Clarke, Mary Cowden ([1851] 1974), 'Viola, the Twin', *The Girlhood of Shakespeare's Heroines*, vol. 3, 265–355, New York: AMS Press.

Cloud, Random [Randall McLeod] (1982), 'The Marriage of Good and Bad Quartos', *Shakespeare Quarterly*, 33 (3): 422–31.

Clubb, Louise George (1989), *Italian Drama in Shakespeare's Time*, New Haven: Yale University Press.
Cobb, Keith Hamilton (2020), *American Moor*, New York: Methuen Drama.
Cohen, Jeffrey Jerome, and Yates, Julian, eds (2016), *Object-Oriented Environs*, Goleta: punctum books. Available online: https://punctumbooks.com/titles/object-oriented-environs/ (accessed 12 February 2021).
Cohn, Ruby ([1976] 2015), *Modern Shakespearean Offshoots*, Princeton: Princeton Legacy Library.
Coleridge, Peter (1993), *Disability, Liberation, and Development*, Oxford: Oxfam.
Coppa, Francesca (2006), 'Writing Bodies in Space: Media Fan Fiction as Theatrical Performance', in Karen Hellekson and Kristina Busse (eds), *Fan Fiction and Fan Communities in the Age of the Internet*, 225–243, Jefferson, NC: McFarland.
Cotta, John (1612), *A Short Discouerie*, London, R. Field/William Iones, *EEBO* (accessed 30 March 2022).
Courtright, Paul (2004), 'Horace Hayman Wilson', *Dictionary of National Biography*, Oxford: Oxford University Press. Available online: https://doi.org/10.1093/ref:odnb/29657 (accessed 30 March 2022).
Crane, Mary Thomas (2001), *Shakespeare's Brain*, Princeton, NJ: Princeton University Press.
Criniti, Steve (2004), 'Othello: A Hawk Among Birds', *Literature/Film Quarterly*, 32 (2): 115–21.
Cristi, A.A. (2021), 'Shakespeare's TWELFTH NIGHT to Be Presented At Historic Strawberry Mansion', *Broadway World*, 19 August. Available online: https://www.broadwayworld.com/philadelphia/article/Shakespeares-TWELFTH-NIGHT-to-Be-Presented-At-Historic-Strawberry-Mansion-20210819 (accessed 29 January 2022).
Cross, Lezlie C. (2013), 'Speaking in the Silence: Deaf Performance at the Oregon Shakespeare Festival', in Kathryn M. Moncrief, Kathryn R. McPherson, and Sarah Enloe (eds), *Shakespeare Expressed: Page, Stage, and Classroom in Shakespeare and His Contemporaries*, 7–17, Madison/Teaneck, NJ: Fairleigh Dickinson University Press.
Dadabhoy, Ambereen (2020), 'The Unbearable Whiteness of Being (in) Shakespeare', *postmedieval: a journal of medieval cultural studies*, 11 (2–3): 228–35.

Davenant, William ([1662] 1970), *The Law Against Lovers*, London: Cornmarket Press.

Davis, Jenny L., and Krystal A. Smalls (2021), 'Dis/possession Afoot: American (Anthropological) Traditions of Anti-Blackness and Coloniality', *Journal of Linguistic Anthropology*, 31 (2): 275–282.

Davis, Lennard (2002), *Bending Over Backwards: Disability, Dismodernism, and Other Difficult Positions*, New York and London: New York University Press.

Dawkins, Richard (1976), *The Selfish Gene*, Oxford: Oxford University Press.

Dawson, Anthony (1982), 'Much Ado about Signifying', *SEL: Studies in English Literature 1500–1900*, 22: 210–21.

De Grazia, Margreta (1991), *Shakespeare Verbatim*, Oxford: Oxford University Press.

Deleuze, Gilles, and Félix Guattari ([1975] 1986), *Kafka: Toward a Minor Literature*, Minneapolis: University of Minnesota Press.

Deleuze, Gilles, and Félix Guattari (1987), *A Thousand Plateaus*, Minneapolis: University of Minnesota Press.

Della Gatta, Carla (2020), 'Shakespeare, Race and "Other" Englishes: The Q Brothers' *Othello: The Remix*', *Shakespeare Survey*, 71: 74–87.

Denslow, Kristin (2017), 'Guest Starring Hamlet: The Proliferation of the Shakespeare Meme on American Television', in Christy Desmet, Natalie Loper, and Jim Casey (eds), *Shakespeare/Not Shakespeare*, 97–110, Lund: Palgrave/Springer.

Derrida, Jacques ([1967] 2013), *Of Grammatology*, trans. Gayatri Spivak, Baltimore: Johns Hopkins University Press.

de Saussure, Ferdinand ([1916] 2011), *Course in General Linguistics*, Perry Meisel and Haun Saussy (eds), New York: Columbia University Press.

Desmet, Christy (2017), 'Alien Shakespeares 2.0', *Actes des congrès de la Société française Shakespeare 35*. Available online: doi: https://doi.org/10.4000/shakespeare.3877 (accessed 30 March 2022).

Desmet, Christy (2018a), 'Emo Hamlet: Locating Shakespearean Affect in Social Media', in Stephen O'Neill (ed.), *Broadcast Your Shakespeare*, 107–22, London: Bloomsbury.

Desmet, Christy (2018b), 'Quoting Shakespeare in Contemporary Poetry and Prose', in Julie Maxwell and Kate Rumbold (eds), *Shakespeare and Quotation*, 231–46, Cambridge: Cambridge University Press.

Desmet, Christy (2019), 'The bedchamber as contested space: *Much Ado About Nothing* in film and social media', *Arrêt sur Scène/Scene Focus* 8: 29–52. Available online: https://ircl.cnrs.fr/productions%20electroniques/arret_scene/8_2019/ASF8_2019_03_desmet.pdf (accessed 7 July 2021).

Desmet, Christy, and Sujata Iyengar (2015), 'Adaptation, Appropriation, or What You Will', *Adaptation*, 11 (1): 10–19.

Desmet, Christy, and David Schiller (2017), 'The Shakespearean World of Music', in Jill Levenson and Robert Ormsby (eds), *The Shakespearean World*, 339–357, London: Routledge.

Desmet, Christy, and Robert Sawyer, eds (1999), *Shakespeare and Appropriation*, London and New York: Routledge.

Desmet, Christy, and Robert Sawyer, eds ([2001] 2002), *Harold Bloom's Shakespeare*, New York: Palgrave Macmillan/SpringerLink.

Desmet, Christy, Sujata Iyengar, and Miriam Jacobson, eds (2020), *The Routledge Handbook to Shakespeare and Global Appropriation*, London and New York: Routledge.

Dickinson, Peter (2002), 'Duets, Duologues, and Black Diasporic Theatre: Djanet Sears, William Shakespeare, and Others', *Modern Drama*, 45 (2): 188–208.

Digges, Leonard (1640), 'Upon Master William Shakespeare', *Poems Written by Wil. Shakespeare*, Folger Shakespeare Library. Available online: doi.org/10.37078/706 (accessed 28 June 2021).

*Dil Chahta Hai* (2001), [Film] Dir. Farhan Akhtar, India: Excel/Eros.

Dionne, Craig, and Parmita Kapadia, eds (2008), *Native Shakespeares: Indigenous Appropriations on a Global Stage*, London and New York: Ashgate.

Dobson, Michael (1992), *The Making of the National Poet: Shakespeare, Adaptation and Authorship, 1660–1769*, Oxford: Oxford University Press.

Donaldson, Peter S. (2006), 'Remediation: Hamlet among the Pixelvisionaries: Video Art, Authenticity, and "Wisdom" in Almereyda's "Hamlet"', in Diana Henderson (ed.), *A Concise Companion to Shakespeare on Screen*, 216–37, Oxford: Blackwell.

Drouin, Jennifer (2014), *Shakespeare in Quebec: Nation, Gender, and Adaptation*, Toronto: University of Toronto Press.

Dryden, John [and William Davenant] (1670), *The Tempest, or, the Enchanted Island*, London: Printed by J.M./Henry Herringman.

Duffett, Thomas (1675), *The Mock-Tempest, Or, the Enchanted Castle*, London: William Cademan.

Dugas, Don-John (2006), *Marketing the Bard: Shakespeare in Performance and Print, 1660–1740*, Columbia: University of Missouri Press.

Dusinberre, Juliet ([1977] 2003), *Shakespeare and the Nature of Women*, London: Routledge.

Ebert, Roger (2000), Review of *Romeo Must Die*, 22 March. Available online: https://www.rogerebert.com/reviews/romeo-must-die-2000 (accessed 30 March 2022).

Edelman, Lee (2004), *No Future*, Durham, NC: Duke University Press.

Edwards, Emily, and Jude Ellison Sady Doyle (2019–2020), [Podcast] 'Fuckbois of Literature: Hamlet'. 9 June. Available online: https://www.fuckboisoflit.com/episodes/2020/6/9/episode-54-hamlet?rq=Hamlet (accessed 23 June 2021).

Edwards, Terra (2018), 'Re-Channeling Language: The Mutual Restructuring of Language and Infrastructure among DeafBlind People at Gallaudet University', *Journal of Linguistic Anthropology*, 28 (3): 273–92.

Elam, Keir (1996), 'The Fertile Eunuch: *Twelfth Night*, Early Modern Intercourse, and the Fruits of Castration', *Shakespeare Quarterly* 47 (1): 1–36.

Engler, Balz (2018), 'On Gottfried Keller's *A Village Romeo and Juliet* and Shakespeare Adaptation in General', *Borrowers and Lenders: The Journal of Shakespeare and Appropriation*, 11 (2). Available online: https://borrowers-ojs-azsu.tdl.org/borrowers/article/view/254/505 (accessed 29 March 2022).

Erickson, Peter (1994), *Rewriting Shakespeare, Rewriting Ourselves*, Berkeley: University of California Press.

Erne, Lukas (2003), *Shakespeare as Literary Dramatist*, Cambridge: Cambridge University Press.

Estill, Laura (2014), 'Digital Bibliography and Global Shakespeare', *Scholarly and Research Communication*, 5 (4): 1–13. Available online: doi.org/10.22230/src.2014v5n4a187 (accessed 19 April 2022).

Fabiszak, Jacek (2015), 'Kenneth Branagh's Multicultural and Multi-ethnic Filmed Shakespeare(s)', *Multicultural Shakespeare*, 12 (27): 75–86. Available online: doi: 10.1515/mstap-2015-0007 (accessed 10 July 2021).

Fanon, Frantz ([1952] 2008), *Black Skin, White Masks*, London: Pluto Press.
Fazel, Valerie (2016), 'Researching YouTube Shakespeare: Literary Scholars and the Ethical Challenges of Social Media', *Borrowers and Lenders: The Journal of Shakespeare and Appropriation*, 10 (1). Available online: https://borrowers-ojs-azsu.tdl.org/borrowers/article/view/281/559 (accessed 4 April 2022).
Fazel, Valerie, and Louise Geddes, eds (2017), *The Shakespeare User*, New York: Palgrave.
Fazel, Valerie, and Louise Geddes, eds (2021), *Variable Objects: Shakespeare and Speculative Appropriation*, Edinburgh: Edinburgh University Press.
Fazel, Valerie, and Louise Geddes (2022), *The Shakespearean Multiverse: Fandom as Literary Praxis*, London and New York: Routledge.
Ferri, Federico (2020), 'The dark side(s) of the EU Directive on copyright and related rights in the Digital Single Market', *China-EU Law J*. Available online: doi: 10.1007/s12689-020-00089-5 (accessed 21 September 2021).
Fine, Ben and Alfredo Saad-Filho (2016), *Marx's 'Capital'*, vol. 1, 6th edn, London: Pluto Press.
Finn, K.M. and McCall, J. (2016), 'Exit, pursued by a fan: Shakespeare, fandom, and the lure of the alternate universe', *Critical Survey*, 28(2), 27–38.
Fish, Stanley (1982), *Is There a Text in This Class?*, Cambridge, MA: Harvard University Press.
Fischlin, Daniel, ed. (2014), *OuterSpeares: Shakespeare, Intermedia, and the Limits of Adaptation*, Toronto: University of Toronto Press.
Fischlin, Daniel (2020), 'Flipping the Turtle on its Back', in Christy Desmet, Sujata Iyengar, and Miriam Jacobson (eds), *The Routledge Handbook of Shakespeare and Global Appropriation*, 127–38, London and New York: Routledge.
Fitzherbert, John (1530), *Book of husbandry*, London: Peter Treuerys.
Foucault, Michel ([1969] 1977), 'What is an Author?', in Donald F. Bouchard and Sherry Simon (eds and trans.), *Language, Counter-memory, Practice: Selected Essays and Interviews*, 113–138, Ithaca, New York, Cornell University Press.
*Forbidden Planet* (1956), [Film] Dir. Fred Wilcox, USA: Metro-Goldwyn-Mayer.

Fortier, Mark (2014), 'Beyond Adaptation', in Daniel Fischlin (ed.), *OuterSpeares: Shakespeare, Intermedia, and the Limits of Adaptation*, 372–86, Toronto, University of Toronto Press.

Fraile-Marcos, A. M., ed. (2014), *Literature and the Glocal City: Reshaping the English Canadian Imaginary*, New York: Routledge.

Francis, Jonathan (2014), 'On Appropriation: *Cariou v. Prince* and Measuring Contextual Transformation in Fair Use', *Berkeley Technology Law Journal*, 29: 681–716.

Franco, Patricia Alejandra Gonzales (2021), 'Interpreting King Lear's Character Transformation Through Stage Directions', unpublished essay, University of Georgia.

Frazer, Kirk-Hendershott (2018), 'Juliet, Tumbld: Fan Renovations of Shakespeare's Juliet on Tumblr', in Stephen O'Neill (ed.), *Broadcast Your Shakespeare: Continuity and Change Across Media,* 141–59, London: Arden Bloomsbury.

Freud, Sigmund ([1899] 2010), *The Interpretation of Dreams*, trans. James Strachey, New York: Basic Books.

Freud, Sigmund (1922), *Beyond the Pleasure Principle*, trans. C.J.M. Hubback, London and Vienna: International Psycho-Analytical Press.

Frost, Robert James (1983), 'The Shakespearean Performances of John Gielgud', PhD diss., The Shakespeare Institute, University of Birmingham.

Fuchs, Christian (2016), 'Dallas Smythe and Digital Labor', in Richard Maxwell (ed.), *The Routledge Companion to Labor and Media*, 51–62, New York and London: Routledge.

Furness, Henry Howard, ([1892] 2018), *A New Variorum Edition of Shakespeare*, HathiTrust. Available online: https://hdl.handle.net/2027/mdp.39015081463138 (accessed 19 July 2021).

Gaba, Jeffrey M (2011), 'Copyrighting Shakespeare: Jacob Tonson, Eighteenth Century English Copyright, And The Birth Of Shakespeare Scholarship', *Journal of Intellectual Property Law*, 19 (1): 21–63.

Galey, Alan (2014), *The Shakespearean Archive: Experiments in New Media From the Renaissance to Postmodernity*, Cambridge: Cambridge University Press.

Gallivan, Brian (2010), 'Sassy Gay Friend: *Romeo and Juliet*'. Available online: https://www.youtube.com/watch?v=lwnFE_NpMsE (accessed 27 January 2022).

Garbus, Martin (1999), 'Lolita and the Lawyers', *New York Times*, 26 September. Available online: https://archive.nytimes.com/

www.nytimes.com/books/99/09/26/bookend/bookend.html (accessed 22 September 2021).

García-Periago, Rosa M (2016), 'In Search of a Happy Ending: The Afterlife of Romeo and Juliet on the Asian Screen', *Atlantis*, 38 (1): 185–200.

Genette, Gérard ([1982] 1997), *Palimpsests: Literature in the Second Degree*, trans. Channa Newman and Claude Doubinsky, Lincoln: University of Nebraska Press.

Gibson, Mary Ellis, ed. (2011), 'Horace Hayman Wilson', in *Anglophone Poetry in Colonial India, 1780–1913: A Critical Anthology*, xcv–ci, Athens: Ohio University Press.

Gibson, Prudence (2018), 'Conclusion: On Rhizomes and Dead Trees', in *The Plant Contract: Art's Return to Vegetal Life*, 163–70, Boston, MA: BRILL.

Gilbert, Sandra, and Susan Gubar (1979), *The Madwoman in the Attic*, New Haven: Yale University Press.

Gilreath, Philip (2020), '"The Art Itself is Nature": Dissolution of the Human Form in Shakespeare's Green Worlds', *ISLE: Interdisciplinary Studies in Literature and Environment*, isaa199, https://doi.org/10.1093/isle/isaa199 (accessed 11 July 2021).

Gilreath, Philip (2021), '"Cloud Capped Towers" Made of Sand: Dissolving Barriers to Female Authorship in Julie Taymor's *Tempest*', *Adaptation*, apaa037. Available online: https://doi.org/10.1093/adaptation/apaa037 (accessed 11 July 2021).

Gilroy, Paul (1993), *The Black Atlantic: Modernity and Double Consciousness*, London: Verso.

Go, Kenji (2012), 'Montaigne's "Cannibals" and The Tempest Revisited', *Studies in Philology*, 109 (4): 455–73.

Goldberg, Jonathan, ed. (1994), *Queering the Renaissance*, Durham, NC: Duke University Press.

Goldhill Global (2021), [Streaming video] *The Complete Works of Shakespeare*, by Seydina Diop. Available online: https://nftstars.app/en/nft/0x3a10b673a043746633918797a32ec5432c7c2281/1636835015396947/ (accessed 18 January 2022).

Goldman, Nick, Paul Bertone, Siyuan Chen, Christophe Dessimoz, Emily M. LeProust, Botond Sipos, and Ewan Birney (2013), 'Towards practical, high-capacity, low-maintenance information storage in synthesized DNA', *Nature* 494: 77–80. Available online: 10.1038/nature11875 (accessed 18 January 2022).

*Goliyon Ki Raasleela Ram-leela (A Play of Bullets)* ([*Ram-leela*] 2013), [Film] Dir. Sanjay Leela Bhansali, India: Eros International.

Gottlieb, Christine Marie (2018), '"Unaccommodated Man": Dismodernism and Disability Justice in King Lear', *Disability Studies Quarterly*, 38 (4): 1–16. Available online: http://dsq-sds.org/article/view/6079/5133 (accessed 30 March 2022).

Gower, John ([1386–90] 2006), *Confessio Amantis*, vol. 1, book 8, ed. Russell A. Peck, Kalamazoo, MI: TEAMS Middle English Texts. Available online: https://d.lib.rochester.edu/teams/text/peck-gower-confessio-amantis-book-8 (accessed 21 February 2022).

Grady, Hugh (1991), *The Modernist Shakespeare*, Oxford: Clarendon.

Greenaway, Peter (1991), *Prospero's Books: A Film of Shakespeare's 'The Tempest'*, New York: Four Walls Eight Windows.

Greenhalgh, Susanne (2011), '"A stage of the mind": Hamlet on Post-War British Radio', *Shakespeare Survey* 64: 133–44.

Greetham, David (1995), 'Phylum-Tree-Rhizome', *Huntington Library Quarterly* 58 (1): 99–126.

Gross, George C. (1972), 'Mary Cowden Clarke, "The Girlhood of Shakespeare's Heroines," and the Sex Education of Victorian Women', *Victorian Studies*, 16 (1): 37–58.

Gruber, Elizabeth (2008), 'Practical Magic: Empathy and Alienation in Harlem Duet', *LIT: Literature, Interpretation, Theory*, 19 (4): 346–66.

Hall, Stuart (1994), 'Cultural Identity and Diaspora', in Patrick Williams and Laura Chrisman (eds), *Colonial Discourse and Post-Colonial Theory: A Reader*, 392–403, New York: Columbia University Press.

Hamburger, Maik (2012), 'Translating and Copyright', in Ton Honselaars (ed.), *Shakespeare and the Language of Translation*, 148–166, London: Bloomsbury Publishing Plc.

*Hamlet* ([2006] 2016), ed. Ann Thompson and Neil Taylor, Arden Shakespeare, 3rd series, London: Bloomsbury.

*Hamlet: The Texts of 1603 and 1623* (2006), ed. Ann Thompson and Neil Taylor, Arden Shakespeare, 3rd series, London: Bloomsbury.

*Hamlet* ([1948] 2006), [Radio broadcast] *BBC Third Programme*, 26 December, repr. (abridged), online [Hong Kong], Naxos.

*Hamlet* (1957), [Vinyl audiodisc] Perf. Old Vic Company, UK: RCA Victor.

*Hamlet* (2000), [Film] Dir. Michael Almereyda, USA: Miramax.

*Hamlet* (2020), [Streaming audio play] Dir. Anna Maria Campoy, Seattle Shakespeare Company. Apple Podcasts (accessed 23 June 2021; link no longer available).

Hammersley, Ben (2004), 'Audible revolution', *The Guardian*, 12 February. Available online: https://www.theguardian.com/media/2004/feb/12/broadcasting.digitalmedia (accessed 22 June 2021).

Hanratty, Conor (2017–21), [Streaming audio] *The 'Hamlet' Podcast*. Available online: https://www.thehamletpodcast.com/episodes (accessed 23 June 2021).

Haraway, Donna ([1965] 2016), *A Cyborg Manifesto*, Minneapolis: University of Minnesota Press.

Harris, Jeremy (2020), *Slave Play*, New York: Dramatists Play Service.

Harris, Jonathan Gil (2009), *Untimely Matter*, Philadelphia: University of Pennsylvania Press.

Harris, Jonathan Gil (2010), *Shakespeare and Literary Theory*, Oxford: Oxford University Press.

Hartley, Andrew, and Peter Holland, eds (2020), *Shakespeare and Geek Culture*, London: Arden Bloomsbury.

Hartley, Andrew, ed. (2018), *Shakespeare and Millennial Fiction*, Cambridge: Cambridge University Press.

Hatchuel, Sarah (2019), 'Shakespeare's Humanizing Language in Films and TV Series', *Borrowers and Lenders: The Journal of Shakespeare and Appropriation*, 12 (2). Available online: https://borrowers-ojs-azsu.tdl.org/borrowers/article/view/233/463 (accessed 5 April 2022).

Hawkes, Terence (1992), *Meaning By Shakespeare*, London: Routledge.

Hawkes, Terence ([2001] 2002), 'Bloom With a View', in Desmet, Christy, and Robert Sawyer (eds), *Harold Bloom's Shakespeare*, 27–31, New York: Palgrave Macmillan/SpringerLink.

Hellinga, Lotte ([2007] 2019), 'The Gutenberg Revolutions', in Simon Eliot and Jonathan Rose (eds), *A Companion to the History of the Book*, 2nd edn, 377–92, New York and London: Wiley-Blackwell.

Hellot, Marie-Christiane, and Michel Garneau (2009), 'Le poète qui traduit: Entretien avec Michel Garneau' (Interview with Michel Garneau), *Jeu*, 133: 83–8.

Henderson, Diana (2006), *Collaborations with the Past: Reshaping Shakespeare across Time and Media*, Ithaca, NY: Cornell University Press, 2006.

Hendricks, Margo (2006), 'Gestures of Performance: Rethinking Race in Contemporary Shakespeare', in Ayanna Thompson (ed.), *Colorblind Shakespeare: New Perspectives on Race and Performance*, 187–203, London and New York: Routledge.

Higginbotham, Evelyn Brooks (1993), *Righteous Discontent: The Women's Movement in the Black Baptist Church, 1880–1920*, Harvard: Harvard University Press.

Higgins, Dick (2001), 'Intermedia', *Leonardo*, 4 (1): 49–54.

Hirsch, Brett D. and Janelle Jenstad (2016), 'Beyond the Text: Digital Editions and Performance', *Shakespeare Bulletin*, 34 (1):106–27.

Hobgood, Allison (2021), *Beholding Disability in Renaissance England*, Ann Arbor: University of Michigan Press.

Hoenselaars, Ton, ed. (2012), *Shakespeare and the Language of Translation*, London: Bloomsbury Publishing Plc.

Holderness, Graham (2005), '"Dressing Old Words New": Shakespeare, Science, and Appropriation', *Borrowers and Lenders: The Journal of Shakespeare and Appropriation*, 1 (2). Available online: https://borrowers-ojs-azsu.tdl.org/borrowers/article/view/79/156 (accessed 13 April 2022).

Holderness, Graham (2013), *Nine Lives of William Shakespeare*, London: Continuum.

Holderness, Graham (2014), *Tales from Shakespeare: Creative Collisions*, Cambridge, Cambridge University Press.

Holland, Peter (2000), 'Modernizing Shakespeare: Nicholas Rowe and *The Tempest*', *Shakespeare Quarterly*, 51 (1): 24–32.

Holland, Peter (2005), 'Coasting in the Mediterranean: The Journeyings of *Pericles*', *Angles on the English-Speaking World*, 5: 11–29.

Holland, Peter (2015), 'David Garrick: Saints, Temples and Jubilees', in Dominique Goy-Blanquet (ed.), *Shakespeare 450: A Jubilee in Paris*. Available online: https://doi.org/10.4000/shakespeare.3020 (accessed 20 July 2021).

Holland, Sharon (2012), *The Erotic Life of Racism*, Durham, North Carolina: Duke University Press.

Hoydis, Julia (2020), '*Hamlet* Revision: Bhardwaj's *Haider* as Crossmapping and Contact Zone', *Adaptation*, apaa035.

Available online: https://doi.org/10.1093/adaptation/apaa035 (accessed 15 July 2021).

Hsu, Spencer S. (2018), '30 years after theft, FBI recovers Chagall painting stolen from New York couple's apartment', *Washington Post*, 12 April. Available online: https://www.washingtonpost.com/local/public-safety/marc-chagall-painting-stolen-from-new-york-apartment-recovered-by-fbi-after-30-years/2018/04/12/15514510-3da9-11e8-a7d1-e4efec6389f0_story.html (accessed 14 September 2021).

Hughes, Bill (2007), 'Being disabled: towards a critical social ontology for disability studies', *Disability & Society*, 22 (7): 673–84.

*The Hurly Burly Shakespeare Show!* (2017), [Podcast] Dir. Aubrey Whitlock and Jess Hamlet. Available online: https://hurlyburlyshakespeareshow.com/podcast/2017/10/23/episode-001-hamlet-101 (accessed 17 June 2021).

Hutcheon, Linda ([2006] 2013), *A Theory of Adaptation*, 2nd edn, epilogue by Siobhan O'Flynn, London and New York: Routledge.

Huxley, Aldous (1932), *Brave New World*, London: Chatto and Windus.

Ick, Judy Celine (2017), 'The Augmentation of the Indies: An Archipelagic Approach to Asian and Global Shakespeare', in Bi-qi Beatrice Lei, Judi Celine Ick, and Poonam Trivedi (eds), *Shakespeare's Asian Journeys*, 19–36, London: Routledge.

Innis, Harold ([1951] 1999), *The Bias of Communication*, Toronto: University of Toronto Press.

Irigaray, Luce ([1977] 1985), *This Sex Which is Not One*, trans. Catherine Porter with Carolyn Burke, Ithaca, NY: Cornell University Press.

Irvington Theatre (2021), 'A fresh take on Shakespeare's Classic'. Available online: https://www.irvingtontheater.com/twelfthnight (accessed 29 January 2022).

Iser, Wolfgang ([1976] 1980), *The Act of Reading*, Baltimore, MD: Johns Hopkins University Press.

Iyengar, Sujata (2001), 'Shakespeare in HeteroLove,' *Literature/Film Quarterly*, 29 (2): 122–127.

Iyengar, Sujata (2014a), 'Upcycling Shakespeare: Crafting Cultural Capital', in Daniel Fischlin (ed.), *Outerspeares: Shakespeare, Intermedia, and the Limits of Adaptation*, 347–371, Toronto: University of Toronto Press.

Iyengar, Sujata (2014b), 'Some Historical, Theatrical, and Critical Backgrounds', in Sujata Iyengar and Frédérique Fouassier-Tate, *'Not Like an Old Play': 'Love's Labour's Lost' de William Shakespeare*, 17–68, Paris: Editions Fahrenheit.

Iyengar, Sujata (2016), 'Woman-Crafted Shakespeares: Appropriation, Intermediality, and Womanist Aesthetics', in Dympna Callaghan (ed.), *A Feminist Companion to Shakespeare*, 507–16, London: Wiley-Blackwell.

Iyengar, Sujata (2017a), 'Shakespeare Transformed: Copyright, Copyleft, and Shakespeare After Shakespeare', *Actes des congrès de la Société française Shakespeare*, 35. Available online: https://doi.org/10.4000/shakespeare.3852 (accessed 15 September 2021).

Iyengar, Sujata (2017b), 'Shakespeare's Anti-Balcony Scene', *Arrêt sur scène/Scene Focus* 6: 135–145. Available online: https://ircl.cnrs.fr/productions%20electroniques/arret_scene/arret_scene_focus_6_2017.htm#sommaire (accessed 30 March 2022).

Iyengar, Sujata (2021), 'Beds, Handkerchiefs, and Moving Objects in *Othello*', in Valerie Fazel and Louise Geddes (eds), *Variable Objects*, 21–36, Edinburgh: Edinburgh University Press.

Iyengar, Sujata, and Christy Desmet (2012), 'Rebooting Ophelia', in Deanne Williams and Kaara Peterson (eds), *The Afterlife of Ophelia*, 59–78, Houndmills, UK: Palgrave.

Jakobson, Roman [1959] (2006), 'On Linguistic Aspects of Translation', in Daniel Weissbort, and Astradur Eysteinsson (eds), *Translation: Theory and Practice*, 330–336, Oxford: Oxford University Press.

Jankowski, Theodora (2000), *Pure Resistance*, Philadelphia: University of Pennsylvania Press.

Jardine, Lisa (1983), *Still Harping on Daughters*, Sussex: Harvester Press.

Jayendran, Nishevita (2020), '"Set Me Free": Spaces and the Politics of Creativity in Margaret Atwood's *Hag-Seed* (2016)', *Journal of Language, Literature, and Culture*, 67 (1): 15–27.

Jenkins, Henry (1988), '*Star Trek* Rerun, Reread, Rewritten: Fan Writing as Textual Poaching', *Critical Studies in Mass Communication*, 5: 85–107.

Jenkins, Henry (2008), *Convergence Culture: Where Old and New Media Collide*, New York: New York University Press.

Jenkins, Henry, Sam Ford, and Joshua Green (2015), *Spreadable Media: Creating Value and Meaning in a Networked Culture*, New York: New York University Press.

Jensen, Michael P. (2017), 'The Case for Audio Shakespeare', in Robert Ormsby and Jill Levenson (eds), *The Shakespearean World*, 405–17, London and New York: Taylor and Francis.

Jensen, Michael P. (2018), *The Battle of the Bard: Shakespeare on US Radio in 1937*, Amsterdam: ARC, Amsterdam University Press.

Johnson, Eric (2003), *Open-Source Shakespeare: An Experiment in Literary Technology*, MA diss, George Mason University. Available online: https://www.opensourceshakespeare.org/info/moby_shakespeare.php (accessed 18 January 2022).

Johnson, Samuel ([1765] 2009), 'Preface to Shakespeare', in Peter Martin (ed.), *Samuel Johnson: Selected Writings*, 353–394, Cambridge, MA: Harvard University Press.

Jones, Leisha (2011), 'Contemporary Bildungsromans and the Prosumer Girl', *Criticism* 53 (3): 439–69.

Joubin, Alexa Alice (2016), 'Boomerang Shakespeare', in Bruce R. Smith (ed.), *The Cambridge Guide to the Worlds of Shakespeare*: vol. 2, 1094–1101, Cambridge: Cambridge University Press.

Joubin, Alexa Alice (2020), 'Screening Social Justice: Performing Reparative Shakespeare against Vocal Disability', *Adaptation*. Available online: https://doi.org/10.1093/adaptation/apaa031 (accessed 11 July 2021).

Joubin, Alexa Alice, and Elizabeth Rivlin, eds (2014), *Shakespeare and the Ethics of Appropriation*, Houndmills, UK.: Palgrave Macmillan.

Kakutani, Michiko (1999), '"Lo's Diary": Humbert Would Swear This Isn't the Same Lolita', *New York Times*, 29 October. Available online: https://archive.nytimes.com/www.nytimes.com/library/books/102999pera-book-review.html (accessed 22 September 2021).

Kapil, Aditi Brennan (2018), *Imogen Says Nothing*, London. Samuel French.

Karas, Helena (2021), 'Therapy as Emotional Vulnerability in Cheek By Jowl's *Périclès, Prince de Tyr* (2018)', unpublished paper, University of Georgia.

Keam, Angela (2006), 'The "Shakesteen" Genre: Claire Danes's Star-Body, Teen Female Fans, and the Pluralization of Authorship', *Borrowers and Lenders: The Journal of Shakespeare and Appropriation*, 2 (1). Available online: https://borrowers-ojs-azsu.td.org/borrowers/article/view/37/72 (accessed 30 April 2022).

Keenan, Tim (2009), 'Adapting the Adaptors: Staging Davenant and Dryden's Restoration *Tempest*', *Journal of Adaptation in Film and Performance*, 2 (1): 65–77.

Kennedy, Dennis, ed. (1993), *Foreign Shakespeare: Contemporary Performance*, Cambridge: Cambridge University Press.

Keyishian, Harry (2007), 'Shakespeare and Movie Genre: The Case of *Hamlet*', in Russell Jackson (ed.), *The Cambridge Companion to Shakespeare on Film*, 72–84, Cambridge: Cambridge University Press.

Kidnie, Margaret Jane (2009), *Shakespeare and the Problem of Adaptation*, London and New York: Routledge.

Kilbourne, Frederick Wilkinson ([1906] 1973), *Alterations and Adaptations of Shakespeare,* New York: AMS Press.

King, Helen (1998), *Hippocrates' Woman,* London: Routledge.

*The King is Alive* (2001), [DVD] Dir. Kristian Levring, USA: MGM/IFC Films.

*King Lear* (1953), [Kinescope recording] Adapted by Peter Brook, Dir. Andrew McCullough, USA: CBS/Films on Demand.

*King Lear* (1997), ed. R. A. Foakes, Arden Shakespeare, 3rd series, London: Bloomsbury.

*King Lear* (2018), [Streaming film], Dir. Richard Eyre, USA: Amazon Prime.

Kittler, Friedrich ([1985] 1990), *Discourse Networks*, trans. Michael Meteer, Stanford: Stanford University Press.

Klomp, Neal Robert (2016), 'Warm Bodies in Plague and Shakespeare's "Womb of Death"', in Jeffrey Jerome Cohen and Julian Yates (eds), *Object-Oriented Environs*, 47–56, Goleta, CA: punctum books.

Knutson, Susan (2012), '"Tradaptation" *Dans le Sens Québécois*: A Word for the Future', in Laurence Raw (ed.), *Translation, Adaptation, and Transformation,* 112–22, London and New York: Continuum.

Koblin, John (2021), 'Nielsen Now Knows When You are Streaming', *New York Times,* June 17. Available online: https://www.nytimes.com/2021/06/17/business/media/nielsen-streaming-metrics-netflix-youtube.html (accessed 19 January 2022).

Kristeva, Julia ([1980] 1982), *Desire in Language*, ed. Leon S. Roudiez, trans. Thomas Gora, Alice Jardine, and Leon S. Roudiez, New York: Columbia University Press.

Kuso (2022), 'Kuso Head Facial Tissue Box Holder . . . (Shakespeare Face)'. Available online: https://www.amazon.com/Kuso-dispenser-

VintageTissue-Rectangular-Shakespeare/dp/B07DL3PX5N (accessed 19 May 2022)

Lacan, Jacques ([1973] 2018), *The Four Fundamental Concepts of Psychoanalysis*, ed. and trans. Jacques-Alain Miller, London and New York: Taylor and Francis.

Lakoff, George, Jane Espenson, Adele Goldberg, and Alan Schwartz ([1989–91] 1991), 'Master Metaphor List', 2nd edn, Berkeley, CA: Cognitive Linguistics Group/University of California, meta. Available online: http://araw.mede.uic.edu/~alansz/metaphor/METAPHORLIST.pdf (accessed 29 January 2022).

Lakoff, George, and Mark Johnson ([1980] 2003), *Metaphors We Live By*, Chicago: University of Chicago Press.

Lamb, Charles, and Mary Lamb ([1807] 1886), *Tales from Shakespeare*, London: Macmillan.

Langlitz, Nicolas (2022), 'We need a less moralistic humanities', *The Chronicle Review*, 19 January. Available online: https://www.chronicle.com/article/we-need-a-less-moralistic-humanities (accessed 12 April 2022).

Lanham, Richard A. (2007), *The Economics of Attention: Style and Substance in the Age of Information*, Chicago: University of Chicago Press.

Lanier, Douglas (2002), *Shakespeare and Modern Popular Culture*, Oxford: Oxford University Press.

Lanier, Douglas (2007), 'William Shakespeare, Filmmaker', in Deborah Cartmell and Imelda Whelehan (eds), *The Cambridge Companion to Literature on Screen*, 61–74, Cambridge, Cambridge University Press.

Lanier, Douglas (2010), 'Recent Shakespeare Adaptation and the Mutations of Cultural Capital', in Susan Zimmerman and Garrett Sullivan (eds), *Shakespeare Studies*, 38: 104–113.

Lanier, Douglas (2014), 'Shakespearean Rhizomatics: Adaptation, Ethics, Value', in Alexa Alice Joubin and Elizabeth Rivlin (eds), *Shakespeare and the Ethics of Appropriation*, 21–40, Houndmills, UK: Palgrave.

Lanier, Douglas (2018), 'The Hogarth Shakespeare Series: Redeeming Shakespeare's Literariness', in Andrew Hartley (ed.), *Shakespeare and Millennial Fiction*, 230–50, Cambridge: Cambridge University Press.

Laqueur, Thomas (1990), *Making Sex*, Cambridge, MA: Harvard University Press.

Latour, Bruno (1996), *Aramis*, trans. Catherine Porter, Cambridge, MA: Harvard University Press.

Lau, Jey Han, Trevor Cohn, Timothy Baldwin, and Adam Hammond (2020), 'Deep-speare crafted Shakespearean verse that few readers could distinguish from the real thing', *IEEE Spectrum*, 57 (5): 40–53. Available online: doi: 10.1109/MSPEC.2020.9078455 (accessed 1 April 2022).

Lavender, Andy (2019), 'Theatricalizing Protest: The chorus of the commons', *Performance Research: A Journal of the Performing Arts*, 24 (8): 4–11.

Lees-Jeffries, Hester (2013), '*Greater Shakespeare*: Working, Playing, and Making With Shakespeare', *Shakespeare Survey*, 66: 188–97.

Lehmann, Courtney (2002), *Shakespeare Remains*, Ithaca, NY: Cornell University Press.

Lehmann, Courtney (2006), 'Faux Show: Falling into History in *Love's Labour's Lost*', in Ayanna Thompson (ed.), *Colorblind Shakespeare: New Perspectives on Race and Performance*, 69–80, London and New York: Routledge.

Lehmann, Courtney, and Lisa S. Starks, eds (2002), *Spectacular Shakespeare: Critical Theory and Popular Cinema*, Madison, NJ: Fairleigh Dickinson University Press; London: Associated University Presses.

Lenard, Patti Tamara, and Peter Balint (2020), 'What Is (the Wrong of) Cultural Appropriation?', *Ethnicities*, 20 (2): 331–52.

Lessig, Lawrence (2004), *Free Culture: How Big Media Uses Technology and the Law to Lock Down Culture and Control Creativity*, New York: Penguin. Available online: http://www.free-culture.cc/freeculture.pdf (accessed 21 May 2016).

Levinas, Emmanuel ([1961] 1991), *Totality and Infinity: An Essay on Exteriority*, trans. Alphonso Lingis, Dordrecht/Boston/London: Kluwer Academic Publishers.

Levine, Lawrence (1988), *Highbrow/Lowbrow*, Cambridge, MA: Harvard University Press.

Levinson, Paul (1997), *The Soft Edge: A Natural History and Future of the Information Revolution*, London: Routledge.

Levy, Deborah (1989), *Ophelia and the Great Idea*, New York: Viking.

Lieblein, Leanore ([2004] 2012), '"Cette Belle Langue": The "Tradaptation" of Shakespeare in Quebec', in Ton Hoenselaars (ed.), *Shakespeare and the Language of Translation*, 255–69, London: Arden Bloomsbury.

Lillo, George (1738), *Marina*, London: John Gray.
Little, Arthur L., Jr. (2016), 'Re-Historicizing Race, White Melancholia, and the Shakespearean Property', *Shakespeare Quarterly*, 67 (1): 84–103.
Ljungberg, Christina (2010), 'Intermedial Strategies in Multimedia Art', in Lars Elleström (ed.), *Media Borders, Multimodality and Intermediality*, 81–98, Houndmills: Palgrave MacMillan.
Loftis, Sonya Freeman (2013), *Shakespeare's Surrogates*, New York: Palgrave Macmillan.
Loftis, Sonya Freeman (2019), 'Autistic Culture, Shakespeare Therapy and the Hunter Heartbeat Method', *Shakespeare Survey*, 72: 256–67.
Loomba, Ania (1998), '"Local-manufacture made-in-India Othello fellows": Issues of Race, Hybridity, and Location in Post-Colonial Shakespeares', in Ania Loomba and Martin Orkin (eds), *Post-Colonial Shakespeares*, 143–63, New York: Routledge.
Loomba, Ania ([1998] 2005), *Colonialism/Postcolonialism*, London and New York: Routledge.
Loomba, Ania, and Jonathan Burton (2007), *Race: A Documentary Companion*, Houndmills, UK: Palgrave.
Love, Genevieve (2006), 'Tsunami in the Royal Botanic Garden', *Borrowers and Lenders*, 2 (2). Available online: https://borrowers-ojs-su.tdl.org/borrowers/article/view/40/78 (accessed 1 May 2022).
Luhmann, Niklas (1993), 'Deconstruction as Second-Order Observing', *New Literary History*, 24 (2): 763–82.
*Macbeth* (2021), [Film] Dir. Joel Coen, US: A24/IAC Films/AppleTV.
MacDonald, Joyce Green (2020), *Shakespearean Adaptation, Race and Memory in the New World*, New York: Palgrave Macmillan.
Mancewicz, Aneta, and Alexa Alice Joubin, eds (2018), *Local and Global Myths in Shakespearean Performance*, Cham, Switzerland: Palgrave.
Marino, James (2011), *Owning Shakespeare, Owning William Shakespeare: The King's Men and their Intellectual Property*, Philadelphia: University of Pennsylvania Press.
Marion, Isaac (2011), *Warm Bodies*, New York: Atria Books.
Markham, Gervase (1613), *Hobsons Horse-Load of Letters: Or A President for Epistles*, London: T. Snodham/Richard Hawkins, *EEBO* (accessed 30 March 2022).

Marsden, Jean I., ed. (1991), *The Appropriation of Shakespeare: Post-Renaissance Reconstructions of the Works and the Myth*, New York: St. Martin's Press.

Marsh, Anne [Anne Caldwell-Marsh] (1849), *Mordaunt Hall*, 3 vols., London: Henry Colburn.

Marx, Karl ([1848] 1996), 'Manifesto of the Communist Party', in Terrell Carver (ed. and trans.), *Marx: Later Political Writings*, 14–16, Cambridge and New York: Cambridge University Press.

Marx, Karl ([1887] 1990), *Capital: A Critical Analysis of Capitalist Production*, in Hanna Behrend, Marion Duparré, Hella Hahn, and Frank Zschaler (eds), Berlin/Boston: De Gruyter Akademie Forschung.

Massai, Sonia (2005), 'Subjection and redemption in Pasolini's *Othello*', in Sonia Massai (ed.), *World-Wide Shakespeares: Local Appropriations in Film and Performance*, 95–103, London: Routledge.

Massai, Sonia (2013), 'Two Gentlemen of Verona for/by Zimbabwean Communities', in Susan Bennett and Christie Carson (eds), *Shakespeare Beyond English: A Global Experiment*, 157–60, Cambridge: Cambridge University Press.

Massai, Sonia (2017), 'Editing Shakespeare in Parts', *Shakespeare Quarterly*, 68 (1): 56–79.

Masten, Jeffrey (1997), 'Is the Fundament a Grave?', in David Hillman and Carla Mazzio (eds), *The Body in Parts*, 129–146, New York: Routledge.

Mayer, Tom (2013), 'The History of Patrick Mcgoohan's Forgotten Directorial Effort, "Catch My Soul" (A.K.A. "Santa Fe Satan")', 4 parts, *The Unmutual Prisoner Article Archive*. Available online: https://www.theunmutual.co.uk/catchmysoul1.htm (accessed 13 April 2022).

McDonough, William, and Michael Braungart (2002), *Cradle to Cradle: Remaking the Way We Make Things*, New York: North Point.

McEachern, Claire (1988), 'Fathering Herself: A Source Study of Shakespeare's Feminism', *Shakespeare Quarterly*, 39: 269–90.

McLuhan, Marshall ([1962] 2011), *The Gutenberg Galaxy*, Toronto: University of Toronto Press.

McLuhan, Marshall, and Eric McLuhan (1988), *The Laws of Media*, Toronto: University of Toronto Press.

McLuskie, Kathleen (1999), 'Shakespeare and the Millennial Market: The Commercial Bard', *Renaissance Drama*, 30: 161–81.

McLuskie, Kathleen (2015), 'Afterword', in Paul Prescott, and Erin Sullivan (eds), *Shakespeare on the Global Stage: Performance and Festivity in the Olympic Year*, 323–338, London: Arden Shakespeare.

McQueen, Amanda (2016), 'The Lost Cult of *Catch My Soul*', *Cinematheque*, 2 November. Available online: https://cinema.wisc.edu/blog/2016/11/02/lost-cult-catch-my-soul (accessed 30 September 2021).

McRuer, Robert (2006), *Crip Theory*, New York: New York University Press.

Mehdizadeh, Nedda (2020), 'Othello in Harlem: Transforming Theater in Djanet Sears's "Harlem Duet"', *Journal of American Studies*, 54:12–1.

Menke, Richard (2019), *Literature, Print Culture, and Media Technologies, 1880–1900: Many Inventions*, Cambridge, Cambridge University Press.

Menon, Madhavi (2008), *Unhistorical Shakespeare: Queer Theory in Shakespearean Literature and Film*, New York: Palgrave.

Menon, Madhavi, and Farhan Akhtar (2007), 'Working Notes: An Interview', *South Asian Popular Culture*, 5 (1): 77–85.

Meyer, Allison (2015), 'Multiple Histories: Cultural Memory and Anne Boleyn in *Actes and Monuments* and *Henry VIII*', *Borrowers and Lenders: The Journal of Shakespeare and Appropriation*, 9 (2). Available online: https://borrowers-ojs-azsu.tdl.org/borrowers/article/view/293 (accessed 16 February 2019).

Miller, James ([1737] 1969), *The Universal Passion*, London: Cornmarket Press.

Minton and Company (1830–1870), '"Miranda" from William Shakespeare's "The Tempest" after John Bell', Parian ceramic, Calke Abbey, Derbyshire. Available online: https://www.nationaltrustcollections.org.uk/object/285165 (accessed 23 April 2022).

Mitchell, Elvis (2000), '"Romeo Must Die": Hip-Hop Joins Martial Arts but Lets Plot Muscle In', *New York Times*, 22 March. Available online: https://archive.nytimes.com/www.nytimes.com/library/film/032200romeo-film-review.html (accessed 30 March 2022).

Mohammad, K. Silem ([2009] 2022), 'Held, Le Flesh Lengthens; Undertook, Le Flesh Holds; Fed Me, Me, Me, Me, Me, Me, Me, Me, *Me*!', from 'The Sonnanagrams [in progress]', unpublished mss., personal communication.

Montaigne, Michel de ([1580] 1603), 'Of the Cannibals', in John Florio, trans. *The Essayes . . . of . . . Michaell de Montaigne*, British Library, shelfmark C.21.e.17, K2v-K6r. Available online: https://www.bl.uk/collection-items/montaignes-essays-translated-by-florio (accessed 1 March 2022).

Montrose, Louis (1991), 'The Work of Gender in the Discourse of Discovery', *Representations*, 33: 1–41.

Mookherjee, Taarini (2019), 'Theorizing the Neighbor: *Arshinagar* and *Romeo and Juliet*', *Borrowers and Lenders: The Journal of Shakespeare and Appropriation*, 12 (2). Available online: https://borrowers-ojs-azsu.tdl.org/borrowers/article/view/230 (accessed 23 April 2022).

Mooneeram, Roshni (2009), *From Creole to Standard: Shakespeare, Language, and Literature in a Postcolonial Context*, Amsterdam: Rodopi.

Morgan, Michael L. (2011), *The Cambridge Introduction to Emmanuel Levinas*, New York: Cambridge University Press (accessed 10 December 2021).

Morrison, Toni, and Rokia Traouré (2012), *Desdemona*, introd. Peter Sellars, London: Oberon Books.

Mowat, Barbara A. (1994), 'Rogues, Shepherds, and the Counterfeit Distressed: Texts and Infracontexts of *The Winter's Tale* 4.3', *Shakespeare Studies*, 22: 58–76.

*Much Ado About Nothing* (2019), [Live-streamed Performance] Dir. Kenny Leon, New York City: Delacorte Theatre, Central Park.

'Much Ado Connect Four' (2021), Game Board, by Stuart Scott. Available online: http://www.collaborativelearning.org/muchadoconnectfour.pdf (accessed 10 July 2021).

Muir, Kenneth (1957), *Shakespeare's Sources*, London: Methuen.

Nagel, Thomas (1974), 'What Is It Like to Be a Bat?', *The Philosophical Review*, 83 (4): 435–450.

Ndiaye, Noémie (2021), '*Pericles* and Us', Program Notes, *Pericles*, Red Bull Theater, 25 October 2021. Available online: https://www.redbulltheater.com/pericles-reading (accessed 22 February 2022).

Nellis, Ashley (2016), 'The Color of Justice: Racial and Ethnic Disparity in State Prisons', *The Sentencing Project*. Available online: https://www.sentencingproject.org/publications/color-of-justice-racial-and-ethnic-disparity-in-state-prisons/ (accessed 2 September 2021).

Nichols, Charles Washburn (1929), 'A Reverend Alterer of Shakespeare', *Modern Language Notes*, 44 (1): 30–32.

Nida, Eugene ([1964] 2006), 'From "Towards a Science of Translating"', in Daniel Weissbort and Astradur Eysteinsson (eds), *Translation: Theory and Practice*, 346–51, Oxford: Oxford University Press.

Nochimson, Martha P (2001), 'The King Is Alive', *Film Quarterly*, 55 (2): 48–54.

*Nothing Much to Do* (2014), [Streaming video series] The Candle Wasters, *YouTube*. Available online: https://www.youtube.com/channel/UCFkxbSqhdwL8OjrTCwwELpQ (accessed 11 July 2021).

Novy, Marianne ([1990] 2000), *Women's Re-Visions of Shakespeare*, Champaign-Urbana: University of Illinois Press.

Nunn, Hillary M. (2015), '"The King's Part": James I, the Lake-Ros Affair, and the Play of Purgation', in Sujata Iyengar (ed.), *Disability, Health, and Happiness in the Shakespearean Body*, 127–41, New York: Routledge.

O'Dair, Sharon ([2001] 2002), 'On the Value of Being a Cartoon, in Literature and in Life', in Desmet, Christy, and Robert Sawyer (eds), *Harold Bloom's Shakespeare*, 81–96, New York: Palgrave Macmillan/SpringerLink.

Olive, Sarah (2013), 'Representations of Shakespeare's Humanity and Iconicity: Incidental Appropriations in Four British Television Broadcasts', *Borrowers and Lenders: The Journal of Shakespeare and Appropriation*, 8 (1). Available online: https://borrowers-ojs-azsu.tdl.org/borrowers/article/view/125 (accessed 23 April 2022)

O'Neill, Stephen (2014), *Shakespeare and YouTube: New Media Forms and the Bard*, London: Arden Bloomsbury.

O'Neill, Stephen, ed. (2018), *Broadcast Your Shakespeare*, London: Bloomsbury.

Orgel, Stephen ([1988] 2002), 'The Authentic Shakespeare', *The Authentic Shakespeare and Other Problems of the Early Modern Stage*, London and Abingdon: Routledge, 231–56.

Orgel, Stephen (1996), *Impersonations*, Cambridge: Cambridge University Press.

O'Rourke, Ash, and Kendall Shaw [Wheezy and Spoons] (2021), [Podcast] 'That Pretentious Book Club: *Hamlet*', 22 March. Available online: https://podcasts.apple.com/us/podcast/hamlet/id1555980345?i=1000513992126 (accessed 23 June 2021).

Osborne, Laurie (2002), 'Cutting Up Characters: The Erotic Politics of Trevor Nunn's *Twelfth Night*', in Courtney Lehmann and Lisa S. Starks (eds), *Spectacular Shakespeare: Critical Theory and Popular Cinema*, 89–109, Madison, NJ: Fairleigh Dickinson University Press; London: Associated University Presses.

Osborne, Laurie (2003), 'Mixing Media and Animating Shakespeare Tales', in Richard Burt and Lynda E. Boose (eds), *Shakespeare, the Movie, II: Popularizing the Plays on Film, TV, Video, and DVD*, 140–53, New York: Routledge.

Osborne, Laurie (2008), 'A Local Habitation and a Name: Television and Shakespeare', *Shakespeare Survey*, 61: 213–26.

Osborne, Laurie (2011), 'Serial Shakespeare: Intermedial Performance and the Outrageous Fortunes of *Slings & Arrows*', *Borrowers and Lenders: The Journal of Shakespeare and Appropriation*, 6 (2). Available online: https://borrowers-ojs-azsu.tdl.org/borrowers/article/view/205 (accessed 23 April 2022).

O'Sullivan, Michael (2000), 'Despite Jet Li, "Romeo" Doesn't Fly', *Washington Post*, 24 March. Available online: https://www.washingtonpost.com/wp-srv/entertainment/movies/reviews/romeomustdieosullivan.htm (accessed 30 March 2022).

*Othello* ([2016] 1997), ed. E.A.J. Honigmann, rev. ed. Ayanna Thompson, Arden Shakespeare, 3rd series, London: Bloomsbury.

Owusu-Bempah, Akwasi, Maria Jung, Firdaous Sbaï, Andrew S. Wilton, and Fiona Kouyoumdjian (2021), 'Race and Incarceration: The Representation and Characteristics of Black People in Provincial Correctional Facilities in Ontario, Canada', *Race and Justice*. Availble online: https://doi.org/10.1177/21533687211006461 (accessed 2 September 2021).

Oxford Academic (2021), 'Rights and Permissions.' Available online: https://global.oup.com/academic/authors/author-guidelines/copyright-permissions/?lang=en&cc=gb (accessed 21 September 2021).

Oxford University Press (2021), 'Film and TV Image Permissions', *Adaptation*. Available online: https://academic.oup.com/

adaptation/pages/film_and_tv_image_permissions (accessed 21 September 2021).
Pai, Anant, ed. ([1967] 1979), *Malati and Madhava*, Amar Chitra Katha 129, Bombay [Mumbai]: India Book House.
Palfrey, Simon, and Tiffany Stern (2007), *Shakespeare in Parts*, Oxford: Oxford University Press.
Paster, Gail Kern (1993), *The Body Embarrassed*, Ithaca, NY: Cornell University Press.
Patricia, Anthony (2017), *Queering the Shakespearean Film*, London: Bloomsbury.
Patton, Chloe (2014), 'Defacing Levinas: Vision, Veiling and the Ethics of Republican Citizenship in France', *Social Identities*, 20 (2–3): 186–198.
Pennacchia, Maddalena (2017), 'Shakespeare's Puppets: *The Tempest* and *The Winter's Tale* in the *Animated Tales*', in Sarah Hatchuel and Nathalie Vienne-Guerrin (eds), *Shakespeare on Screen*: The Tempest *and Late Romances*, 133–46.
Pepycase (2022), 'Milk Shakespeare Toilet Seat Cover'. Available online: https://pepycase.com/products/milk-shakespeare-toilet-seat-cover-mat-3-pcs?currency=USD&variant=42468068032769&utm_medium=cpc&utm_source=google&utm_campaign=Google%20Shopping&srsltid=AWLEVJyMmIDqb73AdrwHx7SJGrCro3oM4Yp94jOJrlJ7Yxw7Vl0h-K0FmZA (accessed 30 March 2022).
*Pericles* ([1963] 1986), ed. F. D. Hoeniger, Arden Shakespeare, 2nd Series, London: Methuen Drama.
*Périclès, Prince de Tyr* (2018), [Live capture recording] Dir. Declan Donnellan.
*Pericles* (2020), ed. Susanne Gossett, Arden Shakespeare, 3rd Series, London: Bloomsbury, 2020.
[Pericles (2021)] *The Adventures of Pericles* (2021), [Podcast] Trans., Ellen McLaughlin, Play On / Next Chapter podcasts. Available online: https://ncpodcasts.com/pericles (accessed 25 April 2022).
*Pericles: A Modern Verse Translation* (2022), trans. Ellen McLaughlin, Tempe: Arizona Center for Medieval and Renaissance Studies.
Pisan, Christine de (1521), *Here begynneth the booke whiche is called the body of polycye*, London: Without Newe Gate.
Plastow, Jane (2013), *Shakespeare in and out of Africa*, Woodbridge, Suffolk: Currey.

Pomeroy, Anne Fairchild (1994), *Marx and Whitehead: Process, Dialectics, and the Critique of Capitalism*. Albany: State University of New York Press.
Pritchett, Frances W. (1995), 'The World of Amar Chitra Katha', in Lawrence A. Babb, Joint Committee on South Asia, and Susan S. Wadley (eds), *Media and the Transformation of Religion in South Asia*, 76–134, Philadelphia: University of Pennsylvania Press.
Propp, Vladimir (1968), *Morphology of the Folktale*, trans. Laurence Scott and introd. by Svatava Pirkova-Jakobson, Austin: University of Texas Press.
*Prospero's Books* (1991), [DVD] Dir. Peter Greenaway. UK/US: Miramax.
*Protactile 'Romeo and Juliet': Theatre By/For the DeafBlind* (2018), [Film] Dir. Jill Bradbury, USA: NEA/Gallaudet University. Available online: https://www.youtube.com/watch?v=btB_nePm860, transcript available online: https://my.gallaudet.edu/deafblind-theater-institute/project-documentary/protactile-romeo-and-juliet-documentary-transcript-and-image-descriptions (accessed 24 March 2022).
Qaiyum, Gregory, Jeffery Quaiyum [the Q Brothers], and Barbara Bogaev (2017), [Podcast and transcript], 'Something Then in Rhyme', *Shakespeare Unlimited*, Folger Shakespeare Library. Available online: https://www.folger.edu/shakespeare-unlimited/q-brothers-othello (accessed 2 September 2021).
Q Brothers [Gregory and Jeffery Quaiyum] (2018), *Othello: The Remix*, New York: Dramatists' Play Service.
Rackin, Phyllis (2005), *Shakespeare and Women*, Oxford: Oxford University Press.
Radway, Janice (1984), *Reading the Romance*, Chapel Hill: University of North Carolina Press.
Rajewsky, Irina O. (2005), 'Intermediality, Intertextuality, and Remediation: A Literary Perspective on Intermediality', *Intermédialités* 6: 43–64. Available online: http://cri.histart.umontreal.ca/cri/fr/intermedialites/p6/pdfs/p6_rajewsky_text.pdf (accessed 14 April 2022).
Ralegh, Sir Walter (1596), *The Discoverie of Guiana*, London.
*Ram-Leela* [*Goliyon Ki Rasleela Ram-Leela (A Play of Bullets)*] (2013), [DVD] Dir. Sanjay Leela Bhansali, India: Eros International.

Rankine, Claudia (2014), *Citizen: An American Lyric*, Minneapolis, MN: Graywolf.

Rapetti, Valentina (2018), 'Beyond *Othello*: Performing Stages of Resistance to Racial Surveillance in Djanet Sears' *Harlem Duet*', *Journal of Adaptation in Film & Performance*, 11 (3): 271–93.

Rapetti, Valentina and Djanet Sears (2018), 'Catching *Othello*'s echoes in *Harlem Duet*: A Conversation on Shakespearean Adaptation, Blackness, and African Diaspora Theatre with Djanet Sears', *Journal of Adaptation in Film & Performance*, 11 (3): 295–313.

Reisz, Matthew (2016), 'Shakespearean Twitter War', *Times Higher Education*, 9 June, repr. *Inside Higher Education*. Available online: https://www.insidehighered.com/news/2016/06/09/two-scholars-engage-debate-twitter-and-elsewhere-over-king-lear (accessed 24 March 2022).

Reynolds, Bryan (2003), *Performing Transversally*, Houndmills, UK: Palgrave Macmillan.

Reynolds, Bryan (2006), 'Transversal Poetics and Fugitive Explorations', in Bryan Reynolds (ed.), *Transversal Enterprises in the Drama of Shakespeare and His Contemporaries*, 1–26, Houndmills, UK: Palgrave.

Reynolds, Bryan, and Donald Hedrick, eds (2000), *Shakespeare Without Class: Misappropriations of Cultural Capital*, Houndmills, UK: Palgrave Macmillan.

Rich, Adrienne (1980), 'Compulsory Heterosexuality and Lesbian Existence', *Signs*, 5 (4): 631–660.

Richards, I. A. ([1936] 1965), *The Philosophy of Rhetoric*, New York: Oxford University Press.

Rivlin, Elizabeth (2014), 'Adaptation Revoked: Knowledge, Ethics, and Trauma in Jane Smiley's *A Thousand Acres*', in Alexa Alice Joubin and Elizabeth Rivlin (eds), *Shakespeare and the Ethics of Appropriation*, 73–87, Houndmills, UK: Palgrave Macmillan.

Roach, Joseph. ([1996] 2022), *Cities of the Dead*, New York: Columbia University Press.

Robertson, Roland (1994), 'Globalization or Glocalization?', *Journal of International Communication*, 1 (1): 33–52.

*Romeo and Juliet* (2012), ed. René Weis, Arden Shakespeare Editions, 3rd series, New York and London: Bloomsbury.

*Romeo and Juliet* (1968), [Film] Dir. Franco Zeffirelli, Italy/UK: BHE/Paramount.

*Romeo Must Die* (2000), [DVD] Dir. Andrzej Bartkowiak, US: Silver/Warner.

Ross, Robert J. S. (2013), 'Bread and Roses', *WorkingUSA* 16: 59–68. Available online: https://doi.org/10.1111/wusa.12023 (accessed 30 September 2021).

Rubin, Gayle (1975), 'The Traffic in Women: Notes on the 'Political Economy' of Sex', in Rayna Reiter (ed.), *Towards an Anthropology of Women*, 157–210, London and New York: Monthly Review Press.

Rushdie, Salman (1992), *Imaginary Homelands*, London: Penguin.

Said, Edward (1978), *Orientalism*, New York: Pantheon.

Said, Edward ([1982] 2014), 'Traveling Theory', in David Damrosch (ed.), *World Literature in Theory*, 115–133, London: Wiley-Blackwell.

Salisbury, Eve (2018), 'Black Gower', *The Gower Project*, 17 December. Available online: https://thegowerprojects.wordpress.com/author/evesalisbury (accessed 30 April 2022).

Sanchez, Melissa (2019), *Shakespeare and Queer Theory*, London: Bloomsbury.

Sánchez Prado, Ignacio M. (2021), 'Commodifying Mexico: On *American Dirt* and the Cultural Politics of a Manufactured Bestseller', *American Literary History* 33 (2): 371–393.

Sanders, Julie ([2006] 2015), *Adaptation and Appropriation*, rev. ed, London and New York: Routledge.

Sanders, Julie (2011), 'The Sonnets as an Open-source Initiative', *Shakespeare Survey*, 64: 121–32.

Sawyer, Robert (2003), *Victorian Appropriations of Shakespeare*, Madison and Teaneck, NJ/ London: Fairleigh Dickinson University Press/Associated University Presses.

Sawyer, Robert (2021), 'Bitcoin, Blockchains, and the Bard', in Valerie Fazel and Louise Geddes (eds), *Variable Objects: Shakespeare and Speculative Appropriation*, 59–81, Edinburgh: Edinburgh University Press.

Schaar, Claes (1982), '"*The full voic'd quire below*": Vertical Context Systems in "*Paradise Lost*"', Lund, Sweden: Gleerup.

Scheil, Katherine West (1997), 'Sir William Davenant's use of Shakespeare in *The Law Against Lovers* (1662)', *Philological Quarterly*, 76 (4): 369–387.

Schiebinger, Londa (1989), *The Mind Has No Sex?*, Cambridge, MA: Harvard University Press.

Schleiner, Winfried (2000), 'Early Modern Controversies About the One-Sex Model', *Renaissance Quarterly*, 53: 180–91.

Schoenbaum, Samuel ([1970] 1991), *Shakespeare's Lives*, Oxford: Oxford University Press.

Schröter, Jens (2012), 'Four models of intermediality', in Bernd Herzogenrath (ed.), *Travels in Intermedia[lity]: Reblurring the Boundaries*, 15–36, Hanover, NH: Dartmouth College Press.

Scott, Robert Dawson (2005), 'Hope from the depths', Review of *Children of the Sea*, *The Times* (United Kingdom), 11 August, Arts and Sports, 22.

Scott-Douglass, Amy (2013), 'This Tempest's Hers: Metropolitan Opera's *The Enchanted Island* and the Feminism of Bel Canto Shakespeare Adaptation', *Borrowers and Lenders: The Journal of Shakespeare and Appropriation*, 8 (1). Available online: https://borrowers-ojs-azsu.tdl.org/borrowers/article/view/126 (accessed 15 April 2022).

Schwartz, Beth C. (1991), 'Thinking Back Through Our Mothers: Virginia Woolf Reads Shakespeare', *ELH*, 58 (3): 721–46.

Sears, Djanet (1997), *Harlem Duet*, Winnipeg, Canada: J. Gordon Shillingford.

Sears, Djanet (2018), Programme Notes to *Harlem Duet*, Toronto, Ontario: Tarragon Theatre. Available online: https://indd.adobe.com/view/58714fe1-d329-4c6c-88c9-87deb27b8af8 (accessed 11 July 2021).

Sellars, Peter (2012), 'Foreword', in Toni Morrison and Rokia Traouré, *Desdemona*, 8–11, London: Oberon Books.

Semenza, Gregory M. Colón (2008), 'Teens, Shakespeare, and the Dumbing Down Cliché: The Case of *The Animated Tales*', *Shakespeare Bulletin*, 26 (2): 37–68.

Sexton, Joyce (1978), *The Slandered Woman in Shakespeare*, Victoria, BC: English Literary Studies, University of Victoria.

Shadwell, Thomas, William Shakespeare, William D'Avenant, and John Dryden ([1674] 1735), *The Tempest: or, the Enchanted Island [Enchanted Island], by Mr. Dryden*, London: Jacob Tonson.

*Shakespeare in Love* (1999), [DVD] Dir. John Madden, USA/UK: Miramax/Universal.

Shakespeare, Tom (2014), *Disability Rights and Wrongs Revisited*, 2nd edn, London: Routledge.

Shakespeare, Tom (2018). *Disability: The Basics*, New York: Routledge.

Shannon, Laurie (2013), *The Accommodated Animal: Cosmopolity in Shakespearean Locales,* Chicago: University of Chicago Press.

Shaw, George Bernard (1901), 'Preface', in *Three plays for Puritans: The devil's disciple, Cæsar and Cleopatra, & Captain Brassbound's conversion*, V–xxxvi, London: G. Richards.

*She's The Man (*2006), [DVD] Dir. Andy Fickman, US: Dreamworks/Paramount.

Shifman, Limor (2013), *Memes in Digital Culture*, Cambridge, MA: MIT Press.

Shohet, Lauren (2010), 'YouTube, Use, and the Idea of the Archive', *Shakespeare Studies*, 38, 68–76, Madison/Teaneck/Cranbury, NJ: Fairleigh Dickinson University Press/Associated University Presses.

Singh, Jyotsna (2019), *Shakespeare and Postcolonial Theory*, London: Arden Bloomsbury.

Singh, Jyotsna G., and Abdulhamit Arvas (2015), 'Global Shakespeares, Affective Histories, Cultural Memories', *Shakespeare Survey*, 68: 183–96.

Smiley, Jane (1991), *A Thousand Acres*, New York: Knopf.

Smiley, Jane (1996), 'Shakespeare in Iceland', *Shakespeare and the Twentieth Century: Selected Proceedings of the International Shakespeare Association World Congress*, 41–59, Newark: University of Delaware Press.

Smiley, Jane (1998), 'Taking It All Back', *The Washington Post*, 21 June, X01.

Smith, Ali ([2019] 2020), *Spring*, New York: Anchor.

Smith, Bruce R. (1999), *The Acoustic World of Early Modern England: Attending to the O-Factor*, Chicago: University of Chicago Press.

Smith, Corinn (2021), 'Director's Statement: *Twelfth Night*', unpublished essay, University of Georgia.

Smyth, Albert H. (1898), 'Shakespeare's *Pericles* and Apollonius of Tyre', *Proceedings of the American Philosophical Society*, 37 (158): 206–312.

Sokolova, Boika, and Katy Stavreva (2020), '"To be/not to be": *Hamlet* and the Threshold of Potentiality in Post-Communist Bulgaria', in Christy Desmet, Sujata Iyengar, and Miriam Jacobson (eds), *The Routledge Handbook of Shakespeare and Global Appropriation*, 280–89, New York: Routledge.

SparkNotes (2021a), *No Fear Shakespeare: Measure for Measure*. Available online: https://www.sparknotes.com/nofear/shakespeare/measure-for-measure/page_100/ (accessed 19 June 2021).

SparkNotes (2021b), *No Fear Shakespeare: Much Ado About Nothing*. Availble online: https://www.sparknotes.com/nofear/shakespeare/muchado/page_60/ (accessed 19 June 2021).

SparkNotes (2022), *No Fear Shakespeare: Pericles: Plot Summary*. Available online: https://www.sparknotes.com/shakespeare/pericles/section4/ (accessed 2 February 2022).

Spivak, Gayatri Chakravorty (1988), 'Can the Subaltern Speak?', in Cary Nelson and Lawrence Grossberg (eds), *Marxism and the Interpretation of Culture*, 271–313, Basingstoke: Macmillan.

Steinhöwel, Heinrich (1510), *Kynge Appolyn of Thyre*, trans. Robert Copland, London: Wynkyn de Worde.

Stern, Tiffany (2013), 'Sermons, Plays, and Note-takers: *Hamlet* Q1 as a "Noted" Text', *Shakespeare Survey*, 66: 1–23.

Stern, Tiffany, and Simon Palfrey, (2007), *Shakespeare in Parts*, Oxford: Oxford University Press.

Straub, Christina (2020), 'David Garrick's Two Tempests and Shakespeare Adaptation in the London Georgian Theater', *Borrowers and Lenders: The Journal of Shakespeare and Appropriation*, 13 (2). Available online: https://openjournals.libs.uga.edu/borrowers/article/view/2118/2619 (accessed 12 July 2021).

Stryker, Susan (2008), 'Transgender History, Homonormativity, and Disciplinarity', *Radical History Review*, 100: 145–57.

Sweet Theatre (n.d), 'Shakespeare's Leading Ladies Chocolate Bars: Miranda Sea-Salt'. Available online: https://www.sweettheatre.com/t2rq4aozfoqi7bz463jmcwlymah5po (accessed 22 July 2021).

Syme, Holger (2016a), 'The Text is Foolish: Brian Vickers's *The One King Lear*', *LA Review of Books*, 6 September. Available online: https://lareviewofbooks.org/article/text-foolish-brian-vickerss-one-king-lear/# (accessed 13 December 2021).

Syme, Holger (2016b), '"King Lear" at the Stationers, Again: A Response to Brian Vickers', *LA Review of Books*, 18 December. Available online: https://lareviewofbooks.org/article/king-lear-stationers-response-brian-vickers/ (accessed 24 March 2022).

Takaki, Ronald (1994), *From Different Shores*, Oxford: Oxford University Press.

Tate, Nahum ([1681] 1965), *King Lear*, in Christopher Spenser (ed.), *Five Restoration Adaptations*, 202–273, Urbana: University of Illinois Press.
Taylor, Charles ([1990] 1994), 'The Politics of Recognition', in Amy Gutmann (ed.), *Multiculturalism* (eds), 25–73, Princeton, NJ: Princeton University Press.
Taylor, Gary, ([1986] 1997), 'General Introduction', *William Shakespeare: A Textual Companion*, 1–67, New York: Norton.
Taylor, Gary (1989), *Reinventing Shakespeare*, London: Weidenfeld and Nicholson.
Taylor, Gary, and Michael Warren, eds (1983), *The Division of the Kingdoms*, Oxford: Clarendon Press.
Teague, Fran (2011), 'Using Shakespeare with Memes, Remixes, and Fanfic', *Shakespeare Survey* 64: 74–82.
*The Tempest* ([1999] 2011), ed. Virginia Mason Vaughan and Alden T. Vaughan, Arden Shakespeare, 3rd series, London: Bloomsbury.
*The Tempest* (2016), Dir. Greg Doran, Stratford-upon-Avon: Royal Shakespeare Company.
Thompson, Ayanna, ed. ([2006] 2016), *Color-Blind Shakespeare*, London and New York: Routledge.
Thompson, Ayanna (2021), *Blackface*, London and New York: Bloomsbury.
Traub, Valerie (1992), *Desire and Anxiety: Circulations of Sexuality in Shakespearean Drama*, New York: Routledge.
*The Treasurie of Auncient and Moderne Times* (1613), London: William Jaggard.
Trevien, Kenan (2021), personal communication (e-mail), January 18.
Trier, Lars von and Thomas Vinterberg (1995), 'The Vow of Chastity', *Dogme95*. Archived *Dogme95.dk – A Tribute to the official Dogme95*, http://www.dogme95.dk/the-vow-of-chastity/ (accessed 3 January 2022).
Trivedi, Poonam (2000), 'Interculturalism or Indigenization: Modes of Exchange, Shakespeare East and West', in Edward J. Esche (ed.), *Shakespeare and His Contemporaries in Performance*, 73–88, Aldershot, England: Ashgate.
Trivedi, Poonam, and Dennis Bartholomeusz, eds (2005), *India's Shakespeare: Translation, Interpretation, and Performance*, Newark: University of Delaware Press.

Trivedi, Poonam, and Paromita Chakravarti, eds (2019), *Shakespeare and Indian Cinemas: 'Local Habitations'*, London: Routledge.
*Twelfth Night* (2008), ed. Keir Elam, Arden Shakespeare, 3rd series, London: Bloomsbury.
*Twelfth Night* (1969), [Television Broadcast] Dir. John Sichel, UK: ATV/ITC/ITV.
*Twelfth Night* (1996), [DVD] Dir. Trevor Nunn, UK/US: Renaissance Films/Fine Line.
*Twelfth Night* (2013), [DVD] Dir. Ian Russell, UK: Globe On Screen/Opus Arte.
Twine, Laurence ([?1594] 1966), *The Patterne of Painefull Adventures*, in Geoffrey Bullough (ed.), *Narrative and Dramatic Sources of Shakespeare*, 8 vols., 7: 423–82, New York and London: Columbia University Press/Routledge.
United States, Department of Labor (n.d.), "Accommodations." Available online: https://www.dol.gov/agencies/odep/program-areas/employers/accommodations (accessed 30 March 2022).
United States, Federal Bureau of Investigation (2018), 'Stolen Art Returned', 12 April. https://www.fbi.gov/news/stories/chagall-oil-painting-recovered-nearly-30-years-after-heist-041218 (accessed 14 September 2021).
Valeonti, Foteini, Antonis Bikakis, Melissa Terras, Chris Speed, Andrew Hudson-Smith, and Konstantinos Chalkias (2021), 'Crypto Collectibles, Museum Funding and OpenGLAM: Challenges, Opportunities and the Potential of Non-Fungible Tokens (NFTs)', *Applied Sciences*, 11 (21): 9931. Available online: https://doi.org/10.3390/app11219931 (accessed 19 January 2022).
Van Vliet, Claire (1986), *The Tragedie of King Lear*, by William Shakespeare, Bangor, ME: Theodore Press.
Venuti, Lawrence (1995), *The Translator's Invisibility*, London and New York: Routledge.
Verrone, William (2011), *Adaptation and the Avant-Garde: Alternative Perspectives on Adaptation Theory and Practice*, London and New York: Continuum.
Vickers, Brian (2016a), *The One King Lear*, Cambridge, MA: Harvard University Press.
Vickers, Brian (2016b), 'A Response to Holger Syme', *LA Review of Books*, 6 November. Available online: https://lareviewofbooks.org/article/response-holger-syme/ (accessed 24 March 2022).

Vogel, Paula ([1994] 1996), *Desdemona: A Play About a Handkerchief*, in Rosemary Keefe Curb (ed.), *Amazon All-Stars: Thirteen Lesbian Plays*, 435–70, New York and London: Applause.

Wade, Elizabeth Ilona (1995), 'History and fortune in Heinrich Steinhoewel's "Appolonius"', PhD diss, University of Illinois at Urbana-Champaign, *ProQuest Dissertations Publishing*, 9543759.

Wald, Christina (2020), *Shakespeare's Serial Returns in Complex TV*, Lund: Palgrave/Springer.

Walker, Lynne (2005), 'EDINBURGH: Theatre – CHILDREN OF THE SEA Royal Botanic Gardens', *Independent* [London, England], 25 August, 44, *Gale OneFile: News*. Available online: https://link.gale.com/apps/doc/A135442835/STND?u=uga&sid=STND&xid=e890ee4b (accessed 25 November 2020).

*Warm Bodies* (2013), [Film] Dir. Jonathan Levine, USA: Mandeville Films.

Webb, Sidney, and Beatrice Webb (1921), *The Consumers' Co-Operative Movement*, London: Longman.

Weinberger, David (2015), 'Shakespeare as Network', in Margaret Jane Kidnie and Sonia Massai (eds), *Shakespeare and Textual Studies*, 398–414, Cambridge: Cambridge University Press.

Weir, R. Stanley (1913), 'The Super-Dreadnoughts', *The Christian Register*, 8 May, 445, repr. Google Books [catalogued as *English Mechanics and the World of Science*, vol. 92]. Available online: https://www.google.com/books/edition/English_Mechanics_and_the_World_of_Scien/oOEfAQAAMAAJ?hl=en&gbpv=0 (accessed 27 January 2022).

Weissbort, Daniel, and Astradur Eysteinsson, eds (2006), *Translation: Theory and Practice*, Oxford: Oxford University Press.

Wells, Stanley, Gary Taylor, John Jowett, and William Montgomery (1986), *William Shakespeare: The Complete Works*, Oxford: Oxford University Press.

Welsh, James ([2005] 2007), 'What is a Shakespeare Film Anyway?', in James Welsh and Peter Lev (eds), *The Literature/Film Reader*, Lanham, MD: Scarecrow, 105–115.

Werstine, Paul (2010), 'The Science of Editing', in Andrew Murphy (ed.), *A Concise Companion to Shakespeare and the Text*, 109–127, London: Wiley-Blackwell.

Werstine, Paul (2012), *Early Modern Playhouse Manuscripts and the Editing of Shakespeare*, Cambridge: Cambridge University Press.

*West Side Story* (1957), [Musical] by Jerome Robbins, music by Leonard Bernstein, lyrics by Stephen Sondheim, book by Arthur Laurents, USA.

*West Side Story* (1961) [Film], Dir. Jerome Robbins and Robert Wise, screenplay by Ernst Lehman, USA: Mirish/Seven Arts/United Artists.

*West Side Story* (2021), [Film] Dir. Stephen Spielberg, screenplay by Tony Kushner, USA: Amblin/TSC/Twentieth-Century.

'When That I Was And a Little Tiny Boy' (2022), by William Shakespeare, Poetry Foundation. Available online: https://www.poetryfoundation.org/poems/50427/song-when-that-i-was-and-a-little-tiny-boy-with-hey-ho-the-wind-and-the-rain (accessed 27 January 2022).

Wilkins, George ([1608] 1953), *The Painefull Aduentures of Pericles Prince of Tyre*, ed. Kenneth Muir, Liverpool, UK: University Press of Liverpool.

*William Shakespeare's Romeo + Juliet* (1996 [1999]), [Film/DVD] Dir. Baz Luhrmann, US: Twentieth-Century.

Williams, Deanne (2014), 'Prospero's Girls', *Borrowers and Lenders: The Journal of Shakespeare and Appropriation*, 9 (1). Available online: https://borrowers-ojs-azsu.tdl.org/borrowers/article/view/153 (accessed 21 September 2021).

Williams, Katherine Schaap (2021), 'Disability Studies', in Evelyn Gajowski (ed.), *The Arden Research Handbook of Contemporary Shakespeare Criticism*, 265–78, London and New York: Arden Bloomsbury.

Wilson, Horace Hayman, trans. ([1901] 2007), *Malati and Madhava; or, The stolen marriage*, by Bhavabhuti, Calcutta/Toronto, H.C. Das/Elysium Press/Internet Archive. Available online: https://archive.org/details/malatimadhavaors00bhavuoft/page/n1/mode/2up (accessed 29 March 2022).

Wilson, Jeffrey (2019), 'Historicizing Presentism: Towards the Creation of a Journal of Public Humanities', *Profession*, New York: Modern Language Association. Available online: https://profession.mla.org/historicizing-presentism-toward-the-creation-of-a-journal-of-the-public-humanities/ (accessed 2 April 2022).

Winckler, Reto (2017), 'This Great Stage of Androids: Westworld, Shakespeare, and the World as Stage', *Journal of Adaptation in Film & Performance*, 10 (2): 169–88.

Woolf, Virginia ([1919] 2018), *Orlando*, eds, Suzanne Raitt and Ian Blyth, Cambridge: Cambridge University Press.

Woolf, Virginia ([1928] 1998), '*A Room of One's Own' and 'Three Guineas*', ed. Morag Schiach, 19–150, Oxford: Oxford University Press.
Woolf, Virginia (1933), 'Shakespeare at the Old Vic', *The New Statesman and Nation*, 30 September, 385–86.
Woolf, Virginia ([1940] 1979), '"Anon" and "The Reader": Virginia Woolf's Last Essays', in Brenda R. Silver (ed.), *Twentieth Century Literature*, 25 (3/4): 356–441, esp. 382–424. Available online: https://doi.org/10.2307/441326 (accessed 19 April 2022).
Worthen, W.B. (2003), *Shakespeare and the Force of Modern Performance*, Cambridge: Cambridge University Press.
Yates, Julian (2006), 'Accidental Shakespeare', *Shakespeare Studies*, 34: 90–122.
Zabus, Chantal (2005), 'The New Wretched of Europe: Shakespeare, Derek Jarman, Peter Greenaway and Flaunting *The Tempest*', in Laura Di Michele (ed.), *Shakespeare: Una 'Tempesta' dopo l'altra*, 255–68, Naples: Liguori.
Zajac, Paul Joseph (2020), 'Prisoners of Shakespeare: Trauma and Adaptation in Atwood's *Hag-Seed*', *Studies in the Novel*, 52 (3): 324–43.
Žižek, Slavoj, *The Sublime Object of Ideology*, London: Verso.

# INDEX

Glossary references in **bold**

Aaliyah, 160–1
Actor-Network Theory, *see* Latour, Bruno
Adaptation
  accidental, 16, 157–61, **177**
  as accommodation, 16, 156, 164–75, **177, 178**, *see also* Cripqueer
  algorithmic reading as, 34, 158, **178, 181**, *see also* Bogost, Ian
  as annotation, 17–20
  as appropriation, *see* Appropriation
  bilingual, 89, 101, 105–8
  as bowdlerization, 18–20
  as collaboration, 8, 56, 68, 79
  as crossover or television tie-in, 18–20
  as cryptocurrency, *see* NFT
  as derivation, 51, 82–6
  'cyborg reading' as, 158–60, *see also* Fazel, Valerie, and Geddes, Louise
  editing as, 68, 76–9, *see also* Editing
  ethics of, 13, 68, 79–80, *see also* Joubin, Alexa Alice, and Rivlin, Elizabeth
  fanwork as, *see* Fandom
  as feminist act, *see* Feminism
  and fidelity, 9, 15–16, 24, 27–32, 34, 69–71, *see also* Editing
  as hybridization, 133–5, 145–52, **179**
  incidental, 155, 157, 169, **179**
  as mashup, 18–20, 94, 127; *see also* Media; Remediation; Remix
  and media, *see* Intermediality; Media; Network; Remediation; Trace
  as offspring, 20, 67–9
  relocation as, 15, 131–40, 147
  as remains or relics, 156, 162–9
  as re-vision, revision, or revisioning, 5, 58, 75, 187
  as rhizomatic growth, 11, 33–5, 115, **182**
  as shoot, seed, fruit, 11, 23–8, 32–3, 101–2, 152, **180**
  student study guides as, 18–19, 142

transcultural, *see* Travelling
    Theory
  as transformation, 27–8,
    111, 118–29, **172**;
    *see also* Copyright
  translation as, *see*
    Translation;
    Tradaptation
Aebischer, Pascale, 98, 167
AAL [African American
    Language], 4, 64–5
Akhtar, Farhan, 10
Albanese, Denise, 7, 182
Aleo, Cindy, 118
Almereyda, Michael, 94, 99
Amberg, Jim, 171
Anti-Stratfordians, 71
Appropriation, 45–66
  in art, 49–51
  as capital, 52–4
  in copyright law, *see*
    Copyright
  cultural, 45–7, 54–5, 79,
    **178** *see also* blackface
  as theft, 54–9, *see also*
    Marsden, Jean I.
  of fanwork, *see* Fandom
  Marxian, 52–4
ASL [American Sign Language],
  *see* Disability
Atwood, Margaret, 37, 40–2, 187
Auden, W. H., 28
Auteur, 32, 162, 184; *see also*
    Dogme 95
Author-function, Shakespeare-
    function as, 7–8, **182**,
    **183**

Babula, William, 39
Balizet, Ariane, 165

Barber, C.L., 3
Bardolatry, 24, 74, 75, 89
Barthes, Roland, 3, 6, 48
Bartholomeusz, Dennis, 134
Bassnett, Susan, 132, 133
Bell, Alexander Graham, 88
Benjamin, Walter
  mechanical reproduction,
    theory of, 91–2
  translation theory of, 144
Bennett, Jane, 110, **181**
Bersani, Leo, 123
Besoondial, Asheesh, 5, 149
Bey, Marquis, 56
Bhabha, Homi, 12, 50, 59–60,
    62, 133, 145
Bhansali, Sanjay 156, 166–7
Bharucha, Rustom, 133, 134,
    145, 146–7
Bicks, Caroline, and Michelle
    Ephraim, 31
Blackface, 47, 54–7, 63
Black Lives Matter, 4
Blackmore, Susan, 14, 109–12,
    180
Bloom, Harold, 12, 68–70, 79,
    83, 174
Bogost, Ian, 10, 158, 161–2,
    **177**
Boland, Alisa, 128, 129
Bolter, Jay David, and Richard
    Grusin, 88, 93–8; *see
    also* Remediation
Boose, Lynda, and Richard
    Burt, 89
Bortolotti, Gary, *see* Hutcheon,
    Linda
Bradbury, Jill, 171, 172–3
Branagh, Kenneth, 9
Brexit, *see* Smith, Ali

Brook, Peter, 78
Brooks, Kinitra, 35
Brown, Anuhea, 106
Browning, Robert, 28
Busch, Elizabeth Kaufer, and William E. Thro, 122
Burt, Richard, 89, 117
Burton, Richard, 117
Busse, Kristina, 80, 111, 155
Butler, Isaac, 168
Byrd, Jodi, 35

Caines, Michael, 24, 26
Calbi, Maurizio, 98, 100
Campbell, Joseph, 5
Campoy, Ana María, 105–8
Candle Wasters, The, 3, 5
Capell, Edward, 35
Carlyle, Thomas, 74
Carney, Jo, 60
Cartelli, Thomas, 29, 89, 98, 100; and Katherine Rowe, 80–1, 84, 85
Casey, Jim, *see* Desmet, Christy, *Shakespeare/Not Shakespeare*
Cavanagh, Sheila, 187
Cavell, Stanley, 125
Césaire, Aimé, 28–9, 35–8
Chagall, Marc, 45–6, 47, 57–8
Chambers, E.K., 56
Charnes, Linda, 70
Cheek By Jowl, 133–4, 141, 143, 150–1
Chess, Simone, 119
Cibber, Colley, 20–1
Clarke, Mary Cowden, 111, 120
Clubb, Louise, 113

Coen, Joel, 111, 114
Cohen, Jeffrey Jerome, and Julian Yates, 110
Cohn, Ruby, 27–9, 91, **180**
Coleridge, Peter, 171
Coleridge, Samuel Taylor, 11
Colonialism, 3, 5, 33, 35–42, 56, 58–60, *see also* Slavery
Commodity, Commodity Fetish, 43, 53
Condell, Henry, *see* John Heminges
Copyright, 48–51, 123, **183**
   creative commons, 48, 51, 52
   *libre* or *gratuit*, 48
Corredera, Vanessa, 58, 187
Cotta, John, 170
COVID-19 pandemic, 100, 101, 103, 105, 128, 153
Cripqueer, 164–7 *see also* Disability
Cristi, A.A., 128
Critini, Steve, 49
Cumberbatch, Benedict, 107

Dadabhoy, Ambereen, 15
Davenant, William, 17–20
Davis, Jenny, and Krystal Smalls, 56
Davis, Lennard, 170
Dawkins, Richard, 14, 109, 180
De Grazia, Margreta, 8, 73
de Saussure, Ferdinand, 2, 4
Deaf, DeafBlind, *see* Disability
Della Gatta, Carla, 64, 65, 182
Deleuze, Gilles, and Félix Guattari, 11, 33, 79,

115, 125, 129, 182, 184
Denslow, Kristin, 110, 113, **180**
Derrida, Jacques, 3, 4, 6, 162, 184
Desmet, Christy, 16, 34, 52, 54, 77, 92, 94, 125, 158–60, 175, **178–82**; *see also* Adaptation
Diaspora, as diaspora, 34–5, 47; *see also* Travelling Theory; Adaptation; Translation
Digges, Leonard, 17
Disability, 16, 125, 165, 170–1, 172–4 *see also* Cripqueer
Dobson, Michael, 17, 24
Dogme95, 80, 82, 85–6
DojaCat and SZA, 126–7
Dominguez, Marquicia, 107
Donaldson, Peter, 94
Doran, Greg, 28, 32
Drouin, Jennifer, 132, 148, **184**
Dryden, John, 23–4, 28, 32, 139
Dusinberre, Juliet, 121

Ebert, Roger, 85, 160
Edelman, Lee, 123
Editing, 70, 72–9, 97–8; *see also* Printing and Publishing
Edwards, Emily, and Jude Ellison Sady Doyle, 105
Elam, Keir, 121
Engler, Balz, 169
Ephraim, Michelle, *see* Bicks, Caroline, and Michelle Ephraim
Erickson, Peter, 5

Fandom, fan fic (fan fiction, fanfic), fan studies, fanwork, 15, 52, 80, 111, 117–28, 166, **178–9**
Fanon, Frantz, 40, 50, 59–60, 63, 69
Fazel, Valerie, and Louise Geddes, 54, 78–81, 110, 111, 112–7, 123, 126, 155, 158, 161, **178, 179, 181, 184, 185**
Feminism, 3, 8, 12, 32, 41, 58–62, 69, 118–25, **179**
Fidelity, *see* Adaptation
Fine, Ben and Alfredo Saad-Filho, 52–3, 93
Fingore, 166
Finn, K.M. and J. McCall, 125
Fischlin, Daniel, 99, 133, 134, **179–80**
Fish, Stanley, 30
Fitzherbert, John, 101–2
Fluxus, *see* Higgins, Dick
Ford, Sam, *see* Jenkins, Henry
Foreman, Michael, 31
Fortier, Mark, 156
Foucault, Michel, 3, 6–8, 182
Franco, Patricia Alejandra Gonzales, 78
Freud, Sigmund, 2, 3, 12, 30, 68, 69–71, 76, 79, 123
Fuchs, Christian, 54, 110

Galey, Alan, 88
Gallivan, Brian, 123

Garbus, Martin, 51
Garfield, Leon, 31
Garland-Thomson, Rosemarie, 171
Garneau, Michel, 15, 131–3, 148, 184
Geddes, Louise, *see* Fazel, Valerie, and Louise Geddes
Genette, Gérard, 16, 29, 77–8,
   hypo- and hyper-text, 16, 29, 167, **179**
   literature in the second degree, 30, 78, 79
   palimpsest, 29–30, 68, 77–8, 166, 168
Gibson, Prudence, 162
Gielgud, Sir John, 38, 101–4, 107
Gilbert, Sandra, and Susan Gubar, 69
Gilreath, Philip, 32
Gilroy, Paul, 35
Globe Theatre (Shakespeare's Globe Theatre), 64, 115–16
Goldberg, Jonathan, 119
Goldman, Nick, 88
Go, Kenji, 35
Good, Jack, 48–9
Gossett, Suzanne, 142
Gottlieb, Christine Marie, 170
Gough, Toby, 133, 149, 150
Gower, John, 134, 135, 137–9
Green, Joshua, *see* Jenkins, Henry
Greenhalgh, Susanne, 98, 100–1, 102, 103, 106
Greg, W.W., 73–5

Greenaway, Peter, 36–42, 51
Greetham, David, 68, 76
Gross, George, 120
Gubar, Susan, *see* Gilbert, Sandra, and Susan Gubar
Guizot, François Pierre Guillaume de, 143

Haddon, Mark, 139–40, 151
Halberstam, Jack, 128–9
Hall, Stuart, 35
Halliwell-Phillips, J.O., 90–2
Hammersley, Ben, 102
Hanratty, Conor, 98, 101, 104
Haraway, Donna, 158
Hard of Hearing (HoH), *see* Disability
Harris, Jeremy, 64
Hawke, Ethan, 99
Hawkes, Terence, 70, 180
Hedrick, Donald, *see* Reynolds, Bryan, and Donald Hedrick
Hellekson, Karen, 80, 155
Hellinga, Lotte, 71
Hellot, Marie-Christiane, 148
Heminges, John, and Henry Condell, 72, 74
Hendershott-Frazer, Kirk, 125
Henderson, Diana, 68, 79
Hendricks, Margo, 160
Higginbotham, Evelyn Brooks, 50
Higgins, Dick, 99, 157, **179**
Hip hop, 64–5, 160, 181–2
Hobgood, Allison, 171
Hoeniger, F. David, 142
Holderness, Graham, 6, 88, 156
Holland, Peter, 15, 24, 131, 179

Holland, Sharon, 58
Hopkins, Anthony, 78
Hughes, Bill, 171
Hugo, Victor, 31
Hutcheon, Linda, 9, 29–32, 35, 99, 113, 133, **177**
Huxley, Aldous, 33

Incarceration, 40–2
Intermediality, 13, 99–101, 103–8, *see also Hamlet*; Media; Remediation; Higgins, Dick
Irigaray, Luce, 3, 69
Irvington Shakespeare Company, 128
Iser, Wolfgang, 30

Jakobson, Roman, 133, 143–5
Jankowski, Theodora, 119
Jardine, Lisa, 121
Jenkins, Henry, 14, 109–10, 158, 182–3
Jensen, Michael, 103, 106
Johnson, Eric, 87
Johnson, Mark, *see* Lakoff, George, and Mark Johnson
Johnson, Samuel, 6, 11, 25–6
Jones, Leisha, 125
Joubin, Alexa Alice, 12, 15, 68, 79, 171

Kapil, Aditi Brennan, 8
Karas, Helena, 151
Keam, Angela, 111
Kennedy, Dennis, 133
Keyishian, Harry, 94
Kidnie, M.J., 54, 62, 76, 77

King, Helen, 123
Kittler, Friedrich, 90, 98
Klomp, Neal, 164, 165
Knight, G. Wilson, 29
Knutson, Susan, 149
Koblin, John, 103
Kristeva, Julia, 3, 77
Kushner, Tony, 167–8, 173

Lacan, Jacques, 3–4, 162
Lakoff, George, and Mark Johnson, see *Metaphor*
Lamb, Charles, 31, 83
  and Mary Lamb, 31
Langlitz, Nicholas, 174
Lanham, Richard, 93, 145
Lanier, Douglas, 11, 33–4, 98, 110, 115, 162, **181**, **182**
  rhizomatic Shakespeare, *see* Adaptation
Laqueur, Thomas, 118
Latour, Bruno, 14, 114–15, *see also* Network
Lau, Jey Han, Trevor Cohn, Timothy Baldwin, and Adam Hammond, 158–9
Lavender, Andy, 4
Lees-Jeffries, Hester, 111, 117
Leon, Kenny, 4
Levinas, Emmanuel, 12, 68, 79, 82–4
Levring, Kristian, 68, 80, 82–6
Lieblein, Leanore, 148, **184**
Li, Jet, 160–1
Lillo, George, 139
Linton, David, 91
Little, Arthur L., 4, 15

Loftis, Sonya, 98, 172, **183–4**
Loomba, Ania, 60, 134, 145–6
Loper, Natalie, *see* Desmet, Christy
Love, Genevieve, 146–7
Luhmann, Niklas, 79, 173–4
Lucas, John, *see* Rankine, Claudia
Luhrmann, Baz, 163

MacDonald, Joyce Green, 5, **181, 184**
Madden, John, 124
Malone, Edmond, 8, 73–4
Malraux, André, 91, 92
Marion, Isaac, 156, 163–5
Markham, Gervase, 170
Marsden, Jean I., 12, 45, 82
Marsh, Anne [Anne Caldwell-Marsh], 111, 113
Martinville, Édouard-Léon Scott de, 88
Marx, Karl, 2, 4, 7, 34, 43, 46, 52–4, 92–3, 178
Massai, Sonia, 51, 76–7, 82–3
Masten, Jeff, 123
Mayer, Tom, 48
McLaughlin, Ellen, 143
McLeod, Randall [Random Cloud], 68, 76
McLuhan, Eric, *see* McLuhan, Marshall
McLuhan, Marshall, 14, 88, 90–3
McLuskie, Kathleen, 78, 117
McQueen, Amanda, 48
McRuer, Robert, 164
Media; *see also* Intermediality; Remediation; Memes
  Audio, 86 (boom box), 100–8, 143
  Cinematic, 31, 48, 82–6, 94, 98, 163–7, 36–42 and *passim*
  Mass, 11, 89, 174, 183, and *passim*
  Myth of 'lossless transfer' in, 13, 87–93
  NFT (non-fungible token), 90–3
  Social, *see also* Media, Streaming
    Facebook, 183
    TikTok, 94–6, 111, 125–7, 183
    Twitter, *see* Editing
  Streaming, 2, 3, 51, 52, 89, 93, 94, 100, 103, 105, 117, 127–8, 161
Memes, 7, 14–15, 111–14, 118, **180**
Menke, Richard, 88
Menon, Madhavi, 10
Metaphor *see also* Lakoff, George, and Mark Johnson
  conceptual metaphor 1, 2, 10–17, 68, 102, 162; *see also* Adaptation
  body or mind are containers, 11, 16, 109–10, 156, 174
  change is motion and caused change is forced motion, 15, 133
  content is encoded in the stimulus, 13, 88, 102

ideas are children, ideas are writing, minds are fertile, 68, 102
ideas make a community, 14, 125–8, 160
morality is clean, pure, or white, 15, 47, 133
qualities, beliefs, and people are possessions, 11, 46–7
Miller, James, 17, 20–1
Minstrelsy, *see* Blackface
Mirren, Helen, 32
Mitchell, Elvis, 160
Mitchell, Margaret, 50
Mohammad, K. Silem, 158–9
Molina, Rafael, 105
Montaigne, Michel de, 11, 35–6
Mookherjee, Taarini, 13, 68, 80, 135
Mooneram, Roshni, 5, 133, 149
Moorhouse, Jocelyn, 78
Moreno, Rita, 168
Morgan, Michael L., 79, 82
Morrison, Toni, and Rokia Traouré, 47, 59–62,
Müller, Heiner, 98

Nabokov, Vladimir, 50–1
Nagel, Thomas, 161
Neely, Carol Thomas, 125
Negritude, *see* Fanon, Frantz
Nelson, Tim Blake, 49
Neo-colonialism, *see* Colonialism, Post-colonialism
Network, 11, 14–15, 90, 92, 114–7, 125–7, 160–1, 180–1, 182–3, 185

Nichols, Charles, 20
Nida, Eugene, 132, 142–5
Nielsen, Asta, 98
Nochimson, Martha, 85–6
Novy, Marianne, 5
Nunn, Hillary, 170
Nunn, Trevor, 112, 114

Olive, Sarah, 155, 157, 169, **179**
OOO [Object-Oriented Ontology], 111, 115–6, 157–60, **181**
O'Neill, Stephen, 89, 92, 94, 127, **183**
Orgel, Stephen, 7–8
O'Rourke, Ash, and Kendall Shaw, 105
Osborne, Laurie, 89, 98
O'Sullivan, Michael, 160
Owusu-Bempah, Akwasi, Maria Jung, Firdaous Sbaï, Andrew S. Wilton, and Fiona Kouyoumdjian, 42

Padilla, Adrian Alonso, 106
Pai, Anant, 169
Palfrey, Simon, and Tiffany Stern, 76
Palmer, C. Dexter, 33
Pasolini, Pier Paolo, 51
Paster, Gail Kern, 98, 123
Pasternak, Boris, 31
Patricia, Anthony, 119
Patton, Chloe, 84
Pennacchia, Maddalena, 31
Pera, Pia, 50–1
Pisan, Christine de, 101
Plastow, Jane, 132

Plowright, Joan, 114
Pollack, Beth, 107
Post-colonialism, 12, 28, 74, 131–3, 146, 167–9, **184**; *see also* Colonialism; Slavery
Pringle, Postell, *see* Q Brothers
Printing and publishing, 53, 71–2; *see also* Editing; Media
Propp, Vladimir, 2, 5
Prosumer, 15, 54, 80, 110, 117, 185

Q Brothers [Gregory and Jeffery Quaiyum], 47, 59, 64–6
Queer Theory, 94–5, 119–29, 164–7, **181**; *see also* Cripqueer; Feminism; Media; Shakespeare, *Twelfth Night*

Rackin, Phyllis, 125
Rajewsky, Irina, 88, 99, **179**
Raleigh, Sir Walter, 37
Randall, Alice, 50
Rankine, Claudia, 50
Remediation, 93–8, 101, 105, 142, **181**; *see also* Adaptation; Intermediality; Media;
Remix, 50, 59–65, 79, 127, 181–2
Reeves, Keanu, 9
Reynolds, Bryan, 79, 110, 115; and Donald Hedrick, 114
Richards, I.A., 10
Roach, Joseph, 96

Ross, Robert, 46
Rowe, Katherine, *see* Cartelli, Thomas, and Katherine Rowe
Rich, Adrienne, 164
Rivlin, Elizabeth, 68, 79, 81–2
Rushdie, Salman, 35

Said, Edward, 35, 135, *see also* Travelling Theory
Salisbury, Eve, 149
Sánchez Prado, Ignacio M., 56
Sanchez, Melissa, 119
Sanders, Julie, 48, 51, 77, 178
Santiago 'Matamoros', 57
Sawyer, Robert, 74, 88, 178
Schiebinger, Londa, 118
Schleiner, Winfried, 118
Schröter, Jens, 99, 108, **179**
Scott, Robert Dawson, 146, 147
Scott-Douglass, Amy, 82
Sears, Djanet, 47, 57–64
Sellars, Peter, 61, *see also* Morrison, Toni and Rokia Traouré
Shakespeare, Tom, 171, **177**
Shakespeare, William, *see also* Adaptation; Editing
*Antony and Cleopatra*, 139
*Hamlet*, 87–108; *see also* Media, Intermediality
First Quarto, 97
Gold Hill Global *Complete Works* NFT, 90–3

*Hamlet (1948)* and
 *Hamlet (1957)*, *see*
 Gielgud, Sir John
*Hamlet (2000)*, *see*
 Almereyda, Michael
*Hamlet* (2020), *see*
 Campoy, Ana María
*Hamlet: Fuckbois of*
 *Literature*, *see*
 Edwards, Emily
*Hamletmachine*, *see*
 Müller, Heiner
'The *Hamlet* podcast', *see*
 Hanratty, Conor
'That Pretentious Book
 Club', *see* O'Rourke,
 Ash
Second Quarto, 97, 103,
 104
Wooster Group, 98, 100
*King Lear*, 67–86;
 *Historie*, 71–3, 75, 78,
 83
 *The King is Alive*, *see*
 Levring, Kristian
 *King Lear ([1681] 1965)*,
 *see* Tate, Nahum
 *King Lear (1953)*, *see*
 Welles, Orson; Brook,
 Peter
 *King Lear (1986)*, *see*
 Taylor, Gary, and
 Stanley Wells
 *King Lear (2018)*, *see*
 Hopkins, Anthony
 *A Thousand Acres*, *see*
 Smiley, Jane
 *A Thousand Acres (1997)*
 *see* Moorhouse,
 Jocelyn

 *Tragedie*, 71–3, 75, 77,
 78 *see also* Van Vliet,
 Claire
*Macbeth*
 *Macbeth (2021)*, *see*
 Coen, Joel
*Measure for Measure*,
 18–19, 170
 *The Universal Passion*,
 *see* Miller, James
*Much Ado About Nothing*,
 3–21
 Connect Four game, 3
 *Dil Chahta Hai (2001)*,
 3, 10
 *Enn ta Senn dan Vid*, *see*
 Virahsawmy, Dev
 *Imogen Says Nothing*, *see*
 Kapil, Aditi Brennan
 *Much Ado About*
 *Nothing (1993)*, *see*
 Branagh, Kenneth
 *Nothing Much to Do*, *see*
 Candle Wasters, The
*Othello*
 *Catch My Soul*, *see* Good,
 Jack
 *Che Cosa Sono Le*
 *Nuvole*, *see* Pasolini,
 Pier Paolo
 *Citizen*, *see* Rankine,
 Claudia
 *Desdemona, or, A Play*
 *About a Handkerchief*,
 *see* Vogel, Paula
 *Desdemona*, *see*
 Morrison, Toni, and
 Rokia Traouré
 *Harlem Duet*, *see* Sears,
 Djanet

O, *see* Nelson, Tim Blake
*Otello*, *see* Verdi, Giuseppe
*Othello (1951)*, *see* Welles, Orson
'Othello and Desdemona', *see* Chagall, Marc
*Othello: The Remix*, *see* Q Brothers
*Santa Fe Satan*, *see* Good, Jack
*Slave Play*, *see* Harris, Jeremy
*Zidane*, *see* Rankine, Claudia, and John Lucas
*Pericles*, 131–53; *see also* Translation, Tradaptation
*Children of the Sea*, *see* Gough, Toby
*Confessio Amantis*, *see* Gower, John
*Countess of Pembroke's Arcadia*, *see* Sidney, Philip, and Mary Sidney Herbert
*Gesta Romanorum*, 135–6
*Marina*, *see* Lillo, George
*Pattern of Painful Adventures*, *see* Twine, Lawrence
*Pericles (1608)*, *see* Wilkins, George
*Périclès (2018)*, *see* Cheek By Jowl
*Pericles (2022)*, *see* McLaughlin, Ellen
*The Porpoise*, *see* Haddon, Mark
*Spring*, *see* Smith, Ali
*Romeo and Juliet*, 7–8,
*Goliyon Ki Raasleela Ram-leela*, *see* Bhansali, Sanjay
*Malati and Madhava*, 168–9
*ProTactile 'Romeo and Juliet'*, 156, 172–4, *see also* ASL; Disability
*Romeo and Juliet (1968)* see Zeffirelli, Franco
*Romeo Must Die*, 160–1
*Tragical History of Romeus and Juliet*, 162
*Warm Bodies (2011)*, *see* Marion, Isaac
*Warm Bodies (2013)*, 156, 163–5
*William Shakespeare's Romeo + Juliet*, *see* Luhrmann, Baz
*West Side Story (1957)*, 167–8
*West Side Story (1961)*, 167–8
*West Side Story (2021)*, *see* Kushner, Tony
*Shakespeare in Love*, *see* Madden, John
*Deep-Speare,* 158–9
*The Sonnanagrams*, *see* Mohammad, K. Silem
*The Sonnets*
*The Tempest*, 23–32, 138
*Brave New World*, *see* Huxley, Aldous

*Dream of Perpetual Motion see* Palmer, C. Dexter
*The Enchanted Island, see* Dryden, John, and William Davenant
*Forbidden Planet, see* Wilcox, Fred
*Hag-Seed, see* Atwood, Margaret
*Prospero's Books, see* Greenaway, Peter
*Une Tempête [A Tempest], see* Césaire, Aimé
*Twelfth Night*, 109–129
   *Orlando, see* Woolf, Virginia
   Queer stage and hybrid productions, 128-9
   *Mordaunt Hall, or a September Night*, see Marsh, Anne [Anne Caldwell-Marsh]
   'The Super-Dreadnoughts', *see* Weir, Stanley
   *Twelfth Night (1969), see* Plowright, Joan
   *She's The Man*, 111, 114, 121–5
   *Twelfth Night (1996), see* Nunn, Trevor
   *Twelfth Night (2013)*, 111, 115–6
   'Viola, The Twin', *see* Clarke, Mary Cowden
   'When People Think Twelfth Night is a Straight Play', *see* DojaCat

Schiller, David, 48–9
Schoenbaum, Samuel, 8, 71
Schwartz, Beth, 120–1
Semenza, Greg, 31
Shannon, Laurie, 170
Shepard, Sam, 99
Shifman, Limor, 14, 109, 112–3
Shohet, Lauren, 51
Sidney, Philip, and Mary Sidney Herbert, 136
Slavery, 58–60, 61–3, 167, 168–9 *see also* Colonialism
Smiley, Jane, 70, 81–2
Smith, Ali, 133, 140, 149–52
Smith, Bruce R., 108
Smith, Corinn, 128
Sokolova, Boika, and Katy Stavreva, 134
Spivak, Gayatri Chakravorty, 3
Steinhöwel, Heinrich, 136, 137
Stern, Tiffany, *see* Palfrey, Simon, and Tiffany Stern
Stiles, Julia, 94, 99
Stryker, Susan, 123
Smyth, Albert, 135–6
Syme, Holger, 70, 78

Takaki, Ronald, 35
Tate, Nahum, 77–8, 82–4
Taylor, Charles, 12, 79
Taylor, Gary, 8, 67, 68, 182, and Stanley Wells, 75; and Michael Warren, 75
Taylor, Neil, *see* Thompson, Ann
Taymor, Julie, 32

Teague, Fran, 14, 113, 117–8, 127, 183
Thompson, Ann, and Neil Taylor, 97
Thompson, Ayanna, 56, 57, 63
Trace, 30, 160, 167–9, **184**, *see also* Palimpsest
  postcolonial, 169, *see also* Singh, Jyotsna
  of slavery, 184, *see also* MacDonald, Joyce Green
Traouré, Rokia, *see* Morrison, Toni, and Rokia Traouré
Tradaptation, 131–3, 148–52, **184**
Translation, 5, 6, 15, 20, 31, 36, 50, 131–4, 140–7
Trans Shakespeare, *see* Queer Theory; Feminism
Traub, Valerie, 119, 125
Travelling Theory, 35, 134–5, *see also* Said, Edward
Trevien, Kenan, 151
Trivedi, Poonam, 131, 133, 134, 145–6
Twine, Lawrence, 136, 137, 138, 139, 140

Valeonti, Fonteini, et al., 90
Van Vliet, Claire, 77–8
Venuti, Lawrence, 132, 133, 144–5
Verdi, Giuseppe, 49

Virahsawmy, Dev, 5
Vickers, Brian, 70, 75, 78
Vogel, Paula,

Wald, Christina, 32, 155
Warren, Michael, *see* Taylor, Gary
Washington, Denzel, 9
Weinberger, David, 116–7
Weir, Stanley, 111, 113–14
Welles, Orson, 63–4, 78
Welsh, James, 5
Werstine, Paul, 73–6
Whishaw, Ben, 32
Wilcox, Fred, 33
Wilkins, George, 16, 131–6, 140
Wilkins, George, 16, 129, 131, 136, 140, 141
Williams, Katherine Schaap, 164
Wilson, Horace Hayman, 168
Wilson, Jeffrey, 9, 180
Winckler, Reto, 32, 48, 157, 158, 183
Womack, Craig, 82, 83
Woolf, Virginia, 120–1
Worthen, W.B., 96–7

Yates, Julian, 16, 110, 115, 157

Zabus, Chantal, 40
Zeffirelli, Franco, 163
Žižek, Slavoj, 162
Zombies, 163–5